AF606892

# King Ranch

Publication of this book was assisted by a
generous gift from King Ranch, Inc.

KING RANCH

Number 24

**Joe and Betty Moore Texas Art Series**

William E. Reaves and Linda J. Reaves, General Editors

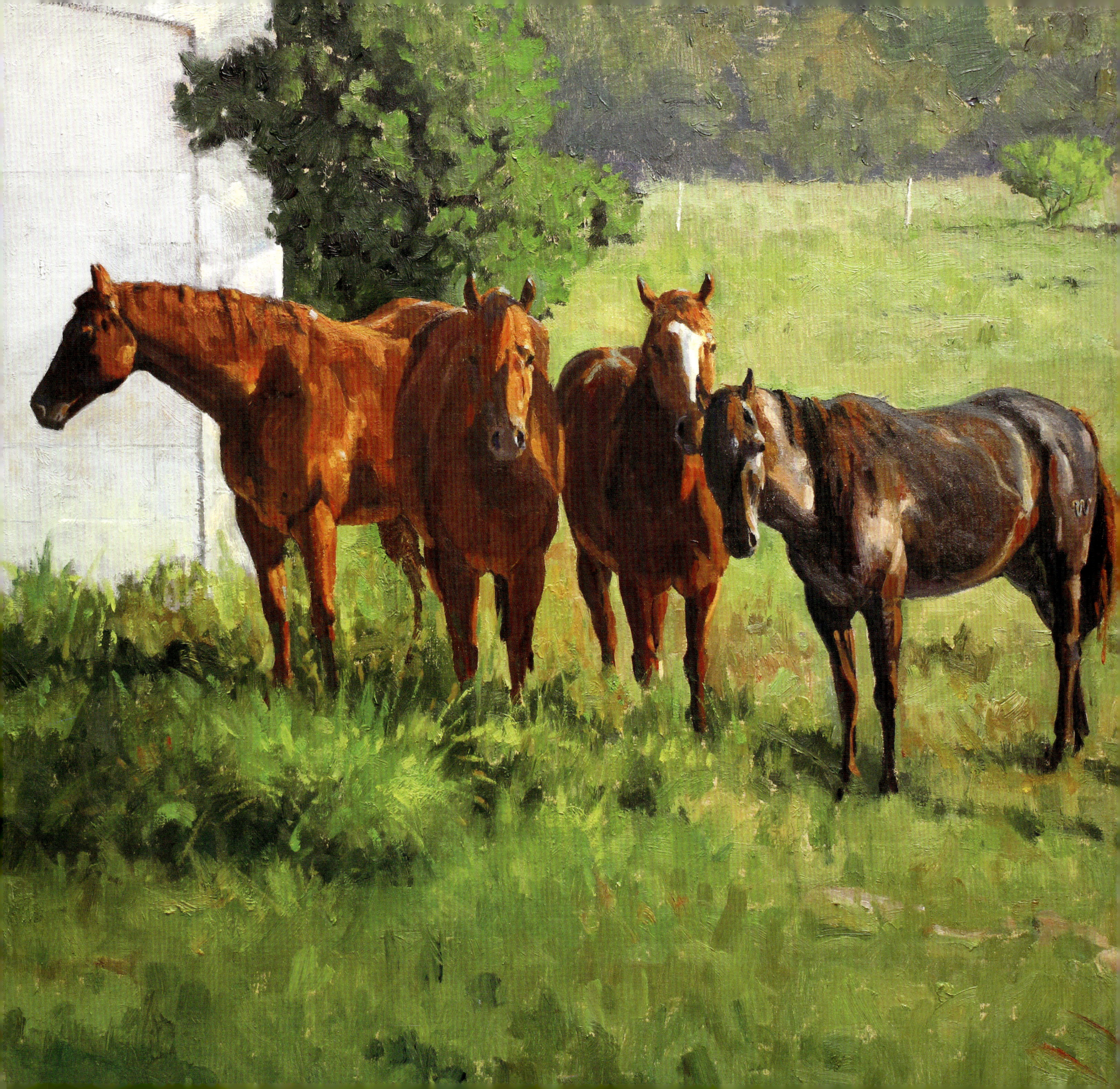

# King Ranch
## *A Legacy in Art*

**NOE PEREZ**

Edited by
Bob Kinnan, William E. Reaves, and Linda J. Reaves

With contributions by
Ron Tyler and Bruce M. Shackelford

TEXAS A&M UNIVERSITY PRESS | COLLEGE STATION

Third printing, 2025

∞ This paper meets the requirements of ANSI/NISO Z39.48-1992 (Permanence of Paper).
Binding materials have been chosen for durability.
Manufactured in China by Martin Book Management.

Library of Congress Cataloging-in-Publication Data

Names: Perez, Noe, 1958– artist, writer of added commentary. | Kinnan, Bob, editor, writer of introduction. | Reaves, William E., editor. | Reaves, Linda J., editor.
Title: King Ranch : a legacy in art / by Noe Perez ; edited by Bob Kinnan, William E. Reaves, and Linda J. Reaves.
Other titles: Joe and Betty Moore Texas art series ; no. 24.
Description: First edition. | College Station : Texas A&M University Press, [2021] | Series: Joe and Betty Moore Texas art series ; number 24 | Includes index.
Identifiers: LCCN 2021019291 | ISBN 9781623499525 (cloth) | ISBN 9781648430039 (hardcover) | ISBN 9781623499532 (ebook)
Subjects: LCSH: Perez, Noe, 1958—Criticism and interpretation. | Landscape painting, American—Texas—King Ranch. | King Ranch (Tex.)—In art. | King Ranch (Tex.)—Biography. | King Ranch (Tex.)—History. | King Ranch (Tex.)—Pictorial works.
Classification: LCC F392.K47 P47 2021 | DDC 976.4/472—dc23
LC record available at https://lccn.loc.gov/2021019291

# Contents

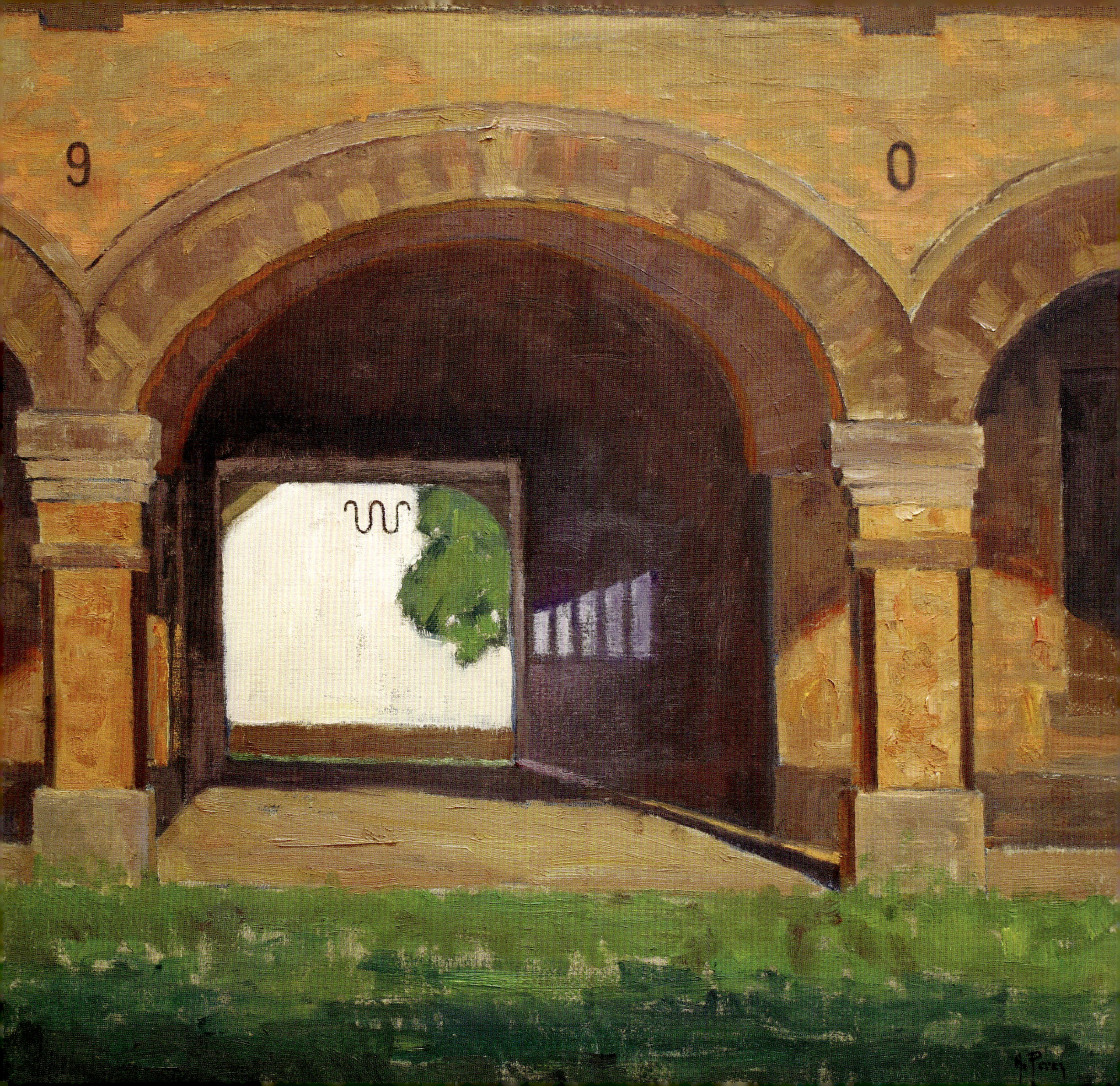
9
0

# Foreword

## Jamey Clement

It is true that you do not miss something until it is gone. Having grown up on King Ranch, I did not fully appreciate its raw beauty until I left to go away to school and ultimately pursue a career. In 1984, I was fortunate enough to join the company. My wife and family jumped at the chance to live on King Ranch, where we had our third child. It was too good to be true—I was home again and raising my children in a wonderful setting. In 1988, however, I was asked to make a corporate move to Dallas, and while living in Dallas has its pleasures, it only made me miss King Ranch and its intrinsic beauty that much more.

During my early years in Dallas, the federal government decided to shut down a bombing range on the island of Vieques, Puerto Rico. It was reported in the *Dallas Morning News* that some thought it would be a great idea to relocate that bombing range to King Ranch! In that article, King Ranch was described as a desolate stretch of land. I was incensed by the suggestion and wrote to the editor that, while King Ranch may be sparsely populated, it was anything but desolate! In fact, there are more flora and fauna in South Texas than in Florida, and that is not by chance. Landowners are always the best stewards of the land because their livelihood depends on it. Sustainability is key.

When I discovered Noe Perez and his art, I immediately became a devotee. His work captures the essence of South Texas, and it instantly made me feel like I was back home again. His art is representative of all that King Ranch means to me.

I have come to realize that King Ranch is my "corner post." The corner post is the foundation of any good fence; without it, the fence is neither strong nor true. In my case, King Ranch is the corner post and the fence is my connection to its legacy.

Noe's landscapes are authentic and serve as a reminder of the beautifully rugged place that is King Ranch. I can think of no better artist to provide an inside view of our family home and convey in a small way why we are so proud of it and its legacy. His paintings are a motivating force for me to live up to the standards set by Captain and Mrs. King, working to preserve this glorious heritage.

---

James H. Clement Jr. serves as Chairman of the Board of King Ranch, Inc., and is a fifth-generation member of the King Ranch Family.

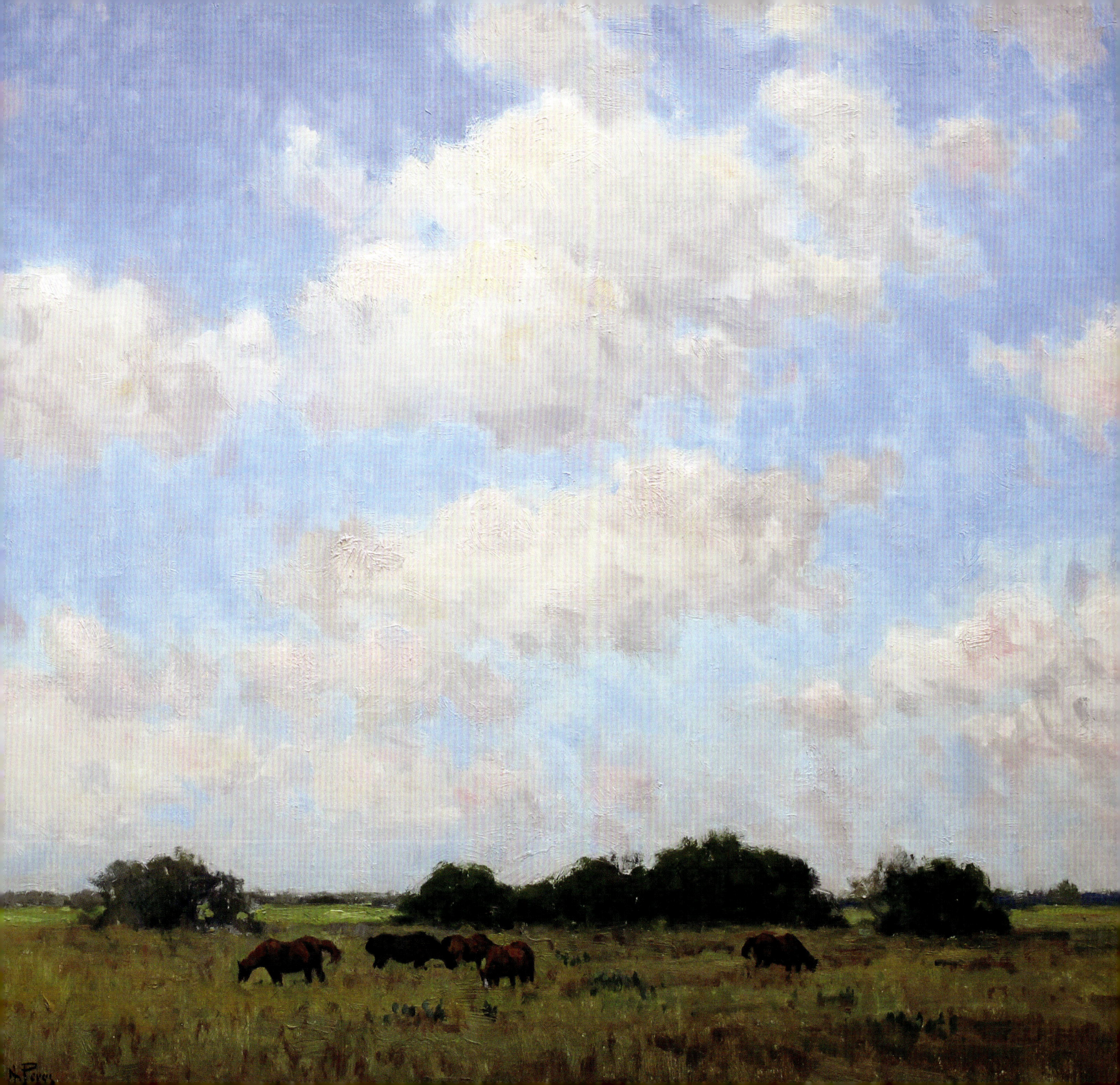

# King Ranch

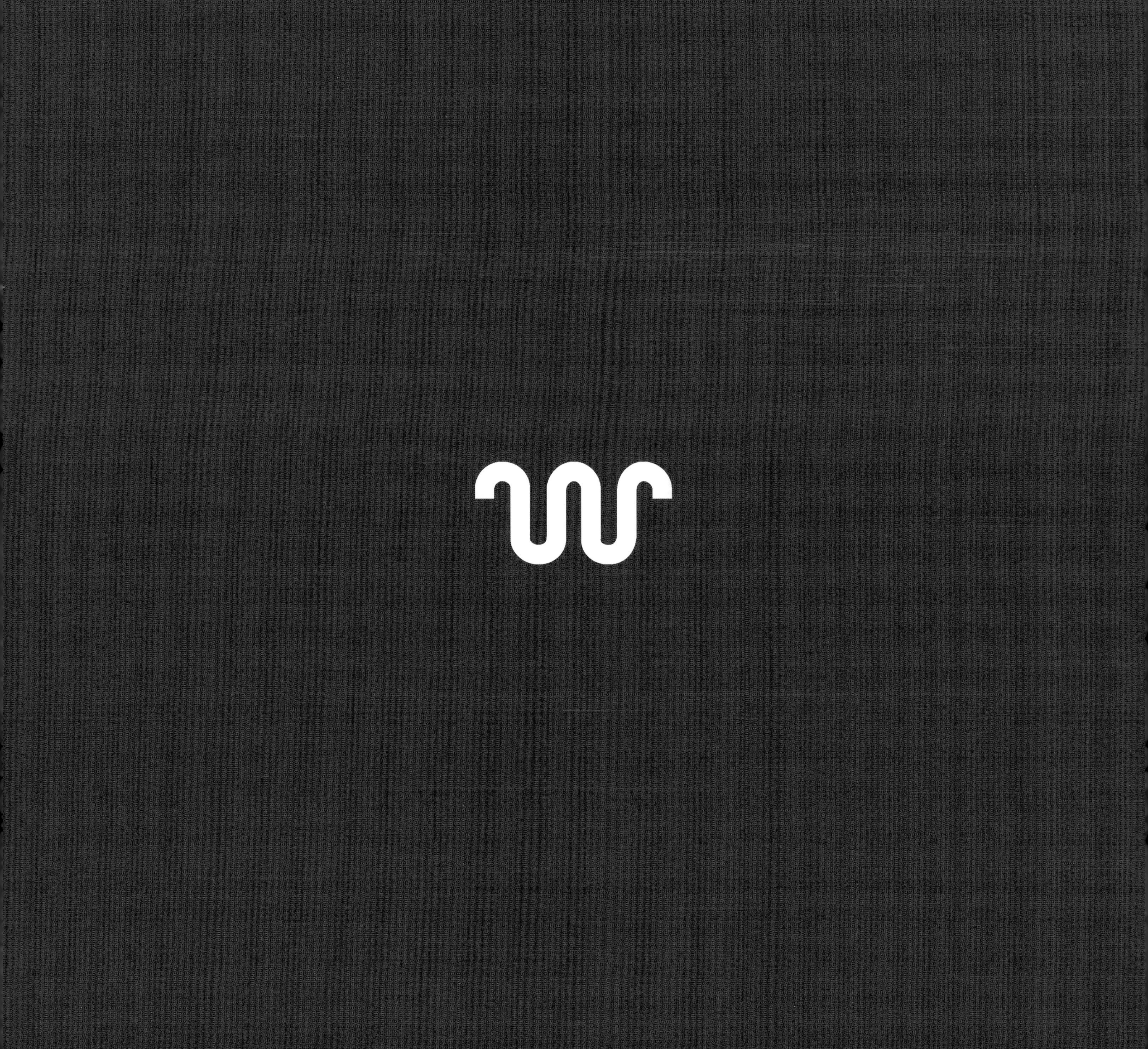

# An Introduction to King's Rancho

## Bob Kinnan

Richard King held the secrets of his childhood within himself. Today, we find only snippets of accounts of his early life, as passed forward by Henrietta King. He was born to Irish immigrants in New York City on July 10, 1824, and beyond that, his ancestral lineage is unknown. At the age of nine, whether by necessity or force, he was signed over to a jeweler as his apprentice. King endured this forced labor for more than two years before making his escape as a stowaway aboard a sailing ship bound for the southern Gulf of Mexico and Mobile Bay. Discovered after the vessel was well out to sea, the ship's captain put the young lad to work as a cabin boy.

King quickly moved beyond cabin-boy status, eventually learning how to pilot shallow-draft steamboats on the southern rivers. His hard work and talent earned him a pilot's license at the age of eighteen and, along with the license, the title of "Captain"—a sobriquet that he embraced for the remainder of his life.

Piloting the southern waterways, Captain King fostered a friendship with one of the trade's most influential boatmen, Mifflin Kenedy. Though they possessed distinctly different personalities, their strong work ethic, ambitions, and mutual trust forged a lasting bond between the two men.

The onset of the Mexican War in 1846 created a high demand for experienced rivermen who could pilot the challenging waters of the Rio Grande to supply the growing needs of the US Army. Mifflin Kenedy answered the call and became part of a large flotilla of steamboats along the river. Kenedy wrote to his friend, Captain King, beckoning him to come to Texas and join the fray. King arrived at the mouth of the Rio Grande during the spring of 1847 and, by June, reported for

---

Bob Kinnan was employed from 2003 through 2016 by King Ranch as Area Manager of the Santa Gertrudis Heritage Society, Main House, and Community Services, during which time he also supervised the King Ranch Visitor Program Services and King Ranch Archives. Since 2016, Kinnan has served as King Ranch Historian and Archival Consultant. He now resides in Mountain Home, Texas.

duty as the pilot of a steamer in service to the army quartermaster's office.

At the end of the war, King was released from duty and in search of new opportunities. The conclusion of US/Mexico hostilities produced attractive prospects for entrepreneurs along the border. The resourceful King purchased a war surplus steamboat, the *Colonel Cross,* and became an independent pilot of his own vessel along the Rio Grande. Around the same time, Kenedy established a trading venture, hauling merchandise from the Rio Grande south to towns in northern Mexico. Another powerful border businessman, Charles Stillman, purchased a number of surplus steamboats and set out to control trade from the mouth of the Rio Grande to ports upriver. However, Stillman's business lacked a boatman who was knowledgeable of the precarious Rio Grande. He chose Kenedy as the man to make his business profitable. Kenedy agreed to the partnership with the stipulation that Capt. Richard King, an experienced river pilot, be brought onboard. An offer was made to King, who accepted with the condition that Stillman's obsolete surplus steamboats be scrapped in favor of newly built ships designed by King himself. Stillman accepted King's proposition, and on March 1, 1850, a partnership was formed between King, Kenedy, and Stillman, known as M. Kenedy & Company. With King's newly designed riverboats, M. Kenedy & Company developed a trading monopoly on the Rio Grande, and Captain King became a prosperous businessman with great influence in the borderlands.

King was aware of the vast regions north of the Rio Grande, but due to the pace of his business interests, his opportunities to explore possibilities in the new State of Texas were restricted. His interest was piqued, however, when the flamboyant founder of Corpus Christi, Henry Kinney, was in Brownsville promoting the undeveloped territory north of the river and inviting the curious to visit and enjoy the Lone Star Fair—a great celebration held in Corpus Christi. Kinney's fair would be the first of its kind in the young state, attracting thousands to

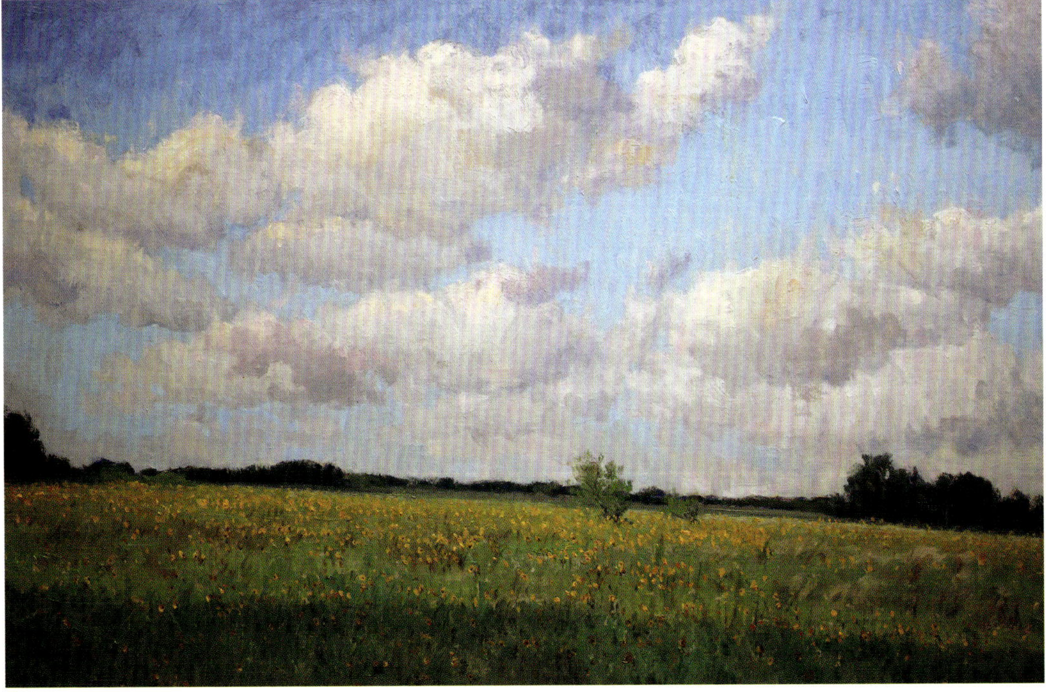

Noe Perez, *Summer Clouds (Norias)*, 2019. Courtesy of the artist.

a region unknown to most Texans. The well-promoted fair offered "luxurious accommodations and lavish entertainment, including agricultural displays and philosophical oratory." The invitation appealed to King, who, after five years on the Rio Grande and in Brownsville, ventured north in 1852, his motivation a combination of adventure, politics, and capitalistic opportunities.

We can only speculate on the details of King's trek across the unforgiving prairie known to Spaniards as El Desierto de los Muertos and dubbed the Wild Horse Desert by English-speaking immigrants. Bound for Henry Kinney's Lone Star Fair in Corpus Christi, King and his companions probably traveled the "Old Road" that had been used by Gen. Zachary Taylor and his army en route to the border and the Mexican War. The expedition traversed the untamed land between the Rio Grande and the Nueces River that had been explored by early Spanish and Mexican adventurers.

The bounty of this vast, open country could not have been lost on King, for it was spring and the coastal prairie was vivid and alive. The beauty of the terrain probably surprised the Captain, with its stirrup high grass, sweeping oak mottes, blooming prickly pear, and abundant wildlife. The land would be perfect for future pastoral efforts, except for the absence of reliable sources of water. For 120 miles north of Brownsville, the scarcity of water made the land almost uninhabitable. A brave traveler would find only rare and occasional water captured in resacas, playas, and bogs scattered along the trail. The dangerous journey across the Wild Horse Desert was not for the ill-prepared or the inexperienced wanderer. Because of the precarious environment, we must assume that King's group traveled in the company of knowledgeable guides familiar with the Old Road. Based on this assumption, it seems logical that King's qualified escort knew of the seep springs along the Santa Gertrudis Creek.

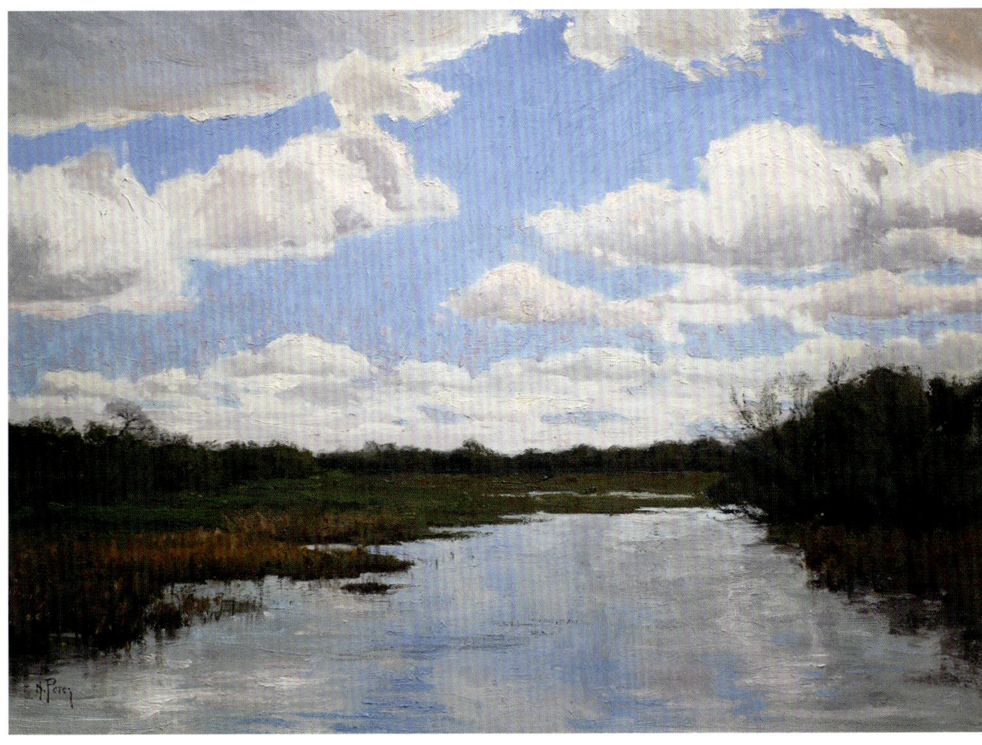

Noe Perez, *Seep Springs (Santa Gertrudis)*, 2019. Courtesy of the artist.

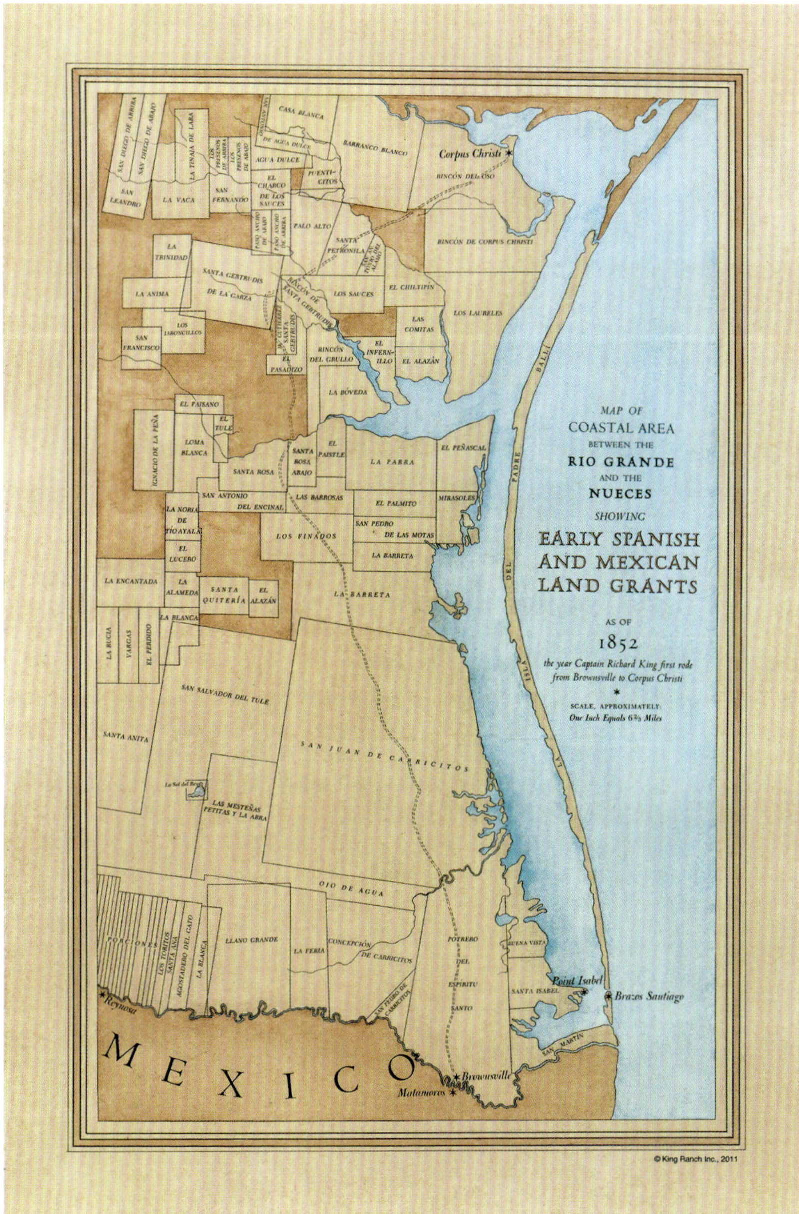


Tom Lea Land Grant Map, 1957. Courtesy of King Ranch, Inc.

After four days on a dry trail, the sweet spring water of the Santa Gertrudis must have been cause for great excitement—an experience not forgotten by Captain King. After their brief respite at this spring-fed oasis, the forty-five-mile journey from Santa Gertrudis to Corpus Christi would be a tranquil passage for King and his companions. Eager anticipation of the awaiting festivities at Kinney's Fair made the miles pass rapidly.

Kinney's Lone Star Fair and its attractions were not-so-subtle enticements for potential settlers and real-estate speculators. Kinney sought to colonize the area around Corpus Christi and the regions south. The fair successfully attracted those seeking entertainment and diversion from the monotony of frontier life, but it failed to entice colonists to settle in the region. The exception was Captain King and an old acquaintance of his, Gideon K. "Legs" Lewis. Inspired by the potential of the region around Santa Gertrudis Creek and persuasive prodding by Lewis, the pair developed a partnership. How long King remained in Corpus Christi is unknown, but certainly it was long enough to set in motion a plan that would give him a foothold where he would begin his ranching endeavor. Upon returning home to Brownsville, Captain King sought out heirs to abandoned Spanish and Mexican land grants along the Santa Gertrudis, which had been unoccupied for more than a generation. By 1854, King and his partner had purchased two land grants, the Rincón de Santa Gertrudis and Santa Gertrudis de la Garza. These lands contained 68,500 acres and became the nucleus of his future ranching empire.

Meanwhile, back in Brownsville, Miss Henrietta Chamberlain, a new arrival to the southernmost tip of Texas, had become King's only distraction other than his businesses, to which he devoted constant attention. Rev. Hiram Chamberlain and his family had arrived in Brownsville in 1850. The first encounter between Richard and Henrietta was not so friendly a meeting, during which she was witness to the Captain's rough and undisciplined demeanor. Smitten by the charming Miss Chamberlain, King quickly reformed his behavior, at least when in the presence of polite society. In the beginning, her feelings were not reciprocal, but soon the challenge of refining such an indecent ruffian grew into a love for and devotion to the Captain. After four years of courtship, Henrietta Chamberlain and Richard King were married. Reverend Chamberlain officiated over his daughter's ceremony in the Brownsville Presbyterian Church, which he had founded in 1850.

Obstacles of the inhospitable frontier lay ahead for the twenty-two-year-old newlywed Henrietta. Like so many other difficulties she had endured as the daughter of an itinerant missionary preacher, she set her mind to the task at hand and relished in the new adventure.

Likely the newlyweds retraced the route taken by Captain King on his first expedition north to the Santa Gertrudis, but this honeymoon journey was quite different. They traveled in a large, closed carriage (or stagecoach) that had been ordered and prepared especially for this trip. For safety and comfort sake, the entourage included mounted guards and a cook. Although the pace was slow, Henrietta was delighted by the wilderness and rejoiced in the new life that lay ahead for the young couple.

At first sight, Rancho de Santa Gertrudis seemed as rough as the men who inhabited it. The cow camp, situated on a rise above the seep springs, consisted of mesquite corrals, small, thatched-roof jacales; and a fortified blockhouse equipped with small brass cannons that served as the camp's stockade. Occupants of the rancho were a cross section formed from the region's inherent cultural diversity. King's partner, Gideon Lewis, and frontiersmen James Richardson and William Gregory protected the rancho and were always on call when danger menaced. The loyal and true James Richardson would serve as King's first headman. From Brownsville,

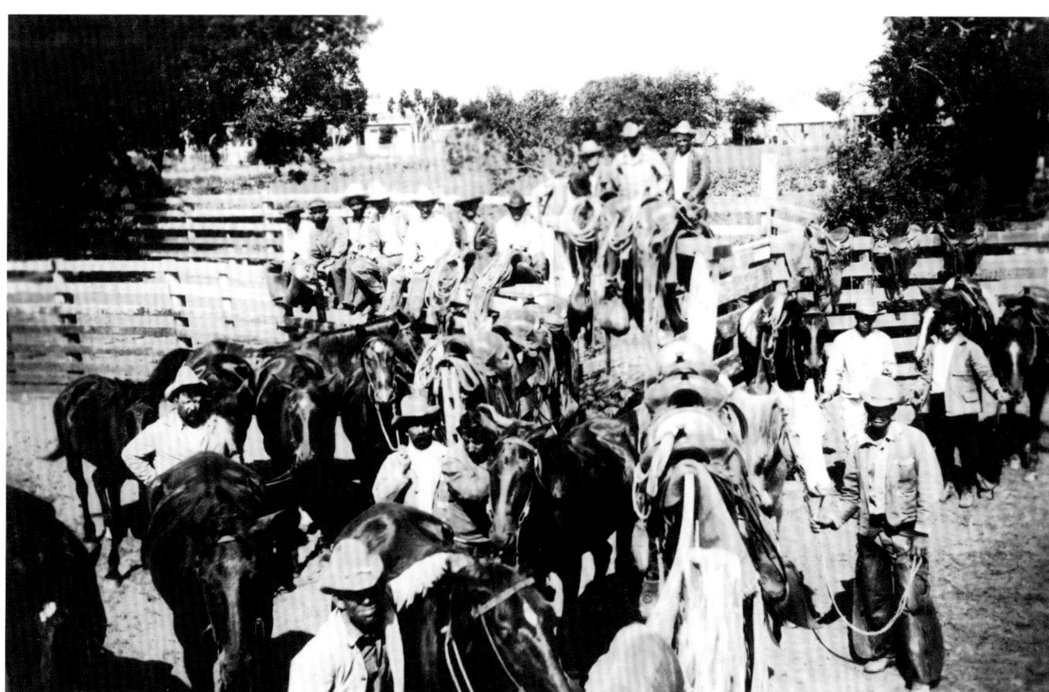

Los Kineños, 1900. Courtesy of King Ranch, Inc.

King brought two trusted men, Faustino Villa and Vicente Patiño. Francisco Alvarado, a resident of the neighboring Rancho Bobedo, came and built the first houses and structures on King's Rancho. The Captain fondly referred to these trusted men as "my friends." Serving alongside these early ranch caretakers came the intrepid los Kineños (King's People) from the small village of Cruillas in northern Mexico. Captain King had found this village while seeking to buy cattle. This group of families rode north from drought-plagued ranchos, accompanying Captain King with the livestock their land could no longer sustain. They traded their homes and livelihoods for the promise of a new life on Rancho de Santa Gertrudis. The loyal and dedicated Kineños became the backbone of King's fledging rancho. Into this society, Henrietta King was greeted and warmly welcomed as La Patrona.

During his years on the Rio Grande, Captain King had developed a reputation for hard work, skill, and innovation, with his knowledge as a riverman and his innovative boat designs. King also had unique and progressive ideas concerning his new ranch, which soon resembled a hacienda in northern Mexico, rather than a farm in the southern United States.

From the beginning of her residency, Henrietta King saw the rancho as her home. La Patrona brought a new sense of decorum and hospitality to this "city of refuge"; her impact was immediate and without compromise. The young couple's first home on the rancho was humble and temporary at best, as Captain King's initial intention was to live as an absentee owner. The Kings divided their time between their home in Brownsville and the rancho, but in the early years, Santa Gertrudis required more of the Captain's time and devotion for the development of his plan. The untimely death of his partner and friend Gideon Lewis required King to redouble his efforts at the rancho and necessitated the search for a new partner. Captain King's priority was that ownership and control of the Santa Gertrudis grants be assured. Following a few missteps, King found his answer and retained a new partner, his respected friend from Brownsville, Capt. James Walworth. With cash on hand, Walworth invested in Rancho de Santa Gertrudis. There is no record as to the exact arrangements of this partnership, but it is clear that King had complete managerial authority.

In 1856, Henrietta King, expecting their first child, was an infrequent visitor to Santa Gertrudis. The birth of their daughter, Henrietta Maria (known as "Nettie"), along with a booming riverboat business kept Captain King close to home in Brownsville. While absent from the rancho, King continued to mold his vision for the future of Rancho de Santa Gertrudis.

In the fall of 1856, Captain King would make the acquaintance of a visiting army officer on temporary duty on the Rio Grande. Captain King's warm and impactful friendship with Lt. Col. Robert E. Lee would influence the King family for the rest of their lives. Lee's counsel would serve to guide King's future, and Lee's sage advice to "buy land and never sell" became King's credo. Conversely, the impact Henrietta King had on Colonel Lee was equally lasting. During his stay in Texas from 1856 to 1861, Lee had the opportunity on a number of occasions to visit Santa Gertrudis and referred to the frontier way station as a "seat of hospitality." Henrietta King's respect and admiration for General Lee would endure for the rest of her life.

From 1857 thru 1859, Richard King proceeded to grow his interests at a dizzying pace. Brownsville was budding and so were the operations of M. Kenedy & Company and Rancho de Santa Gertrudis. Trips to the rancho resumed, with Henrietta and Nettie accompanying the Captain. Activities on the rancho included dam building to capture precious water from seasonal rains. Cattle were being marked with the rancho's first brands—the Ere Flecha and the HK. In addition,

Captain King began to improve his cattle herds and retained all heifer calves to increase his cattle inventory. He pursued a program to improve his mustang horses by purchasing well-bred studs, and the rancho developed a lively and profitable mule market. Ever the innovator, King established hide and tallow plants as early as 1859 and was an early pioneer in the development of wider markets for his livestock, some even outside of Texas. The King family grew again with the birth of their second daughter, Ella Morse, in 1858.

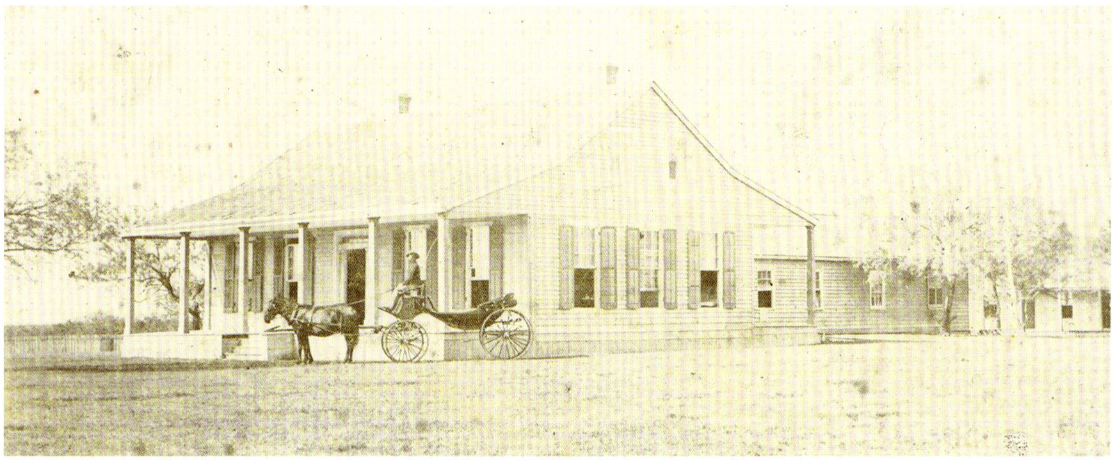

Original Main House, 1869. Courtesy of King Ranch, Inc.

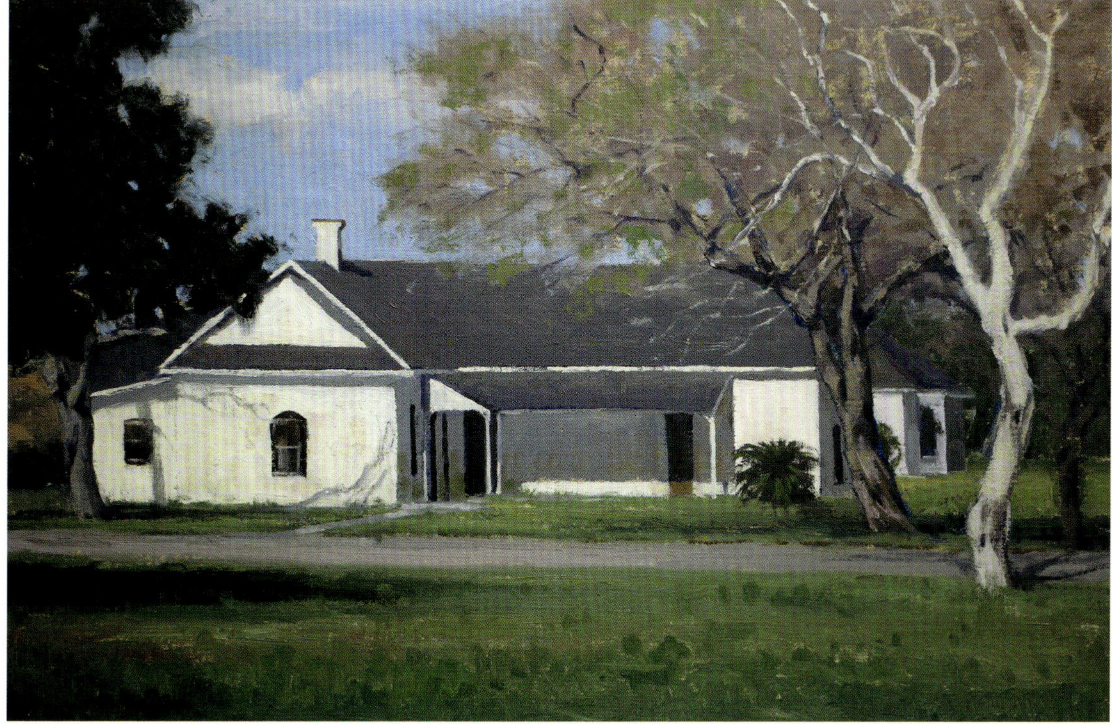

Noe Perez, *Old Colony Casitas* (*Santa Gertrudis*), 2019. Courtesy of the artist.

Captain and Mrs. King also built their first permanent home on the Santa Gertrudis sometime between 1857 and 1859. The modest prairie house consisted of one and a half stories with five rooms and a banister front porch. During this period, the blockhouse stockade was expanded to include the Commissary as well as a kitchen, dining hall, and men's dormitory for visitors and travelers passing by Santa Gertrudis. The headquarters now included stables, wagon sheds, and a busy blacksmith shop. The Kineño colony, just north of the Commissary, continued to expand. The primitive ranch headquarters on the rise above Santa Gertrudis Creek was soon fostering a thriving community, before now an unknown phenomenon in the Wild Horse Desert. We can be certain that around this time, discussion of relocating the King family permanently from Brownsville to Santa Gertrudis had commenced.

A note penned on December 3, 1860, by Reverend Chamberlain gives the first indication of the Kings' relocation to the rancho. The Reverend wrote that Captain King had begun packing for a general move to Rancho de Santa Gertrudis, expressing his sorrow at their pending departure. Reverend Chamberlain closes his letter philosophically, saying it is for the best and that "this is a world of changes." Almost assuredly, the relocation was delayed by the arrival of the Kings' third child, first son, and the Captain's namesake, Richard King II.

Captain King's growing family and his dedication to expanding the rancho inspired his move to Santa Gertrudis. The establishment of a new firm, R. King & Company, pooled the land and assets of Rancho de Santa Gertrudis into a new organization with new ownership that included King, James Walworth, and Mifflin Kenedy. The Captain retained management control of the rancho, while Walworth became engaged in state politics and Kenedy stayed in Brownsville to supervise commercial operations on the Rio Grande. The consequences of the Captain's relocation and the joy that emanated from his family, now residing on the land that they loved, cannot be overstated. Sadly, the Kings' halcyon inhabitance would be short-lived, as the winds of war were swirling all around them.

The family's general move to Santa Gertrudis was probably complete by the time irreconcilable differences between the North and South exploded into war. On February 1, 1861, Texas seceded from the United States of America to join the Southern Confederacy. Soon South Texas and Rancho de Santa Gertrudis would be completely embroiled in the War of the Rebellion.

Southern Texas avoided the conflicts early on, and R. King & Company prospered from the spoils of war. Cotton flooded into Texas from the Southern states, whose ports had been blockaded by the Union Navy. Rancho de Santa Gertrudis became a depot for Confederate cotton and an important way station for wagon trains traveling south. New companies were formed by King, Kenedy, and Charles Stillman, capitalizing on commercial opportunities that ensured safe access for cotton bound for ports at the mouth of the Rio Grande. They went to the extreme of registering their riverboats in Mexico and flew the Mexican flag to avert capture by the Union Navy. Cotton was the lifeblood of the Confederacy, and foreign ships waited off the coast to transport the cash crop to distant textile mills. The Union was determined to halt this flow of goods, which helped sustain the South. In addition to halting the cotton trade, bounties were offered for the apprehension of Confederate profiteers like Richard King.

With much happiness and celebration, the Kings welcomed a new daughter to the family on April 29, 1862. Alice Gertrudis was born in the family's little prairie home at Santa Gertrudis, and her name is a tribute to the place where she was born. The destiny of

Rancho de Santa Gertrudis was secured with the birth of little Alice.

Then the inevitable occurred. Seven thousand Union forces landed between Padre Island and Brazos Santiago, the doorstep of the Rio Grande and Brownsville. The invaders moved swiftly, and three days before Christmas in 1863, a detachment of Union Cavalry was dispatched, capturing Rancho de Santa Gertrudis. Fortunately, when that time came, the Captain was absent from the rancho. Weeks before the raid, he had traveled to Mexico to retrieve stolen cattle. Due to this opportune absence from the rancho, King eluded capture and a likely death sentence. The fate of Henrietta King and her children was exacted quickly, as all were exiled from their home for the duration of the conflict. Henrietta King, pregnant with her fifth child and accompanied by her children and elderly father, Reverend Chamberlain, made it as far as San Patricio on the north side of the Nueces River. There, Mrs. King's second son was born, and whether out of respect or defiance, she named the baby Robert E. Lee King.

In 1866, after the South's surrender, King and Kenedy were granted amnesty and their citizenship was restored. Their pardon was granted more for the commerce they influenced in the United States, rather than as a mark of forgiveness for their allegiances during the war. Captains King and Kenedy moved forward rapidly to put their business interests in order. James Walworth, a partner in R. King & Company, had passed away, and Charles Stillman had withdrawn from M. Kenedy & Company. The void left by these recent circumstances precipitated a reorganization of both companies. In due course, King and Kenedy bought Walworth's interest from his estate, and they were now each half owners in Rancho de Santa Gertrudis. This new incarnation of steamboat operations was considerably more complicated, but soon the new firm King, Kenedy & Company was established, with King and Kenedy owning half of the interest in the company and the other half spread among six Brownsville business associates. Kenedy would assume management over the steamboat operations, and King returned to Santa Gertrudis and devoted his efforts to the future of his beloved rancho, which now encompassed 146,000 acres.

Captain King's departure from Brownsville to Santa Gertrudis marked the end of his active involvement in the affairs on the river. King's future lay with the land and ranching, and as with all of his previous business endeavors, he became totally and tenaciously immersed in every aspect of Rancho de Santa Gertrudis.

King foresaw the end of riverboats as the primary means of trade on the Rio Grande. The difficulties with navigating the shifting course of the river, less reliable contracts, and the impending arrival of the railroad sealed the fate of steamboat transportation. He argued that there was a future with land and livestock, and he soon convinced Mifflin Kenedy to change course and join him in the Wild Horse Desert. Bigger changes lay ahead for the friends and partners.

The assets of King and Kenedy's partnerships were diverse and complicated. Because they both hailed from large families, they saw the importance of the individual ownership of their interests. With this in mind, they determined what was best for each family's future—a friendly division of their holdings. The process began late in 1867, with an agreed inventory of assets and a plan for the division of their herds. By May 1868, the partners signed the "Article of Agreement and Settlement of R. King & Company." Three days after signing the agreement, Mifflin Kenedy bought the Rincón de Los Laureles, which would become the headquarters of his independent ranching interests until 1882, when it was sold to a Scottish syndicate, the Texas Land & Cattle Company. Richard King became the sole owner

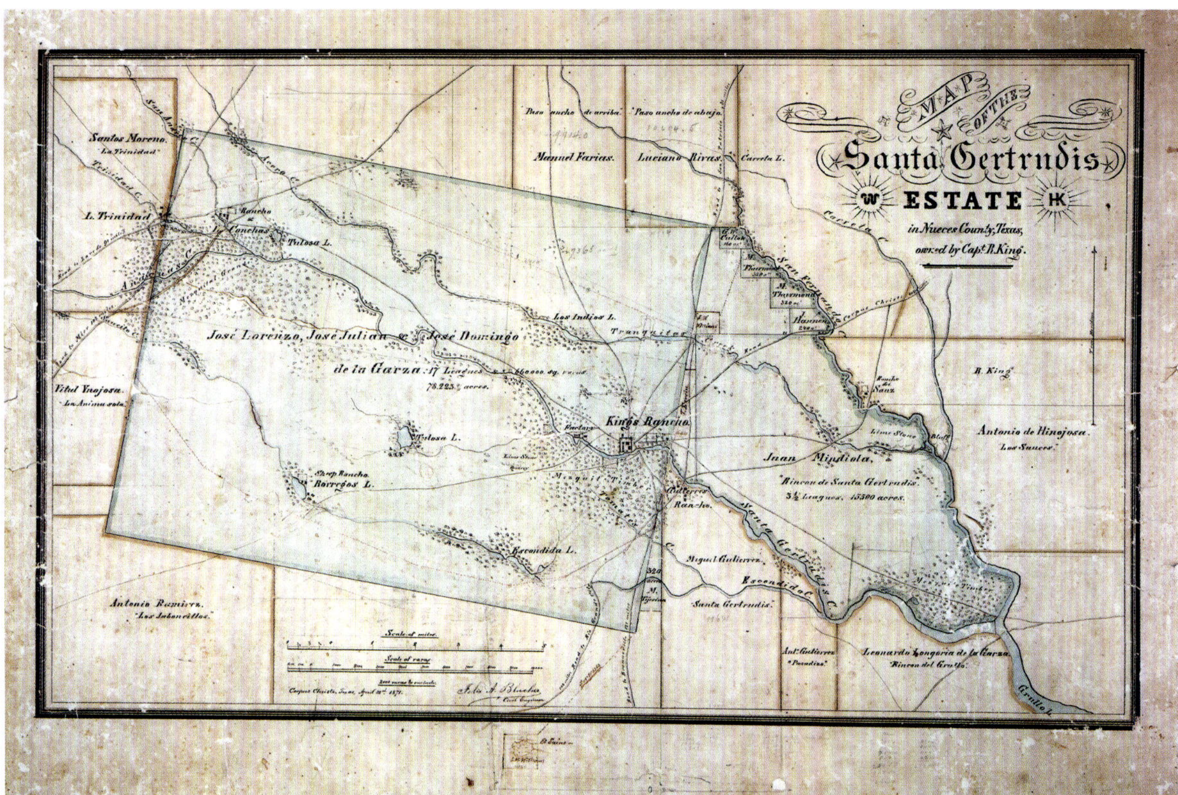


Felix von Blucher Map of Santa Gertrudis Estate, 1871. Courtesy of King Ranch, Inc.

of Rancho de Santa Gertrudis and its improvements on the gentle rise above the seep springs of the Santa Gertrudis Creek.

The division of livestock between King and Kenedy was an occasion for the introduction of a new symbol of the Captain's independent ownership of Rancho de Santa Gertrudis. King chose to mark his cattle with a new brand known as the Running W—a simple design that would come to represent the family's commitment to the land. The Running W was first registered by Captain King in 1869, although it had been in use on the rancho before any legal formality. It was only a matter of time before the Running W became a respected symbol, known from the southern border of Texas to the distant stockyard cities of the north. The origin and meaning of the Running W remain unknown to this day.

Now on his own, Captain King escalated his entrepreneurial efforts at a phenomenal pace. The Captain was intent on doing business his way, and he looked to the future strategically. An important part of his strategic plan was to control his boundaries and herds. Mifflin Kenedy was the first to fence in South Texas on his Laureles property, but King followed right behind and fenced his Santa Gertrudis land grant. The wild long-horned-type cattle, most descended from herds brought to the New World by early Spanish explorers, overpopulated the rancho and interfered with the Captain's plan and upgrading program. In 1869, King began to gather and drive the long-horned cattle to northern markets in Louisiana, Kansas, Missouri, and Illinois. Between 1869 and 1884, King shipped more than 100,000 head of cattle north. Vertically integrated, he maintained large herds of cattle, horses, mules, hogs, sheep, and goats.

King also continued to operate hide and tallow plants to offset downturns in the northern markets. He further diversified his business holdings both in Brownsville and Corpus Christi. During the 1870s, King owned and operated ice plants in both cities, maintained warehouses in Brownsville, and was the owner of the *Corpus Christi Free Press*. King and Kenedy were the primary underwriters of the Corpus Christi, San Diego & Rio Grande Narrow Gauge Railroad, the first rail service of its kind in South Texas. King also invested profits from his cattle drives in International Railroad stock, which later became the International and Great Northern—the first railroad to transport cattle from South Texas to the northern markets. Not satisfied with regional overland transportation, King opened a stage line between Corpus Christi and Brownsville. He spearheaded the Corpus Christi Navigation Company, whose efforts dredged a channel deep and wide enough to make the Corpus port available to larger seafaring commerce. When the new port needed a wharf for cattle, wool, and other goods, King raised the funds to build what was required. The Captain's entrepreneurial initiatives and business investments paved the way for commerce and communities in South Texas.

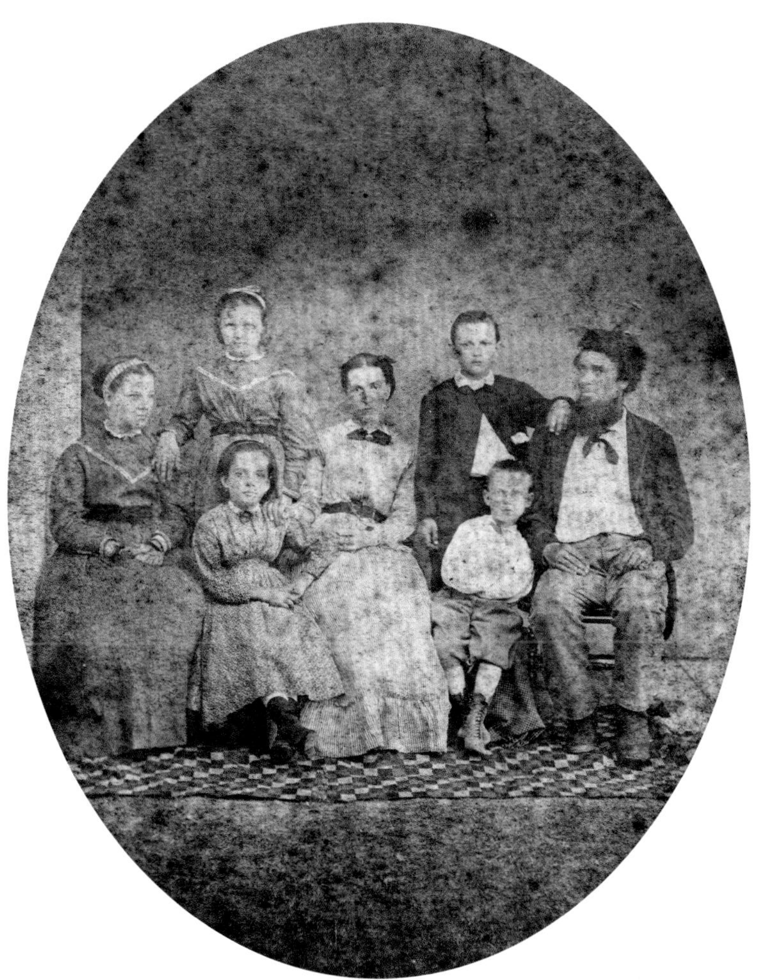

King Family Portrait, 1869. Courtesy of King Ranch, Inc.

Despite his entrepreneurial advances, the 1870s were turbulent times for King's Rancho de Santa Gertrudis. Cattle thieves and border marauders created desperate conditions for livestock operations in South Texas. The lack of adequate law enforcement on the frontier produced uncontrolled banditry and brought the region to a virtual standstill. Santa Gertrudis became an armed camp, as King was determined not to allow the desperadoes to control his travel or trade and continued to conduct business. He referred to his rancho as "the big contentious place," but he and his family remained secure and protected by the brave and loyal Kineños.

As Captain King expanded his business and ranching footprint across South Texas, Henrietta King nurtured and raised the five King children. Totally committed to her Captain and her children, she devoted herself to the development of Santa Gertrudis as a home for her family and los Kineños, as well as a "seat of hospitality" to travelers. Mrs. King's devotion, driven by her deep faith and moral values, brought structure to the Santa Gertrudis community. Under her direction, a small school was built on the rancho, and her love and personal commitment for los Kineños brought great stability to their daily lives. Henrietta King embodied cultural propriety, and her character laid the foundation of the King Ranch Family heritage and community.

Captain King doted on his children and never missed an opportunity to spoil them with material tokens of his love and affection. Likewise, Henrietta's love for her children abounded, and her generous nature and Christian values impacted the children's upbringing. Mrs. King had received the best education available to young women of her time and was intent on providing no less for her children. The Kings found the best Christian and academic source of formal education at Centre College for their boys and Henderson Female Institute for the King sisters, both institutions in Danville, Kentucky. Alice and Lee King later attended schools in St. Louis. Captain King had made horse-buying trips to Kentucky and done considerable business in St. Louis during his cattle-driving days, so both areas were familiar to and comfortable for the family. Life in the north had made Nettie and Ella quite partial to the cosmopolitan lifestyle, but Richard, Lee, and Alice Gertrudis longed for the rancho, and while Richard graduated before returning home, Lee and Alice were never content with the city schools and longed for home and ranch life on Santa Gertrudis.

Business developments, dislocation of family, and constant threats of violence in the region never abated King's expansion of his ranching territory. True to his credo to "buy land and never sell," King continued to move his fences to accommodate his growing boundaries. Part of that expansion included purchases in the San Juan de Carricitos land grant, some sixty miles south of the Santa Gertrudis Rancho. Located in the deep sands and oak mottes of the Wild Horse Desert, the impact of King's first ride across this area and its stirrup high grass must have still been in his memory. Obtaining clear title to Spanish and Mexican land grants was a difficult process, and to ensure that all was legal and proper, King retained the best legal counsel. His primary source of representation was Stephen Powers—lawyer, diplomat, judge, and friend. Powers, a veteran of

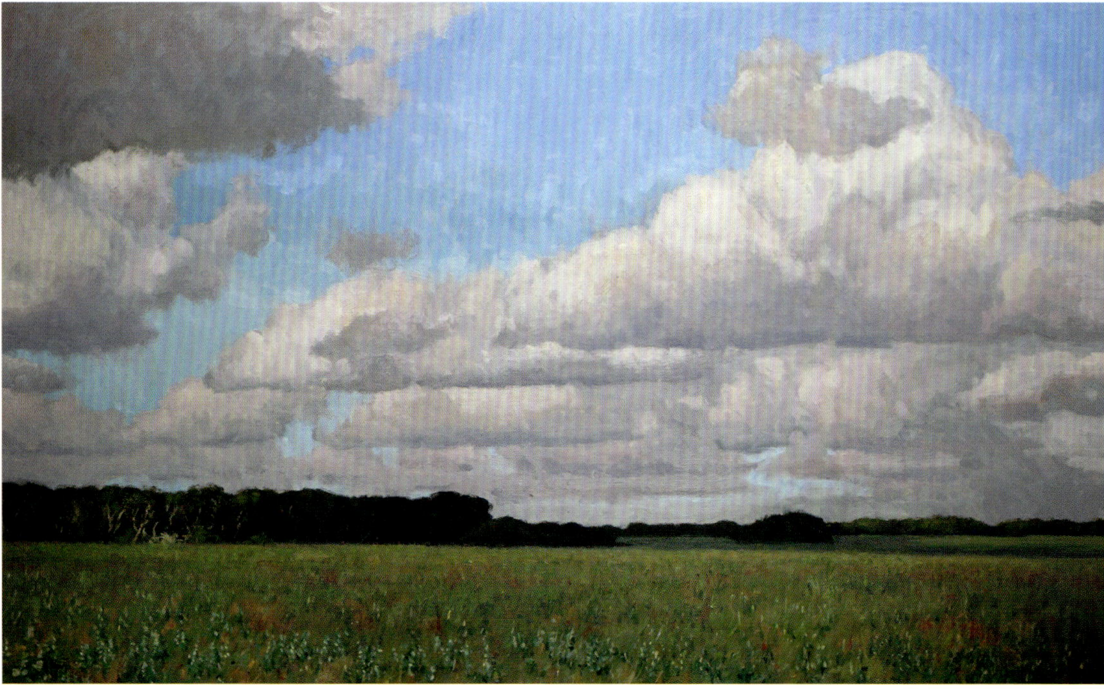

Noe Perez, *Coastal Plains (Norias)*, 2019. Courtesy of the artist.

the Mexican War, began his law practice in Brownsville in 1849. Along with Captain King, Powers did more than any other person to shape South Texas in the nineteenth century. After Powers's death, the mantel of legal authority was passed to James B. Wells, who continued to advise and assist Captain King with all matters concerning his interests. King trusted Powers and Wells above all others, and the formative impact they had on King Ranch was only equaled by los Kineños.

The close of the 1870s and early 1880s were times of great joy and devastating sadness alike. Richard King II had graduated college and was back home on the rancho. Nettie and Ella were married and living the cosmopolitan life they preferred in St. Louis. Lee King, between schools, was on the rancho, and Alice, home from school, became her father's companion and caretaker while Mrs. King was away in St. Louis, tending to the needs of the extended family. Also on the rancho was Mrs. King's half brother, Peter Bland Chamberlain, who had lived with the Kings and had worked for the Captain since he was twelve. Separation was the new normal for the King family, making reunions—whether at Santa Gertrudis or in St. Louis—times of great jubilation.

In 1881, a legal disappointment brought about a fateful meeting that would change the course and direction of Rancho de Santa Gertrudis and the King family. Captains King and Kenedy had filed a lawsuit concerning a disputed easement between their Santa Gertrudis and Laureles ranchos. A young lawyer representing their adversary in the case had skillfully defended his client and won the day over the powerful plaintiffs. That evening, following the judgment, Captain King visited the young lawyer, Robert Justus Kleberg, and offered him a retainer to join as one of his lawyers beginning immediately. King also extended an invitation for Kleberg to visit his rancho.

Robert Kleberg was the son of prominent German immigrants to Texas. His parents, Robert and Rosalie von Röeder Kleberg, came to Texas in 1835 and were patriots in the fight for Texas independence. Rosalie was a descendent of minor Prussian royalty, and Robert held a degree of Doctor Juris from a German institution. The Klebergs were held in high public esteem as influential citizens during the state's early years. Most likely, Captain King was already familiar or acquainted with the Kleberg family and their reputation when he employed young Robert.

Robert Kleberg arrived at Santa Gertrudis in the early morning. Summoned by the Captain, Alice Gertrudis served the guest coffee and cakes. In later years, she related how she thought her father's guest very handsome and went so far as to say it was "love at first sight." Simply stated, this informal meeting of Robert Kleberg and Alice Gertrudis King marked the beginning of a new era and a monumental shift in the destiny of Rancho de Santa Gertrudis.

In 1882, a sequence of deaths occurred that would consume Captain and Mrs. King with overwhelming sadness. On February 7, their lawyer and counselor Stephen Powers died. King wrote to Mifflin Kenedy concerning the death of their dear friend: "There is not a man in this State, less yourself, [who] misses him more than myself." A second tragedy struck Captain King while he was away from the ranch. Shortly after Powers's passing, the Captain was alerted that Bland Chamberlain was suffering an unknown illness and was near death. King returned to the rancho and, with only minutes to spare, asked, "Do you know who this is?" Bland answered, "Yes" and then passed away. Early in 1883, a final blow fell on Captain King's heart with the death of his youngest son. Lee, while in St. Louis at business school, was stricken with pneumonia. The tragic and premature death of Lee had a shattering effect on the

King family. Mrs. King, so distraught with sorrow, fell ill and remained in St. Louis for months. Alice Gertrudis stayed with her father at Santa Gertrudis, doing her best to console the Captain as he mourned the loss of young Lee, who had held so much promise.

Overwhelmed and depressed, Captain King began to question his direction of the rancho going forward. In letters to Mrs. King, he wrote of being tired of the business and complained that he had made a mess of everything. Tempted by the influx of foreign investors buying western ranch lands, King pursued buyers for his rancho. Upon visiting Santa Gertrudis, perspective investors soon realized that the vast acreage and large herds were beyond their expectations and means. Mrs. King's good health eventually returned and abundant summer rains brought new life to the Santa Gertrudis, leading Captain King to dismiss his notion to sell the rancho. He returned to his work, with the promise of better days ahead.

Happiness returned with the marriage of Richard King II to Pearl Ashbrook. Captain and Mrs. King gifted Richard and Pearl King the beautiful Rancho Puerta de Agua Dulce, building them a new home on the land.

Now only one of the King children remained at the Santa Gertrudis home with her parents. Alice, whom the Captain called his "little pet," faithfully remained to support the family and, more importantly, was the surrogate mistress of Santa Gertrudis in her mother's absence.

The challenges of falling cattle prices and rising debt from King's insatiable appetite to buy land loomed over the rancho. The railroad and divided lands on the cattle routes were putting an end to the long drives north. During these trying times, Captain King had come to depend on the good counsel of his new retainer, Robert Kleberg, for more than just legal advice. Kleberg understood the complexities of King's operations and was spending more time dealing with his complicated affairs. Additionally, Robert and Alice's love and affection for each other had grown since their first meeting, and his trips to Santa Gertrudis came more frequently. By 1884, Kleberg was devoting all of his energies to assisting Captain King.

Victorian courtships were tediously slow and required much formality in the process to reach the point of matrimony. There is no question of Robert Kleberg's intentions nor the fondness the King family had for Alice's young suitor, but the Captain was hesitant to offer his final approval. Since the death of Lee, the Captain's health had begun to fail, and his reliance and dependency on Alice's loving care was evermore required. The betrothal would wait until a more appropriate time.

By 1884, the effects of an unknown illness were having an obvious influence on the appearance and demeanor of Captain King. Even with his failing health, King was determined to execute the requirements of his business at a normal pace. He refused to abate his activities, despite his condition. The new year of 1885 found him mortally ill. He had taken his final business trip and was home at Santa Gertrudis in the care of Mrs. King and Alice. In pain and feeling weak, he finally acquiesced to the pleadings of his family and traveled to San Antonio for intensive care. Before his departure, he instructed his lawyer James B. Wells to keep buying land in the San Juan de Carricitos and, with the same determination he had exhibited throughout his life, gave his final order: "Tell him not to let a foot of dear old Santa Gertrudis get away from us." The loyal Kineños loaded their Patrón on the carriage and said a final adios to El Capitán.

In San Antonio at the Menger Hotel, Captain King was in the primary care of Dr. Ferdinand Herff, consulting with a specialist who had traveled from New

Orleans at the request of Mifflin Kenedy to assist with diagnosis and treatment. All agreed that Captain King's illness was caused by cancer of the stomach that had reached the terminal stage.

All the King children—except Nettie, whose husband was ill—gathered at the Menger. Robert Kleberg rushed to San Antonio, leaving the affairs of the family business in Brownsville. Mifflin Kenedy, still in mourning over the death of his wife, joined the family at the Captain's bedside. So many had benefitted from Captain King's accomplishments, and many of those fortunate benefactors came to bid him farewell. On April 14, 1885, Capt. Richard King drew his final breath.

The Captain's last will and testament, his final wishes, were clear. To his dear Henrietta, he bequeathed his entire estate. The fortunes of his labors, the total management of his immense empire were hers with only a simple stipulation: the rancho was "to be by her used and disposed of precisely the same as I might do were I living." King's life's work came down to this—total trust and devotion for the woman who gave him so much in life and dedicated herself to Santa Gertrudis, the land they loved.

Upon the family's return to Santa Gertrudis, Henrietta King appointed Robert Kleberg as her ranch manager. This was an easy decision and one that would have been endorsed by Captain King before his death. This was the beginning of a new era for Rancho de Santa Gertrudis, now with a new moniker, King's Rancho, a memorial to its founder. Robert Kleberg immediately set out to consolidate and transfer the financial obligations of Captain King to Mrs. King and developed a systematic plan to pay off all their debts. This would take time, but Kleberg was up for the challenge.

In 1886, following an appropriate period of mourning, the marriage of Robert Kleberg and Alice King was held at the Santa Gertrudis home. Following the wedding and accompanied by Henrietta King, Robert and Alice Kleberg left the ranch for a honeymoon. Following the trip, Robert and Alice moved into Mrs. King's home on Santa Gertrudis.

The year before the wedding, Robert Kleberg had spent his time familiarizing himself with the operations of the ranch, gaining the trust and loyalty of los Kineños. His hard work and dedication were inspiring to all around him. Kleberg's personality was very different from Captain King's, but he was no less passionate about the rancho. His character was best described by Holland McCombs, a researcher for Tom Lea and his book *The King Ranch*: "Kleberg displayed strong traits of his character. Prussian mettle, with its scientific bent, its passion for orderly method, appears not to be too heavily encumbered with opinionated didacticism. This quality blended with a naturally sanguine temperament and a noticeable streak of sentimentality toward all things dear to him, gave warmth to his personality and made him effective—in spite of his actual inexperience."

Robert Kleberg began to make his mark, developing his own plan for a new and different King's Rancho, but never losing sight of the foundation laid by Captain King and always after the acceptance and approval of Mrs. King. While los Kineños continued to be the backbone of King's Rancho, Kleberg also brought in experienced and trusted subordinates to help manage the massive operation. He bought additional lands for Mrs. King and, within ten years, had settled all debts inherited in the estate. Like Captain King, Kleberg was motivated and inspired by the beauty and bounty of the Wild Horse Desert.

Robert excelled at his duties as ranch manager, assuming significant leadership roles throughout the region. Robert's pragmatic principles were practiced in business as well as civic activities, and these qualities earned him great respect among his peers.

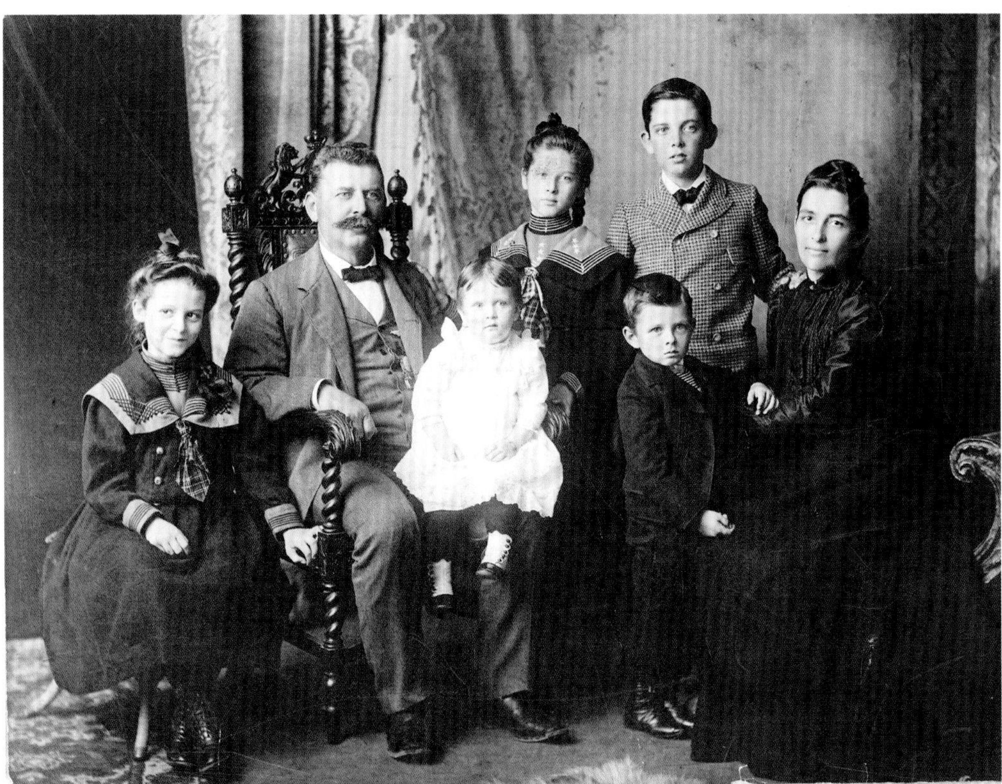

Kleberg Family Portrait, 1900. Courtesy of King Ranch, Inc.

Alice and Robert raised their five children at Santa Gertrudis, and the old house abounded in familial love and happiness. The Kleberg children were raised in the ways of the ranch and taught the customs, culture, and history of the place by los Kineños. Mrs. King built a home in Corpus Christi, where the grandchildren could receive a formal academic education. From these two classrooms—the pastures of King's Rancho and a Corpus Christi schoolhouse—the Kleberg children gained a well-rounded knowledge of the world around them and a love for the land—a heritage to which they would become stewards.

Mrs. King and Alice maintained the "seat of hospitality" at Santa Gertrudis, welcoming and hosting business associates and extended family. The Kleberg children learned the customs of cordiality, which was such an important part of the historic rancho. For the Kleberg children, life on Santa Gertrudis was filled with happiness, whether working alongside the grown-ups at the cow camps or playing with Kineño children at the rancho headquarters. These were formative years, during which they strengthened their bonds with the family and the land.

The beginning of the twentieth century was filled with growth and prosperity on King's Rancho. Mrs. King continued to buy land and broaden the rancho's footprint across South Texas. In 1901, Henrietta King bought 60,000 acres, including the land grants Las Comitas, El Infernillo, and El Chiltipín that had once belonged to Captain Mifflin Kenedy. Finally, in 1906, the 110,000-acre Rincón de Los Laureles was purchased from the Texas Land & Cattle Company. Now King's Rancho encompassed 1,000,000 acres of diverse ranch lands. These were years of great innovation, highlighted primarily with the development of equipment and methods for tapping the rich artesian waters under the dry surface of South Texas. With this discovery, Robert Kleberg began to envision new commercial possibilities for King's Rancho.

Like Captain King, Kleberg realized that transportation was key to the development and colonization of the vast open country between Corpus Christi and Brownsville. Now with sustainable water sources across the region, the time was right to pick up the mantle and move forward with plans for a railroad through the Wild Horse Desert. There was plenty of local and regional support for building a railroad, but companies like Southern Pacific were unenthusiastic about investing in such uncharted territory. With the help of Uriah Lott, Captain King's and Kenedy's old friend and railroad promoter, and with financial backing from landowners across the area, the St. Louis, Brownsville & Mexico Railway became a reality. This was the beginning of the fulfillment of Henrietta King's dream of organized communities across the Wild Horse Desert, and Robert Kleberg, the colonizer, was ready to make her dream a reality.

Donations of rights-of-way through the large ranches in the path of the railroad were obtained, with Mrs. King making the largest commitment of half interest in 75,000 acres through King's Rancho. With land and monies dedicated to the cause, construction commenced in 1903, and the developers and town builders were well ahead of the iron road. Robert Kleberg organized the Kleberg Town and Improvement Company, with title to lands owned by Mrs. King along the route. By July 4, 1904, the first excursion train reached the newly formed town of Kingsville, named in honor of Captain King, and the first incorporated community within the boundaries of King's Rancho now began to take shape. Soon the railroad reached the Rio Grande Valley, and an unprecedented boom of farming and community development spread across the fertile lands of southernmost Texas.

This era of prosperity for King's Rancho and South Texas gave rise to extraordinary generosity by Henrietta King, the philanthropist. Beyond her donation of land and resources for the general development of the region, Mrs. King gave to specific causes with far-reaching beneficial consequences. Her benevolence included gifts of land and capital for the development of churches, schools, universities, hospitals, and businesses within the broad area of her influence. She had no selfish intent or expectation of personal benefit from her philanthropy. Her missionary spirit and dedication to a Christian duty of giving was a fundamental part of her life. Her generosity had a tremendous impact on the developing towns and cities of South Texas. The Kleberg children witnessed these aspects of Henrietta King's generous character and inherited her selfless spirit. This spirit of generosity has continued throughout each successive generation of the King Ranch Family.

On January 4, 1912, a devastating fire destroyed Mrs. King's Santa Gertrudis home. Beyond a few small items and business records removed from the home's office, the house and its contents were a total loss. It is hard to imagine the tremendous loss of historical treasures and personal items devoured by flames. More than fifty years' worth of memories were gone in a matter of hours. Mrs. King, unfazed and grateful that no lives were lost, simply commented, "We can build a new house." Within days, Robert Kleberg began the process of reconstruction. He described his intention to build a home that would be a "monument to Mrs. King's hospitality." Within three years, the new house on Santa Gertrudis was completed—its distinctive design the creation of young architects Carl and Carlton Adams, with exquisite exterior and interior details by Tiffany Studios of New York. The unique beauty was indeed a tribute to La Patrona and her family, who still call it home today. It soon came to be known as the "Main House," a title that has endured for generations.

The Main House was christened with many joyous occasions, starting with the marriage of two Kleberg daughters, Henrietta and Alice, in 1915. Henrietta Rosa married John Larkin of New York and soon moved to a new home far away from Santa Gertrudis. Alice Kleberg married rancher Tom East and moved south to the San Antonio Viejo Ranch. Meanwhile, eldest son Richard (Dick) Mifflin Kleberg had graduated college, was married, and was living with his wife, Mamie, on the Laureles Division of King's Rancho. Robert (Bob) Justus Kleberg Jr. was enrolled at the University of Wisconsin, leaving only little Sarah Spohn Kleberg at home on the ranch.

Amid the familial growth, a catastrophic change was on the horizon that would alter the course for King's Rancho and its extended family. By 1916, Robert Kleberg Sr. was suffering the effects of palsy, which impeded his activities and restricted his excursions on the land. Bob Kleberg came home from college in 1918 to work with his brother Dick and fill the void caused by their father's illness. With the assistance and guidance of their cousin Caesar Kleberg, who managed the southern divisions of King's Rancho, a gradual transition was taking place, and Bob Kleberg was taking over the active management of ranch activities. Bob's management style was a combination of Captain King's energetic pragmatism and Robert Kleberg's scientific bent. He was tireless in his efforts and totally dedicated to the land. Bob was naturally equipped to reinvent a modern King Ranch.

With the future of dear old Santa Gertrudis in mind, Henrietta King set in motion a process that might guarantee the rancho's future. All of the King children had passed on, with the exception of her devoted daughter, Alice Gertrudis Kleberg. In October 1918, Henrietta King gifted the Santa Gertrudis Headquarters to Alice. A separate gift of valuable farmland was given to the Kleberg children, with Bob Kleberg acting as trustee for this disposition. Bob's benevolent influence and guidance, as trustee for his siblings, continued to increase the footprint of King's Rancho. In 1924, both the Stillman property and Ed Lasater's Encino Ranch were purchased and added to the rancho's holdings. These properties were leased to Mrs. King from the Kleberg Trust and came under the management of King's Rancho. In these final years of Mrs. King's life, she was surely satisfied to see the destiny of her rancho in such capable hands.

On March 31, 1925, Henrietta King, the matriarch of King's Rancho, passed away in her home on the gentle rise above the seep springs of the Santa Gertrudis. Her life, dedicated to faith and family for more than ninety years, had reached its end. Henrietta King had amassed an enormous fortune, but her life's worth continues to be measured more by her Christian ethic, rather than material wealth.

Henrietta King's last will and testament called for a ten-year trusteeship prior to the partition of her estate. This progressive act of estate planning helped ensure the perpetuation of her beloved rancho. The trusteeship also allowed Bob Kleberg, as general manager of the ranch, to continue his efforts to produce cattle and horses better suited for the South Texas environs. Another obstacle that affected the future of King's Rancho was the oppressive state and federal estate taxes levied on Mrs. King's estate. Bob and Caesar Kleberg dedicated six months each in Washington, DC, accumulating evidence and negotiating fair values of the estate. Eventually, an amount was agreed upon, and before the end of the estate trusteeship, a means to pay the taxes was found by leasing Mrs. King's ranch lands to Humble Oil and Refining Company of Houston.

The death of Robert Kleberg Sr., Mrs. King's ranch manager, came in 1932. His efforts on behalf of Mrs. King were immeasurable, and his loyalty was unquestioned. Mr. Kleberg guided King's Rancho through the most difficult times with exceptional grace and humility. His scientific and methodical approach to ranching marked his management style from the very beginning. Robert Kleberg was a progressive visionary whose efforts helped secure King's Rancho for generations to come.

Even before his death, Robert Kleberg began a process to develop a plan to keep the ranch together, following the partition of Mrs. King's estate. He negotiated with the heirs outside the Kleberg family to purchase their interests and laid the groundwork for a new ranching structure. In 1934, Alice Kleberg organized a family corporation under the name King Ranch and transferred her ownership share of Mrs. King's estate into the entity. The shares of the new King Ranch were owned equally by the five Kleberg children: Dick, Henrietta, Alice, Bob, and Sarah, with Bob and Dick appointed as trustees for themselves and their three sisters. The establishment of King Ranch, Inc., would ensure the retention and conservancy of their dear Santa Gertrudis.

The way forward was rocky for King Ranch, but the Klebergs persevered. Partition of Mrs. King's estate was made to Alice, her only surviving child, and to Mrs. King's grandchildren. The transition was relatively smooth, with some electing to sell interests to the Kleberg family and others receiving land and establishing independent ranching operations. In the end, ranching operations and boundaries were not radically changed, and there was little disruption of daily routines on the four Kleberg-owned divisions of King Ranch: Santa Gertrudis, Laureles, Norias, and Encino.

The ranch continued to operate with its new identity as a family corporation. Factors such as complex business issues, a demanding environment, and internal as well as external challenges were business as usual for King Ranch. These difficulties were confronted through a combination of diversification, innovation, and improvement—learned, standard operating proce-

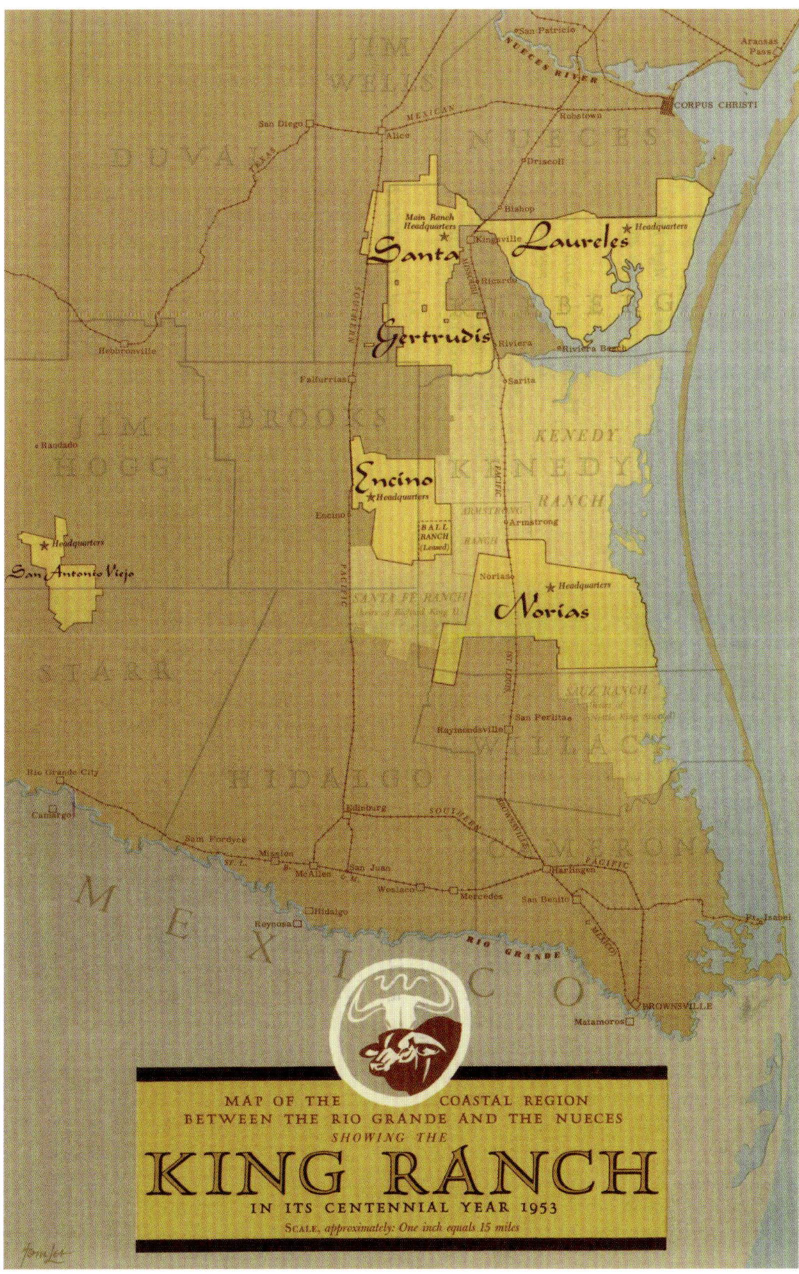


King Ranch Divisions, 1953. Courtesy of King Ranch, Inc.

dure for the King/Kleberg family. Always advancing, never retreating, the third generation moved King Ranch forward, guided by the same sense of duty bestowed on Henrietta King by the Captain to manage the rancho "the same as I myself might do were I living."

For more than fifty years, Bob Kleberg navigated King Ranch into the future, advancing a tradition of invention and stewardship. His energetic and creative mind developed the structure for a modern King Ranch and paved the way for successors who have improved the products and procedures of the past. The history of King Ranch is as much about its future as it is about its past, and the story of its progressive successors moving the contemporary ranch forward has yet to be told.

New challenges have produced a productive partnership between the King Ranch Family and the people of King Ranch. These people, its employees, include generational Kineños and modern visionaries, all loyal to the progressive philosophies of their predecessors. This historic partnership continues to honor and sustain the legacy of King Ranch.

Inspired by the King Ranch Family and their generational commitment to stewardship of their land, this book documents the historic home ranches using both art and the written word. The works of art within these pages are the product of Noe Perez, a native son of the Wild Horse Desert. His passion for the region and the significance of its natural beauty is epitomized with every brushstroke on each canvas. The subject of each painting embodies the splendor of the historic King's Rancho and its distinctive habitat. This book honors the land, the culture, and the heritage of a family bound by a promise to "not let a foot of dear old Santa Gertrudis get away from us."

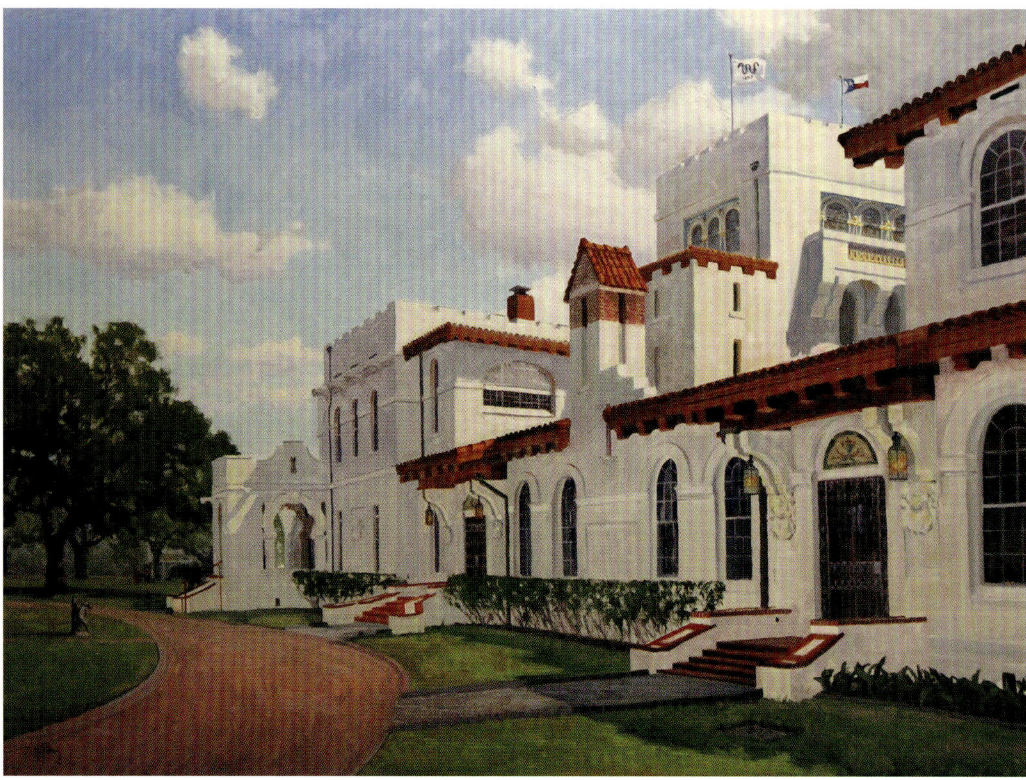

Noe Perez, *King Ranch Main House 2015*. Collection of King Ranch, Inc. Courtesy of the artist.

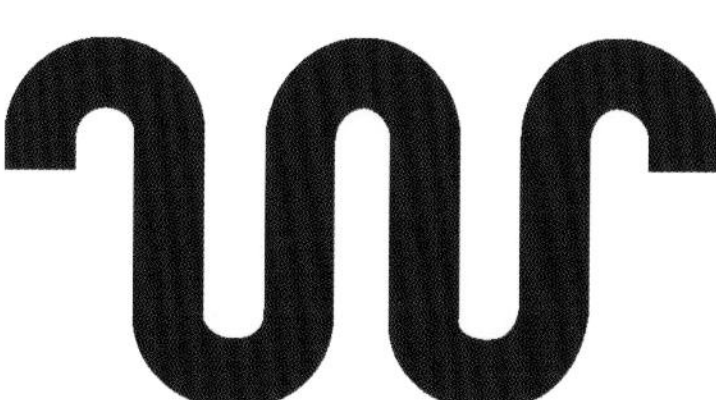

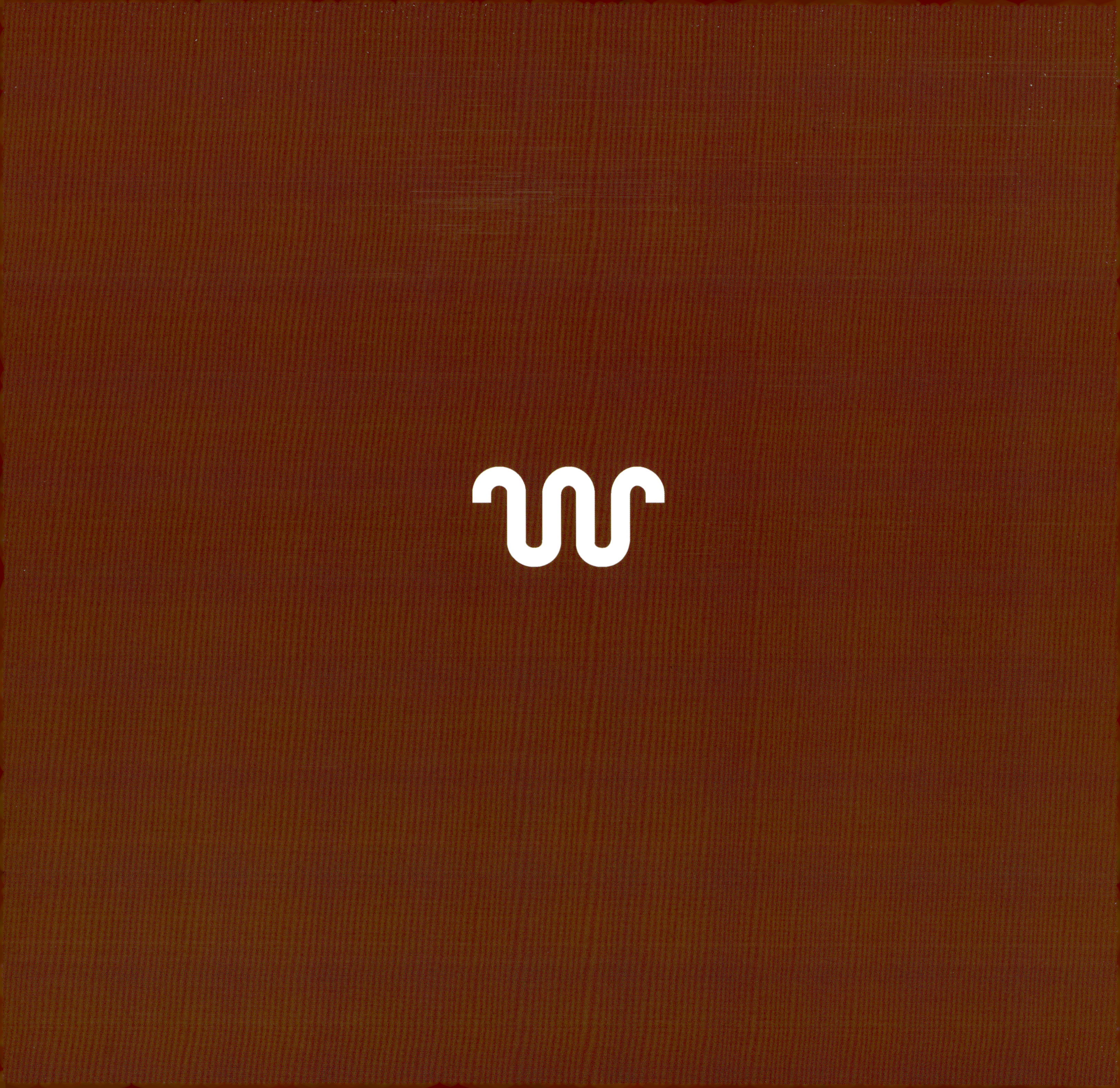

# A Vision

## *From Ranch House to Empire*


### Bruce M. Shackelford


A successful rancher is a judge. The rancher judges which bulls and mother cows to keep, which yearlings to sell, when the grass is too short or too long, when supplies are running low, and who works on the ranch and what they do. Ventures are often made and lost from these decisions, affecting the employees of the ranch as well as the livestock. The future of the entire ranch is based on the successes of the rancher's judgments, and the family lives on the timing of the land, not a clock. The environment and the creatures therein dictate the schedules of the people living off the land. Weather and its effects can determine the time for a roundup or a break from work. A stretch of dry weather can change the future, as can a hurricane. All factors must be taken into account by a rancher and the ranching family.

Ranch judgment necessarily requires skill in "seeing" —seeing the physical conformation (i.e., physical advantages) of a bull or stallion and understanding their abilities, qualities, and flaws. The ranch operator sees the impact of the weather on the land, sees what land will produce and what it won't, and knows how to respond to what he sees. While successful ranchers are often risk takers, they also must develop and aspire toward a long-term vision for the success of their operation. Like an artist, the rancher's "seeing" involves close attention to detail and the ongoing application of cumulative experience toward a larger vision. These skills have been passed down through family generations at King Ranch, as has the history of pastures or the characteristics and conformation knowledge of a horse or bull that lived one hundred years ago. The

---


Bruce M. Shackelford is a historian specializing in the trans-Mississippi American west and the cattle industry. He lives in San Antonio, Texas, and has been a curator at the Witte Museum off and on since 1989. His writing includes *The Wests of Texas* (TSHA Press) and *Photography on the South Texas Frontier* (Maverick Publishing), with contributions to *Black Cowboys of Texas* (TAMU Press), *Navajo Saddle Blankets* (Museum of New Mexico Press), and other publications.

family knowledge of the land, its creatures, and the necessary work involved not only have led to the development of an incomparable ranching empire but also have helped cultivate the arts and material culture of an entire region.

As King Ranch grew and the family vision progressed over time, the ranch became known in terms of the practical craftsmanship associated with ranching. Whether via its brands, saddles, and tack, or preference for styles of boots and spurs, dress, and attire, King Ranch helped shape the "look" of the South Texas rancher.

## From Spanish Traditions

When Richard King bought South Texas land in 1853, Spanish traditions formed the basis of cattle ranching. There were Spanish cattle in Texas, and ranching was already underway east of the Rio Grande by the early 1720s. Traditional Spanish open-range cattle ranching spread throughout the Rio Grande area in what is now South Texas. Sheep and goats were also herded to a lesser extent. Some Spanish soldiers came from Queretaro in Central Mexico and brought ranching skills with them to the Spanish frontier settlements on the Rio Grande.

Cattle in northern Mexico were herded and worked from horseback by vaqueros using ropes and sometimes a lance-like tool called an *espiga.* The saddle, dress, and methods of the vaquero would come to be those of the Texas cowboy after Texas statehood in 1845 and the US-Mexican War of 1846. The most prominent addition to Spanish cattle work in Mexico was throwing ropes to catch cattle and using a saddle horn to secure the rope. Both skills probably came from the Mexican vaqueros of the late 1600s or early 1700s.

In the 1840s and 1850s, the vaqueros of South Texas on the Nueces Strip dressed and worked stock as they had since the late 1700s. Author Tom Lea located a report from US Army captain George W. Hughes describing a vaquero in 1846 when Hughes marched with Gen. John Wool to Saltillo, Mexico, from San Antonio, Texas, during the US-Mexican War:[1]

> Dressed in a pair of leather unmentionables [trousers], without suspenders, buttoning from the knee downwards, which are usually left open in warm weather for comfort, and to exhibit the white drawers underneath; a common cotton shirt, often wanting; a red sash tied tightly around the waist; a pair of sandals on his feet, and enormous iron spurs on heel; with a heavy conical felt hat (that would almost resist a sabre cut) on head, and a long pointed aspen goad in hand, and you have the perfect picture of the ranchero, or vachero [*sic*]. Mounted on a spirited pony, with a lasso at his saddle-bow, he is no mean adversary for a single man to encounter. He rides well and fearlessly, and throws the lasso with unerring aim. It is a beautiful sight to see him with his red blanket (worn as a poncho in cold weather) streaming in the wind, his head bent eagerly forward, and lasso whirling in circles high in the air, riding down on some refractory animal that he seldom fails to catch, at the first throw, by the neck or hind foot bringing him violently to the ground. . . . Every Mexican . . . is an expert with a lasso and the throwing of it may be regarded as a national amusement.[2]

Having more eighteenth-century elements than nineteenth century, the vaquero dress detailed by Captain Hughes was already an outdated style when he described it. The dress was so ingrained into the vaqueros' self-image that it was being worn in New Mexico into the 1880s. The dress on King Ranch was what worked in that area and changed as required by the job and the brush. Yet the hats, boots, long pants, and long-sleeved shirts that were the norm for vaqueros are some basic elements that have never changed.

The first supply orders made for King's Rancho were for saddles and tack for the ranch vaqueros. The tools for managing cattle were purchased before there was a ranch house.

## Making a Home on the Ranch

A home and its contents are part of a family vision, and in the case of King Ranch, that vision continues today. In the early days of the ranch, before their marriage, former steamboat entrepreneur Capt. Richard King and Henrietta Chamberlain each lived and worked in Brownsville across the Rio Grande from Matamoros. Shipping and trading were the main endeavors in the 1850s after the US-Mexican War, and much of the business was centered on supplying nearby Fort Brown and other government military operations in Texas. Sailing ships and steamships arrived regularly, carrying both travelers and goods to Brownsville and Matamoros.[3]

Fine, well-furnished houses stood on both sides of the river and hosted both American and Mexican visitors. Madame Farnaber, a widow, lived in a large well-furnished house in Matamoros and entertained wives and friends of officers from Fort Brown, as well as school teachers, ministers, priests, and other members of local society.[4] As the daughter of the local Presbyterian minister, Henrietta Chamberlain likely attended Madame Farnaber's teas and had been a guest in at least a few of these fine homes.

When King and his partner, former Texas Ranger Gideon K. "Legs" Lewis, bought the 15,500-acre Rincón de Santa Gertrudis, the first substantial ranch building constructed was the Commissary. Constructed in a Spanish colonial style, much of the building still stands today near the King Ranch Main House. The Commissary building had a lookout tower that was later echoed in the architecture of the present-day Main House.

Richard King and Henrietta Chamberlain married in 1854 and traveled to the remote ranch on their honeymoon. Their first home on Santa Gertrudis Creek was a Mexican-style log cabin, a *jacal*. Victor Rodríguez Alvarado, a King Ranch vaquero, said, "In order to build his first houses, King went to Bobedo Ranch and got my grandfather, Francisco Alvarado, to build houses or jacals. . . . They made the first houses of wood and dirt with thatched roofs."[5]

Jacals were made by creating walls from long posts stuck into the ground and plastering interwoven sticks with adobe mud to seal them from the weather. The walls were then plastered over, inside and out. The floors of pounded earth were made hard and shined by repeated wetting and sweeping until they had the appearance of polished stone. Tanned deer and buffalo hides were sometimes used for floor coverings. The Kings' jacal stood by the Commissary, their first home so meager that cooking and serving utensils were hung on the outside wall.[6]

Richard King ran the ranch, and Henrietta Chamberlain King ran the family and the home. Caring for a family was not new to Henrietta. Her mother died in 1835 when she was three years old. Her father, Presbyterian minister Hiram Chamberlain, had twelve children by two more marriages, and as the eldest, Henrietta often cared for her younger siblings.[7] She possessed organizational skills and excelled at dealing with family difficulties. Like Saint Gertrude the Great, the namesake of the ranch she had come to call home, Henrietta was steadfast in her own deep religious beliefs.[8] She was also used to a life of self-denial as part of her Presbyterian upbringing.[9]

From the modest jacal, the legacy of permanent homes on King Ranch begins with the "original" house built sometime between 1857 and 1858. The one-story frame house included a half-story dormer in the top attic space and was set on the hill above Santa Gertrudis Creek. At the start of the Civil War in 1861, the King family lived in this frame house close to the Commissary, which served as a place of refuge from bandit raids and attacks from Plains Indian tribes.[10]

In April 1863, a British military visitor wrote that the "ranch is comfortable, [with] well-furnished wooden buildings."[11] What hung on the inside walls of these wooden buildings, if anything, is not known. Henrietta Chamberlain was from an educated family and had traveled to areas outside of Texas, but her family was her top priority, with employees as a close second. What décor she had was probably essential for her family and their basic comfort—not any display of pretension or ostentatiousness.

During the third year of the Civil War, the US government placed a bounty on Captain King for his service to the Confederacy, transporting Southern cotton down the Rio Grande to ships bound for European textile mills. The Santa Gertrudis Ranch became a cotton depot for Confederate cotton. When Union Army troops came to King's Rancho to arrest the Captain on the morning of December 23, 1863, King was away from Santa Gertrudis, retrieving stolen cattle south of the ranch. Henrietta and the children were in the house with employees when the Union Army began firing on them, killing unarmed vaquero Francisco Alvarado in the doorway of the house.[12] The soldiers then ransacked and plundered the home, destroying the furnishings and other buildings around the ranch.

On Christmas morning, a pregnant Henrietta King left the house in a carriage with her children to travel to the village of San Patricio on the Nueces River, where, on February 22, 1864, she gave birth to the Kings' fifth child—a son named Robert E. Lee King. When she was able to travel, she moved to the relative safety of San Antonio for the duration of the war.

The Civil War ended in 1865, and the bounty on King was lifted by a presidential order from Andrew Johnson; the ranch soon went back into full operation.[13] By 1867, a new second story had been added to the original frame house, giving the family the opportunity to acquire furnishings and décor more in keeping with

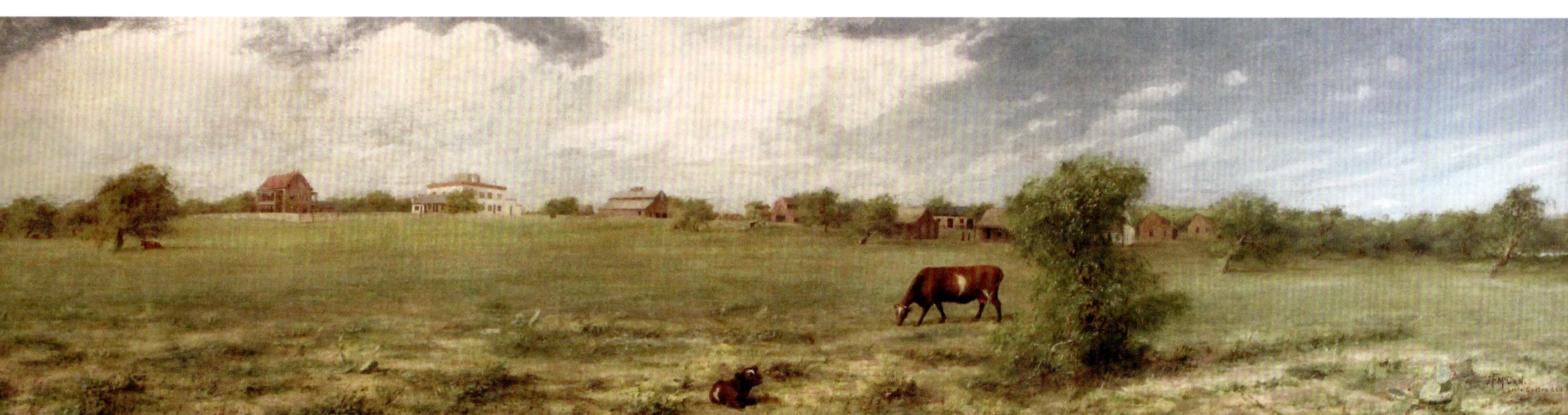

James Ferdinand McCan, *King Ranch,* 1895, oil on canvas, 18 × 64 inches. Courtesy of King Ranch, Inc. McCan was commissioned to paint this pastoral image of the Santa Gertrudis headquarters with the frame house as it appeared before the 1912 fire.

their image as the owners of a successful ranching enterprise, now with more than three hundred employees and huge herds of horses and cattle.

Preserved descriptions of the interior of the larger original house call to mind the décor and style of many fine South Texas ranch houses of today. The two-story, wood-frame home was known throughout the region. The lower entry was paneled in dark wood set with game mounts, in addition to lighting and leather furnishings of the era. Later, a second-story wing and a third story were added to accommodate the growing family and the many visitors to King Ranch. There were ten bedrooms in the rear addition to the house; half of those rooms were lived in by family members most of the time, and the rest were for guests.[14] Over the years, the King home came to be known throughout South Texas as a place of hospitality.

Captain King died in 1885, leaving Henrietta King and their family to manage the ranch. On June 17, 1886, Alice Gertrudis King married Robert J. Kleberg Sr. at the Santa Gertrudis Rancho at six in the morning.[15] Kleberg took over all of the ranching operations. Alice raised their five children, organized the home for the family and guests, and worked with her husband Robert and aging mother Henrietta. Robert drilled water wells across the million-acre ranch and made numerous improvements to both the land and the livestock. By 1900, King Ranch was ready for the new century.

## From the Ashes: A New Home for the Twentieth Century

About 4:00 a.m. in the dark of night on January 4, 1912, the King Ranch family home was set ablaze by a suspected arsonist. The Kleberg family, two guests, numerous employees, and seventy-nine-year-old widow Henrietta Chamberlain King fled from the house and watched with vaqueros and employees as it burned completely down to the ground. As the house was evacuated, Mrs. King told ranch foreman Sam Ragland, "Let nobody get hurt. We can build a new home. We can't replace a life."[16]

The place that had been the King and Kleberg family ranch home for decades was completely gone, as were all their furnishings and family heirlooms. The news of the fire spread across the country. Robert Kleberg Sr. wired famed American poet and ranch visitor Edgar A. Guest:[17]

> THEY MAY DESTROY, THEY MAY BURN THE BUILDINGS OF SANTA GERTRUDIS IF THEY WILL, BUT THE SPIRIT OF HOSPITALITY AND FRIENDSHIP WILL HANG AROUND HER STILL. HER GATES ARE OPEN WIDE AND ALL HER FRIENDS MAY ENTER AND NONE WILL BE DENIED.[18]

Within weeks, plans were underway to build a new, larger ranch house that could accommodate all of the family members, as well as the frequent visits of friends and business associates. Carleton W. Adams (1885–1964) of the San Antonio–based architectural firm Adams and Adams was retained to design the house. The new ranch house was planned completely, down to the last detail, from the interior to all the exterior spaces—patios, landscaped yards, a pool, and fountains—along with all surroundings and utilities, such as water storage. Roads and access plans to the house were updated but reflected those of the original house in some aspects. The style of the new King Ranch home was that of a Mexican hacienda with decorative details from Spain and Morocco. Unlike most ranch houses, with outside-facing windows, this magnificent structure would face a large interior courtyard, open to the sky.

Mrs. King, son-in-law Robert J. Kleberg Sr., and daughter Alice Kleberg described their requirements for the new family home. Mrs. King told the architect, "Build a house that anyone can walk in in boots."[19] She is also said to have asked that the new hacienda be fireproof. The walls of the house were to be constructed of reinforced concrete, hollow tile, and brick. Very little wood paneling or wainscots would be used in the house, to reduce the chance of fire. The floors were terra-cotta throughout, with the exception of the two formal rooms—the dining room, which had floors made of New York bluestone, and the grand salon, where teak and rosewood floors were specified.[20] Robert J. Kleberg Sr. said the house should be "a monument to Mrs. King's hospitality."[21]

As planning progressed, Carleton Adams brought in the world-renowned design firm of Tiffany Studios of New York to submit interior proposals for colors, furniture, and lighting, as well as carpets and paintings.[22] Tiffany Studios also specified all hardware—door hinges and latches and metal corner protectors over the plaster corners—and designed the heart of the home, the grand, two-story, three-section Tiffany art-glass windows in the main stairwell.[23]

Tiffany Studios was commissioned to paint a mural of Mission Concepción above the doorway from the main hall into the grand salon. James Ferdinand McCan (1868–1925) painted a landscape with deer in 1917 for the arch on the opposite side of the doorway. Tiffany Studios also designed the five outside entry doorways, including the iron gates, doors, tile, trim, and fittings.

In addition to the latest conveniences like a commercial washing machine and an elevator, Adams and Adams Architects specified some of the finishes, such as those on the bronze lighting fixtures. Tiffany Studios was also responsible for acquiring, delivering, and installing the furnishings. While some items that appear on Tiffany and King Ranch blueprints were obviously specially

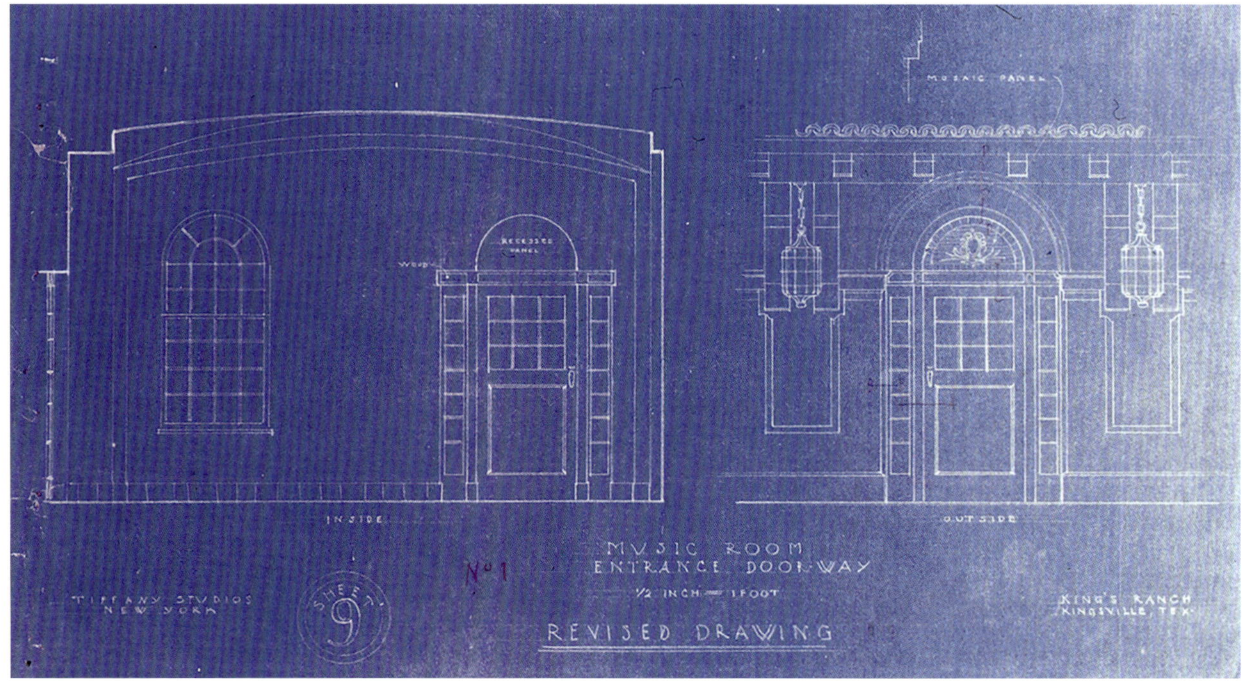


Original blueprints from Tiffany Studios show the music room exterior door as it was revised from the original design. Courtesy of King Ranch, Inc.

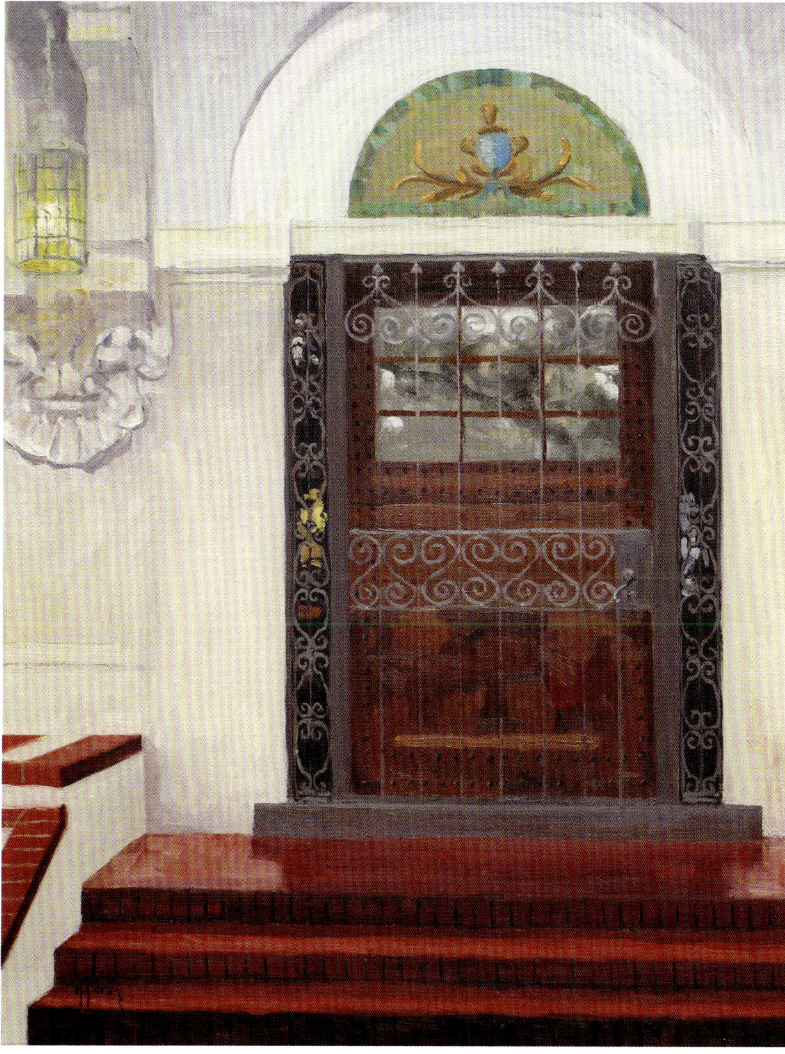

Noe Perez, *Tiffany Gate at the Main House (Santa Gertrudis)*, 2019. Courtesy of the artist. This 2019 painting of the music room exterior entrance shows little change from the blueprints from Tiffany Studios. The decorative lunette over the door is Tiffany art glass set in mortar and is clearly visible in both images.

designed and made for the project, other items (such as furniture) were produced by other manufacturers for Tiffany. Any furnishings left out of the original plans were designed and added as the project progressed, such as the twenty-six spark guards for fireplaces sent by Tiffany Studios for approval in October 1913.[24]

The furniture on the second floor was designed by Tiffany and mainly made of wicker, with larger pieces made of wood in the arts-and-crafts style of the period. The ground-floor rooms were furnished with solid wood furniture in the arts-and-crafts or "mission" style. Some furniture pieces had oak and dark-smoked finishes, like the ornate oak built-in display cabinet in the dining room, while others were lighter in color.

Large floor rugs were produced in a factory in Austria from Tiffany Studios designs. The patterns were taken from geometric Navajo tribal weaving designs and combined with the Running W ranch brand as a design motif.[25]

In early January 1915, three years after the fire demolished the old ranch house, construction was completed and the family moved into the new Main House. The gleaming, white, Spanish-style home immediately became an icon in Texas and the Southwest, and it was nationally known in architectural circles for its design and quality. The Main House is the most widely known structure on the premises, documenting the art and artistic preferences of the family and the "King Ranch style."

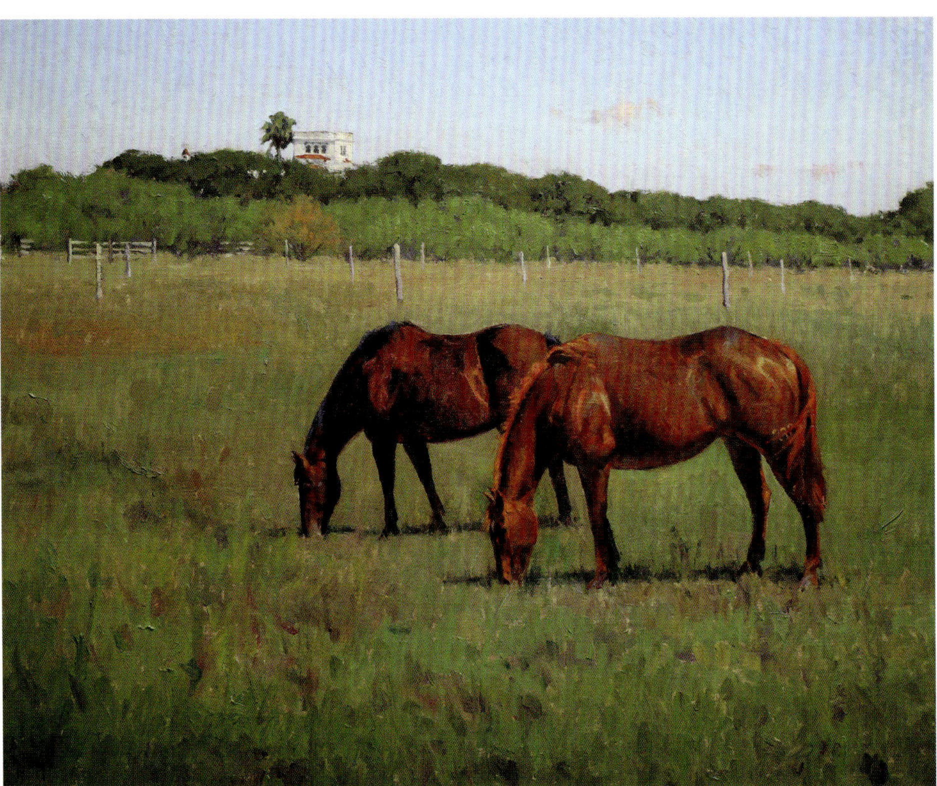

Noe Perez, *Creek Barn Trap Grazers* (*Santa Gertrudis*), 2019. Courtesy of the artist. The tower of the Main House rises above the surrounding trees like a sentinel keeping watch over King Ranch, as it has since 1915.

Henrietta Chamberlain King passed away in 1925, ten years after the new headquarters home was finished. At ninety-two years of age, South Texas mourned the passing of La Patrona, a woman known for her devotion to family, employees, friends, and the land she lived on. She was loved throughout South Texas for her kindness, hospitality, and philanthropy.[26]

## Remembering the Family: Portraits and Paintings through Time

Most of the portraits hanging in the Main House today were painted on contract by two well-known Texas portrait painters of the era, James Ferdinand McCan and Soloman Saloman (1869–1937).[27] These portrait artists created paintings for Mrs. King's home in Corpus Christi, constructed in 1893, and the paintings now hang in the Main House. One of the first portraits painted for Mrs. King was of Richard King, as done by McCan. The painting was created after Captain King's death, using a photograph for reference.

Saloman also painted from photographs, both before and after death, and his painting of Mrs. King was completed during her lifetime. In the Main House today, Saloman's portrait of Henrietta hangs above the McCan likeness of Captain King.[28]

In addition to portraits, both Saloman and McCan created other paintings for the King-Kleberg family. McCan painted a number of game paintings of quail and other birds, and Saloman copied a photograph taken at the last meeting of the Old Texian veterans group in Goliad, Texas, in 1906.[29] The Old Texians were survivors of the 1836 Battle of San Jacinto of the Texas Revolution. Saloman also painted a recreation of Robert E. Lee and Stonewall Jackson's last meeting for Mrs. King.

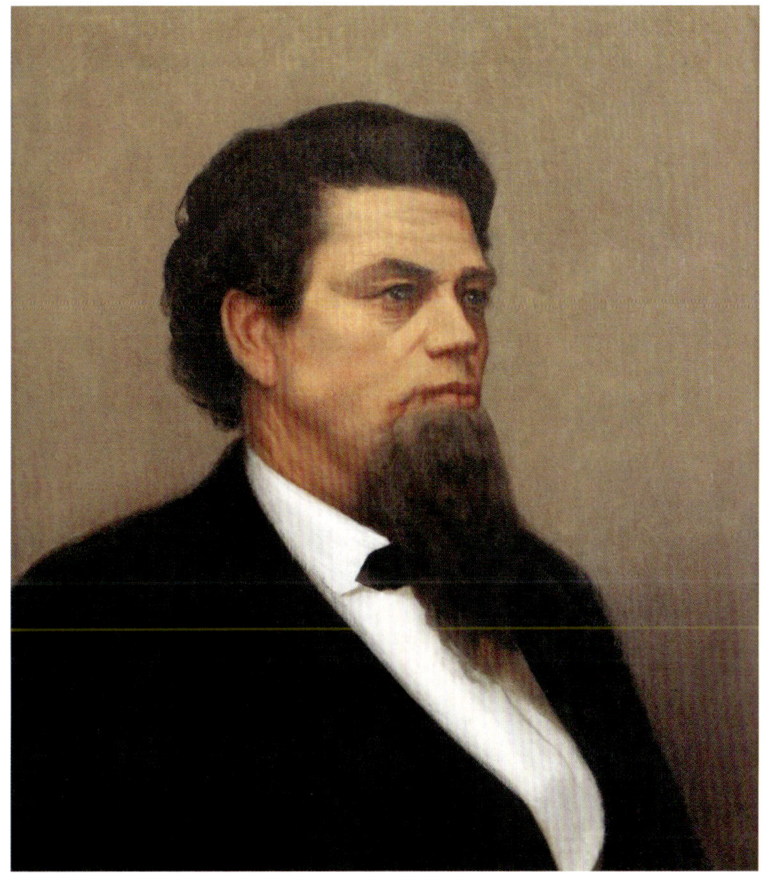

James Ferdinand McCan, *Captain King*, signed, no date, oil on canvas, 28 × 18 inches. Courtesy of King Ranch, Inc. This portrait was painted by James McCan using a photograph long after the death of Richard King.

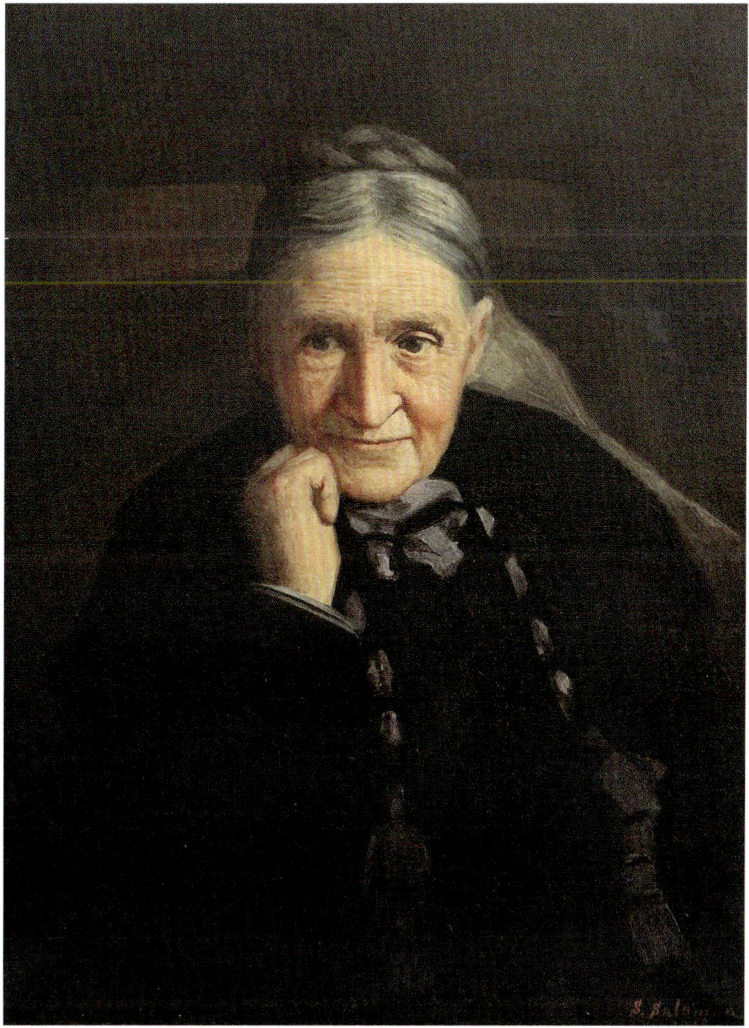

Soloman Saloman, *Mrs. King*, signed, no date, oil on canvas, 28 × 18 inches. Courtesy of King Ranch, Inc. Saloman painted mostly from photographs with some visits to the sitter. His portrait of Mrs. King is in the same format as the McCan portrait of Captain King.

James Louis Lundean (1894–1961) was another painter on the ranch. Born in Council Bluffs, Iowa, and raised in Wyoming, Lundean loved depicting anything to do with horses.[30] He painted cowboys, Plains Indians, polo players, foxhunts, and racehorses, and was a regular visitor to King Ranch, where he depicted action scenes of cowboys at work. The December 1933 Christmas issue of *Fortune* magazine featured a fourteen-page article on King Ranch, with photographs and illustrations of paintings done on the ranch by Lundean. These paintings were family favorites and still hang in guest rooms and hallways throughout the Main House.[31]

Tom Lea (1907–2001) of El Paso drew a series of portraits of the people, places, cattle, and horses of the ranch, included in the two-volume set of cased books *The King Ranch*, published in 1957. The books were researched by Holland McCombs (1901–91) and written and illustrated by Tom Lea under the supervision of Robert J. Kleberg Jr. Lea used pen and ink on paper to create the illustrations for the book. The original pen and ink drawings are now a part of the King Ranch art collection, along with other drawings and paintings by Lea.

Lea's illustrations for *The King Ranch* are on display in the entry hall of the Main House. Paintings by Tom Lea of King Ranch Australia and murals of King Ranch divisions and twentieth-century foreign properties by Tilford Collins (1916–92) now hang in the Main House's "pool house."

## The Photographic Tradition on King Ranch

Photography was a part of the King family history from the 1850s onward. Early photographs of the family were mainly portraits, but the subjects changed in the twen-

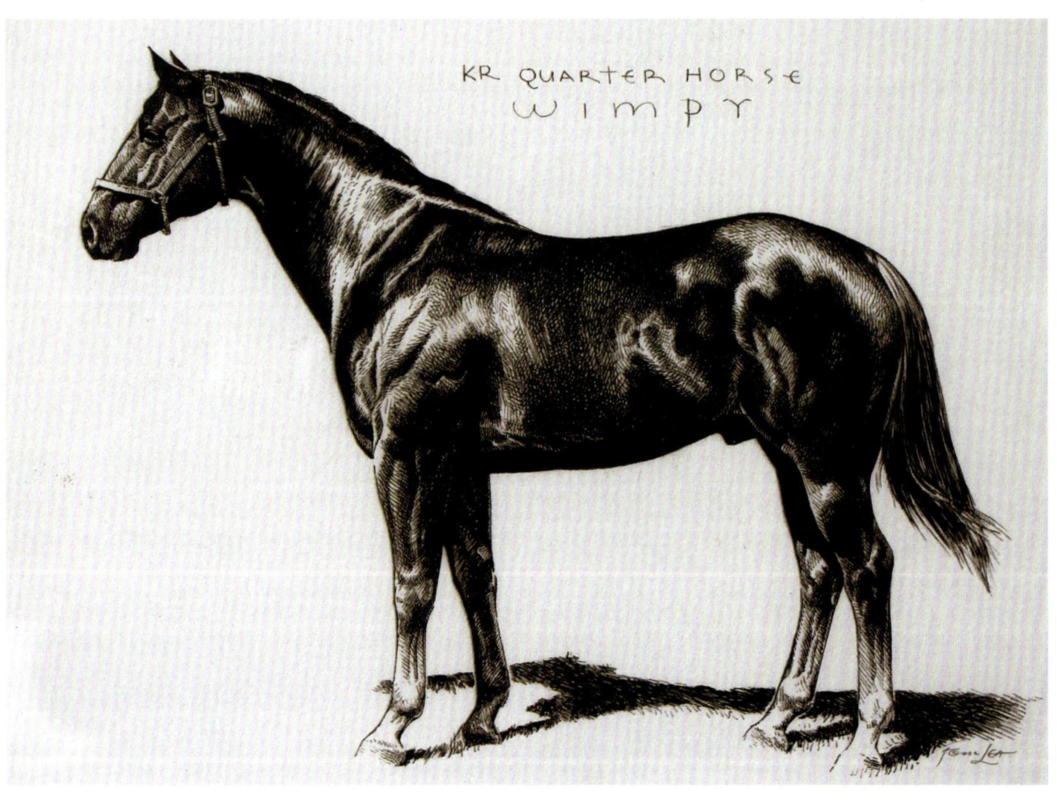


Tom Lea, *Wimpy*, circa 1957, pen and ink, 8 × 10 inches. Courtesy of King Ranch, Inc. Writer and artist Tom Lea drew the famed King Ranch quarter horse Wimpy P-1 for *The King Ranch*, and the original drawing is illustrated in volume 2, page 658. King Ranch commissioned artworks of their fine livestock, as well as family members and friends. Wimpy was one of a long line of fine quarter horses bred for cow work and was honored as the first registered quarter horse in the *American Quarter Horse Stud Book of Registry*.

tieth and twenty-first centuries. The Kings had small personal family photos in the *cartes-de-visite* size, larger cabinet cards, and framed family portraits.

Prussian-born photographer Louis de Planque (1842–1898) was probably one of the first to photograph the Kings as a family in the 1870s. He made the King family portrait illustrated in this book. De Planque practiced photography in Mexico for the duration of the Civil War and in Matamoros and Brownsville in 1866, before moving to Refugio and then to Corpus Christi.[32] He billed himself as "an itinerant Texas photographer" and traveled South Texas and the coastal bend area up to Victoria. By the time he photographed the Kings, he had taken photographs of outlaws and prominent officials like Mexican general Tomas Mejia, who served under Emperor Maximillian of Mexico, and outlaw Juan Cortina, whose criminal activities were a serious problem for Richard King and other South Texas ranchers.[33] Louis de Planque died at fifty-six years of age in Corpus Christi.

New photographers arrived in South Texas in the twentieth century, with innovative skills and equipment. Chiropractor John Frederick "Doc" McGregor (1893–1986) settled in Corpus Christi in 1929, and soon his photography hobby became his main occupation. Although he arrived long after Richard King's era and four years after Henrietta's passing in 1925, McGregor took a significant number of images documenting King Ranch and the Kingsville area. By the time of his death in 1986, McGregor had taken more than 500,000 photographs, and many of them depicted King Ranch and members of the family. "Doc" McGregor was a journalistic photographer, and his work was used by the *Corpus Christi Caller-Times* newspaper and other publications.[34]

James "Jimmie" Andrew Dodd (1917–84) found his way to Kingsville while working for the Missouri Pacific Railroad. In 1935, Robert "Bob" J. Kleberg Jr. loaned Dodd $250 to purchase a used Auto Graphlex camera, and he began to take photographs as a hobby. Dodd worked off his loan by taking pictures on King Ranch, and soon he had the "run of the place." From the mid-1930s through 1950, Dodd photographed the Kleberg family, King Ranch employees, and various daily activities of ranch life. Before his death, Dodd's collection of 23,000 photographs of King Ranch and South Texas was acquired by the Barker Texas History Center at the University of Texas at Austin.[35]

A visitor to the ranch in 1939, photographer Toni Frissell (1907–88), captured the people of King Ranch as they had never been portrayed before. After meeting Frissell at the Saratoga thoroughbred horse racetrack in upstate New York, Robert and Alice Kleberg's son Bob and his wife Helen Campbell Kleberg invited her to visit King Ranch. Frissell was a celebrated New York fashion photographer when she came to the ranch, and she began a series of images of the ranch during her visits that continued until 1944. Already known for her narrative style photography that had been featured in *Vogue* magazine, Frissell's photographic vision was perfect for telling the stories of King Ranch.[36] The resulting photographs made by Frissell were compiled into a book called *The King Ranch 1939–1944: A Photographic Essay*, published by the Amon Carter Museum in 1975.

When Frissell first visited the ranch, she was in awe of the place. Bob's wife Helen took Frissell around the vast property to photograph cattle gatherings, or roundups; the Kineños who worked and lived on the ranch; members of the family; and everything related to life on King Ranch. Frissell's photographs of the family and employees at work are arguably some of the best of her career. By 1960, Frissell had photographed World War II in England and France, world leaders, and celebrities, but her King Ranch images stood out as an important part of her body of work. Today Frissell's negatives of King Ranch are jointly held by the Library of Congress and King Ranch, Inc. Bob and Helen Kleberg's daughter,

Helen Kleberg Groves, and other family members also personally own Frissell photographs of family members.

Frissell's presence at King Ranch soon inspired Helen Campbell Kleberg to sharpen her own skills with a camera. Helen had always carried her Kodak Brownie on the ranch, but during her time with Frissell, she acquired a 35mm Leica camera and set up a darkroom in the household bathroom for developing her film and print photographs.[37] The two women photographed each other on the ranch, working and relaxing. Helen Kleberg's photos show a unique style that is very different from Frissell's, but a style that is just as strong in her depictions of her subjects. To date, two books about life on King Ranch featuring photographs by both women have been published.[38]

Photography on King Ranch has continued to the present time, not only by approved outside photographers but by the family as well. David Stoecklein (1949–2014), an Idaho photographer known for his cowboy and western photographs, created his share of images of King Ranch. Like Frissell, Stoecklein established his career in the fashion, catalog, and magazine industries, shooting for the L.L.Bean catalog, among others, and various magazine covers. While taking photographs on King Ranch, Stoecklein discovered another photographer in the Kleberg family and published her work: Janell Gerald Kleberg. Janell married US congressman Richard "Dick" Kleberg's grandson Stephen "Tio" J. Kleberg in 1969. Tio Kleberg grew up on King Ranch and managed it from 1977 until 1998.[39] Like Helen, Janell carried a camera to work on the ranch with Tio. She attended her first roundup on King Ranch in 1971. She took her skills to the overseas divisions of King Ranch in Argentina, Brazil, Venezuela, and Australia.[40] Like Toni Frissell and Helen Kleberg, Janell Kleberg's photography depicts her own vision of the ranch where she lived. Her photographs are mainly in color and show the family and Kineños at various roundups. Janell also took a special interest in documenting the gear that was used on various King Ranch divisions.

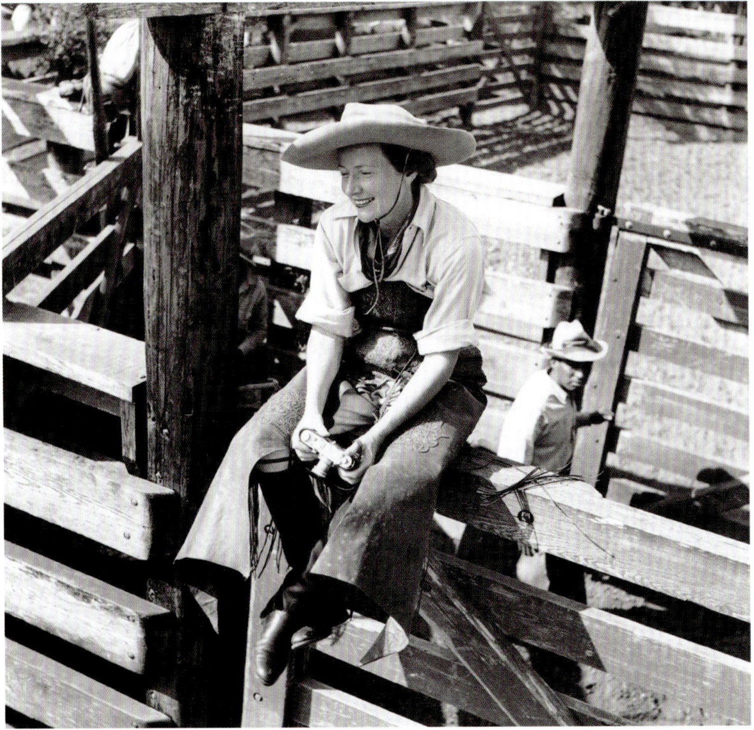

Helen Campbell Kleberg photographed by Toni Frissell, holding her Leica camera while dressed for working cattle on horseback, circa 1940. Toni Frissell Collection, Prints and Photographs Division, Library of Congress, Washington, DC. Courtesy of King Ranch, Inc.

## Artisans of the Ranch

The working tools and equipment used in the field exhibit the personal design choices and skills of the top craftsmen of King Ranch. Captain King and his successors employed craftsmen and artisans to design and create everything from branding irons to weavings for the ranch and the hands, as well as for nearby ranches.

Cattle branding is used to identify the cattle of a ranch or an owner. The original designs of the King

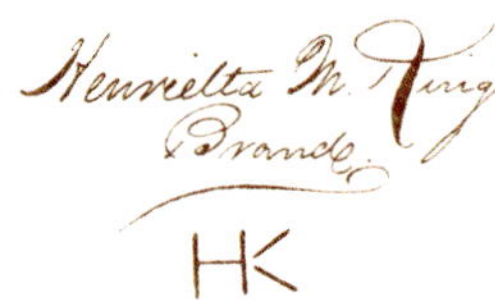


*THE STATE OF TEXAS*
*COUNTY OF NUECES*

Be it remembered *that Mistress Henrietta M. King, wife of Richard King, having deposited her brand in this office for record as described and laid down in the margin, the same was this day recorded in Book "B," of the registry of brands, Nueces County, on page 57.*

*Witness my official signature, at my office in Corpus Christi, this 20th day of March,* a.d. *1859.*

Reuben Holbein, *Clerk,* c. c. n. c.

---

*THE STATE OF TEXAS*
*COUNTY OF NUECES*

Be it remembered *that Richard King, having deposited his brands in this office for Record, as described and laid down in the Margin, the same were this day recorded in Book "B," of the registry of brands, Nueces County, on page 61.*

*Witness my official signature, at my office in Corpus Christi, this 27th day of June* a.d. *1859.*

Reuben Holbein, *Clerk,* c. c. n. c.

---

*THE STATE OF TEXAS*
*COUNTY OF NUECES*

Be it Remembered *that on this The Ninth day of February A.D. 1869, Richard King having deposited his Brand and Ear Mark for Horses & Cattle as described and laid down in the Margin hereof, the same was and is hereby duly Recorded in Book "B" for the Registry of Brands in said Nueces County on page 181.*

*Witness my Official Signature at Office in Corpus Christi, the day and date above written.*

Joseph FitzSimmons, *Clk.* c. c. n. co.

The connected HK, the Ere Flecha or Arrow R, and the LK brands were registered by Captain King in 1859. The now internationally known Running W brand was registered in 1869. Courtesy of King Ranch, Inc.

Ranch brands were rendered by Captain King himself, and the branding irons were forged and handcrafted by King Ranch blacksmiths. The first brand and image related to King Ranch was the Ere Flecha, or Arrow R. The second brand used by Captain King was the connected HK, for Henrietta King. The HK and the Ere Flecha were the first ranch brands to be legally registered in 1859. Another early brand, the LK, was also registered but had limited use after 1859.[41] The legendary Running W brand came into use in the 1860s and was registered on February 9, 1869.[42] These brand images have become definitive symbols of the ranch since they were brought into use for marking livestock. Few images from the 1850s and 1860s can be positively connected to the ranch, but these brand marks certainly can.

The Running W has become more than an identifying mark for livestock. King and his descendants made sure that the mark represented quality—good livestock that came from a good ranching operation, careful land stewardship, a home for the family, and a place of hospitality to visitors. The Running W now marks everything, from cattle to pickup trucks.[43]

Captain King recognized that ranching in South Texas demanded not only good men, horses, and cattle, but also outstanding gear. His account books for the late 1860s, at the end of each year, list the number of saddles, harnesses, and other leather goods made on the ranch, exclusively for the use of los Kineños and other ranch workers. In 1867, King began operating his own saddlery, with artisans crafting the best saddles, harnesses, and other equipment. Throughout the rest of the nineteenth century, Captain King and later Robert Justus Kleberg Sr. continued to hire only the most qualified artisans to make saddles and other tack for the cowboys employed on the ranch. By the 1900s, the saddlery operation was housed on the second floor of the historic Commissary on the Santa Gertrudis Division. The leather goods were all stamped "Santa Gertrudis Make." As the fame of the King Ranch saddles spread, the ranch began to craft a significant number of pieces for outside parties.

The founding of Kingsville in 1904 on land deeded by Henrietta King led to an increased commercial demand for the ranch's leather goods. Robert Justus Kleberg Sr., Captain King's son-in-law who was then managing the ranch, realized that this was an opportunity to serve the needs of both the cattlemen and the public. Kleberg was also president of the Kingsville Lumber Company, and he arranged for that company to take over the ranch's saddle shop operation, creating what is known today as the King Ranch Saddle Shop. During this time, leather goods were marked "SANTA GERTRUDIS MAKE" in an oval cartouche. In 1918, the King Ranch Saddle Shop was moved to the top floor of the Flato building in downtown Kingsville. Here, in a space of forty-by-one hundred feet, the shop began manufacturing saddles and equipment for other ranches in the surrounding area, as well as King Ranch. Harnesses, bridles and halters, horse collars, tapaderos, chaparajos, scabbards, and a full line of outdoor wear and equipment soon followed. Two saddle stamps with "Kingsville Lumber Co." were used between 1918 and 1939. One of the stamps featured the Running W brand with the words "RUNNING-W-Brand"; the other did not use the brand. Both styles also included "KINGSVILLE, TEXAS." A simple oval cartouche with the brand image and no words also came into use in 1918 and is still used today for some products.

By 1923, the King Ranch Saddle Shop had a catalog with more than seventy pages, featuring saddles, chaps, and tack. It served a regular trade territory from the Rio Grande Valley to Laredo and up to San Antonio and Houston. When it was first established, the shop manufactured only a few styles of saddles —those that met the needs of the ranch. After production was taken over by the Kingsville Lumber Company, the Saddle Shop's business expanded steadily and many new styles were added. Among the new styles (and still being made today) were the Dick Kleberg and the Bob Kleberg Working Saddles, named after brothers Dick and Bob Kleberg, grandsons of Captain King. Designed as safe, comfortable working saddles, the Dick and Bob Kleberg Working Saddles are built to protect the horse's back.

With the expanding manufacturing business, it became necessary for the King Ranch Saddle Shop to adopt a trademark. Building off previous designs, starting in 1940, a cartouche came into use with the words "KING RANCH" across the top and "KINGSVILLE, TEXAS" across the bottom. In the center of the mark was the King Ranch brand with the words "RUNNING-W-BRAND" below. Beginning in 1990, the oval cartouche placed on leather goods sold by the Saddle Shop displayed "KING RANCH" across the top, "KINGSVILLE, TEXAS" along the bottom, and the King Ranch brand mark in the center.[44]

When the Saddle Shop moved into the same location as the King Ranch Lumber Company in Kingsville, catalogs were printed, offering saddles, bridles, spurs, boots, hats, and other ranching goods. The hats offered were Stetson; the boots were Justin and Nocona. Many of the bits and spurs shown in the catalogs are clearly the work of (Victoria) Texas spur maker and blacksmith Joe Bianchi. Bianchi forged all of his bits and spurs by hand in his shop and applied any decoration. Whether cowboys on the ranch wore Bianchi spurs is in question, but Dick Kleberg rode wearing them, as did his brother Bob. Many Klebergs and their cousins, the Easts, wore Bianchi spurs, with the signature hook-shaped shank and Mexican coin buttons.[45]

Through the Saddle Shop, King family preferences for saddle styles and other products became available to the general public. Helen Campbell Kleberg designed a purse that is still sold today in an updated leather version. Helen liked the round rope bags of the vaqueros and cowboys on the ranch. She took the short cylindrical design, made it smaller, and had the Saddle Shop make one from white canvas with her initials. The bag found a ready audience among ranch wives in Texas. Many products, like luggage and briefcases, are still developed for the Saddle Shop with family guidance.

The nineteenth-century Kineños brought their own skills to the ranch, in a tradition that has continued into the twentieth century. Established in 1856 by Richard King, the King Ranch weaving shop made many of the necessary wool items for the ranch—mainly wool saddle

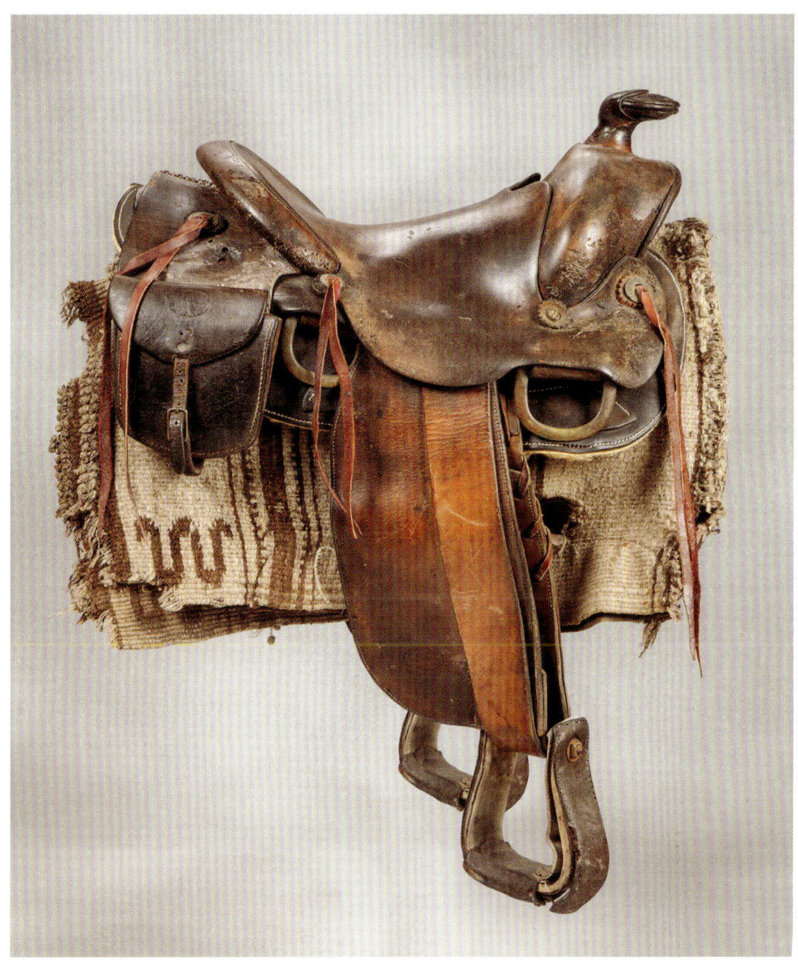

A King Ranch saddle, formerly in the Fort Worth Museum of Science and History; the current location of this saddle is unknown. Courtesy of Brian Lebel's Old West Events. Stamped with the words "King Ranch, Kingsville, Texas, Running-W-Brand" in an oval cartouche, this saddle was probably made in the 1940s in the King Ranch Lumber Company Saddle Shop. Running W wool saddle blankets were woven at King Ranch for use by vaqueros who worked "for the brand."

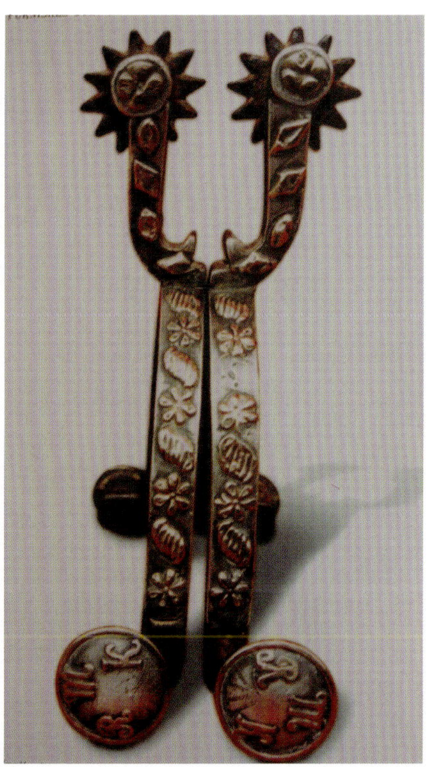

With gold overlaid decoration, these Bianchi spurs were made for Richard "Dick" Mifflin Kleberg Sr. and have his initials, RMK, on the button. Spurs made by Joe Bianchi in Victoria, Texas, were worn by men and women throughout South Texas. Illustration from Kurt House, *Hand Forged for Texas Cowboys* (San Antonio Three Rivers Publishing, 2001), 128. Anonymous collection. Courtesy of Kurt House.

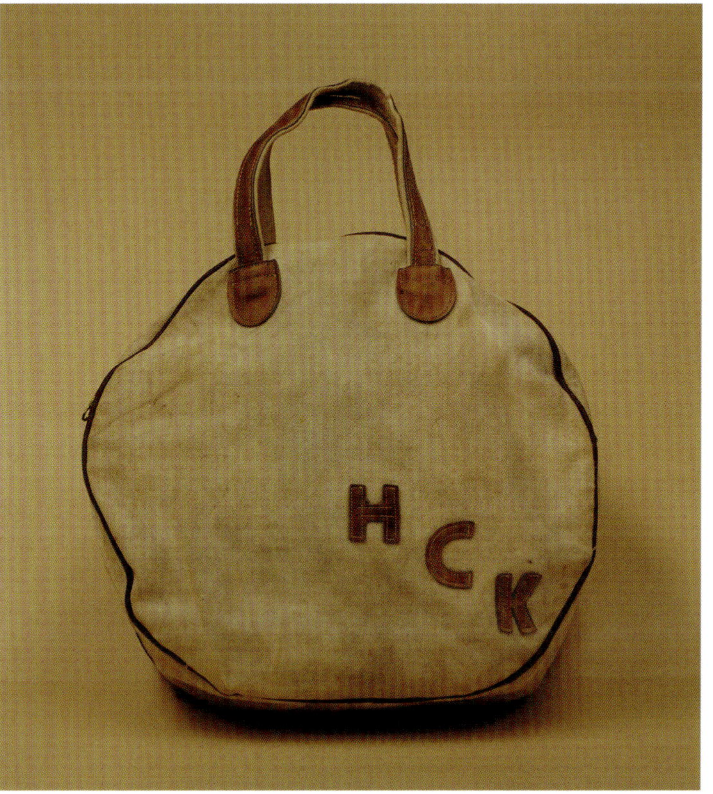


In the 1930s, Helen Campbell Kleberg used the design of a vaquero's rope bag for a canvas and leather purse. The initials on the side are hers. Gift of Helen K. Groves and Family. Witte Museum, San Antonio, Texas.

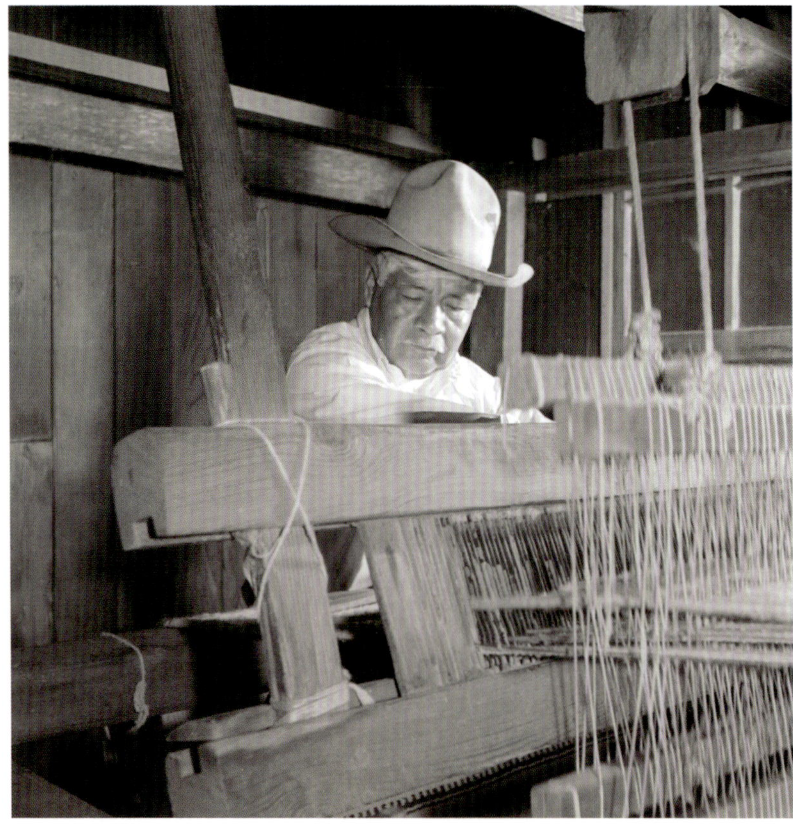

Master weaver Emiliano García was born in Mexico and moved to King Ranch. Photograph by Toni Frissell, circa 1940. Toni Frissell Collection, Prints and Photographs Division, Library of Congress, Washington, DC. Courtesy of King Ranch, Inc.

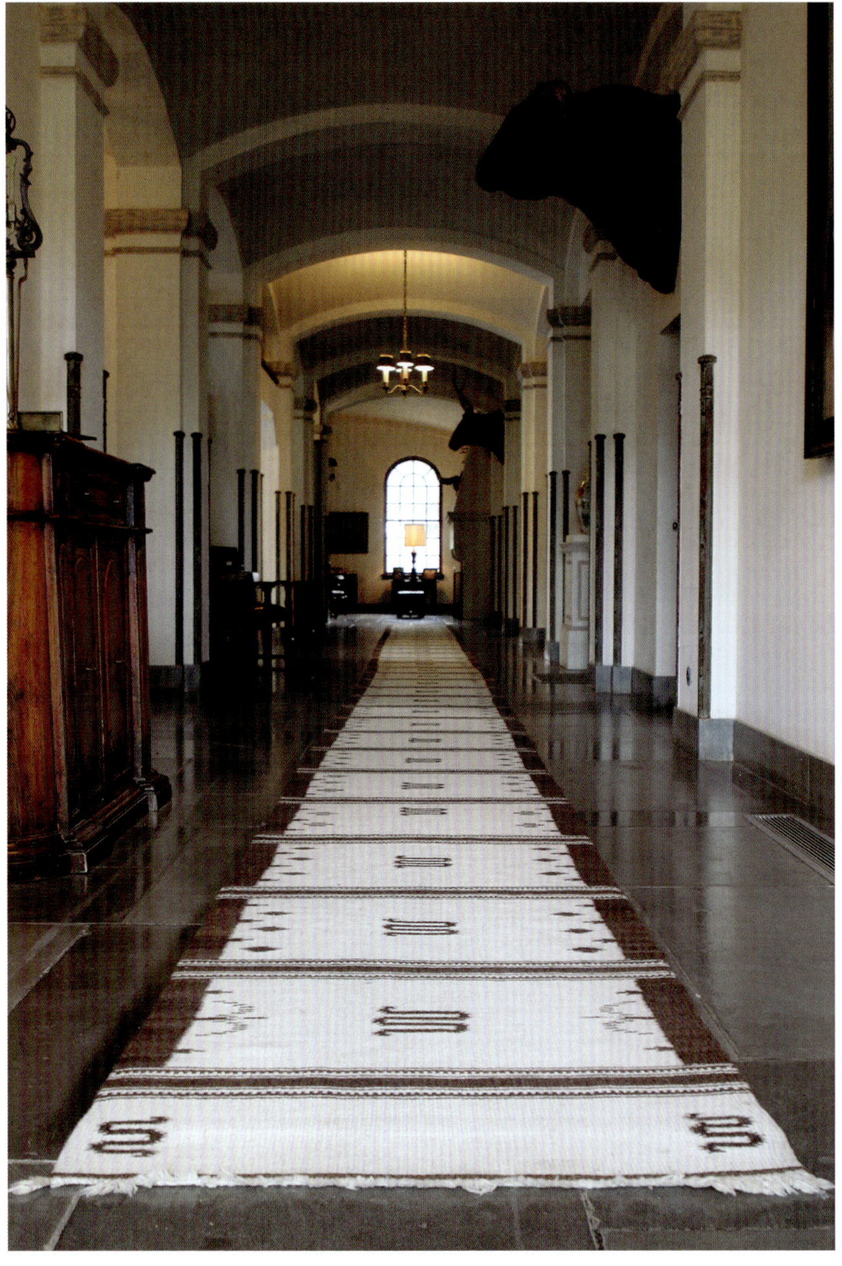

The pattern of a Running W wool saddle blanket was repeated by weaver Emiliano García to create this rug in the entry hall of the Main House, circa 1956. Courtesy of King Ranch, Inc.

blankets, which constantly needed to be replaced. The continuing tradition was still practiced on the ranch well into the twentieth century, and brand-marked saddle blankets were traditionally reserved for riders on the ranch. During her time on the ranch, photographer Toni Frissell captured a striking image of master weaver Emiliano García at his loom, wearing a cowboy hat.

The wool for the weavings came from King Ranch sheep and was completely processed on the ranch. The main colors were a natural cream and a walnut brown. Blankets from the early twentieth century show the Running W brand in the four corners of the textiles. A woven wool floor rug by García lies in the front entry hall of the Main House and measures sixty feet long. The weaving is a repeated pattern of the famed saddle blanket.[46]

## The Emergence of the King Ranch Style

Throughout the late 1800s and the early 1900s, the Kleberg family traveled across the United States and Mexico. Richard and Henrietta King had started their lives amid the influences of New York and Pennsylvania, traveling down the East Coast and then to South Texas and Mexico. During their marriage, they traveled from Mexico to St. Louis regularly and experienced what all those places and the locations in between had to offer. The couple, and later their family, observed their surroundings and brought back new skills and innovative ideas to the ranch to solve problems and make work and life more efficient. As business interests and educational opportunities increased, so did the families' trips. Children and grandchildren widened the scope of travel as well.

After the death of Henrietta King, ranching practices changed under the direction of her son-in-law Robert J. Kleberg Sr. and again later under the management of Robert "Bob" J. Kleberg Jr. Over the years, King Ranch developed many new agricultural techniques (from cattle raising to farming), some of which were experimental, and visitors came from around the world to see the results. The ranch was home to the research that ultimately led to the control of the fever tick, which had plagued the cattle industry since the trail-drive era. New grasses were introduced, and brush control became an important area of focus for researchers. Wildlife research was also carried out under the leadership of Caesar Kleberg. A new breed of cattle, Santa Gertrudis, was developed, and the list goes on—many research contributions and discoveries have been made (and are still being made) at King Ranch.

A big change occurred on the ranch in September 1933, when Humble Oil and Refining Company of Houston signed a lease and partition agreements with the heirs of Henrietta King.[47] The 1939 discovery of oil and gas on the ranch relieved the expanding empire's financial pressures and lowered its debts. The oil and gas activity also brought a steady stream of visitors and business associates to the ranch. New friends and associates brought with them a wide variety of tastes and styles of dress from around the world, but nothing changed the sun, heat, and the environment of the ranch.

So what is "King Ranch style," and how did it originate? The distinct stylistic elements and personal demeanor inspired by King Ranch originate in the ranch's work and social requirements. The King Ranch style has been translated into the arts, architecture, and material craftsmanship. The style is evident in the demeanor and appearance of people associated with this vast ranching empire, even down to specialized automobile designs.

Tom Lea recounts Captain King as wearing boots, often with one pant leg out of the boots and one tucked in, as well as a slouchy dark felt hat and wool pants and coat. He rarely varied from the dress and was known by his profile in town and on the range. Henrietta dressed as a proper woman of the time. She wore long dresses on and off the ranch, and after her husband's death, she wore primarily black.

When Alice's husband, Robert Kleberg Sr., took over the ranch operations, he dressed as he always had—like an attorney in a three-piece suit. Kleberg was not a cowboy but is shown in family photographs wearing boots and a cowboy hat with his suit—a necessity due to the heat and snakes of South Texas. Kleberg did not work on horseback but was often in a wagon. His wife Alice wore the dresses of a lady of the era—long with long sleeves, typically in black or gray.[48]

The family's style began to change in the twentieth century. A mix of fashions as well as new interests led to the changes. The children of Alice Gertrudis King and Robert J. Kleberg Sr. were raised on the ranch with the children of Kineños as friends and playmates. They wore clothes suited to riding horses and being around cattle and the outdoor ranch environment—boots and a hat were always present. Bob Kleberg appears in childhood photos wearing sombreros on and off horses. As a teen, he wore the dress of a King Ranch working cowboy—boots, a hat, "batwing" chaps, lightweight pants, and a long-sleeved shirt—as did his elder brother Dick.

Mamie Searcy, Dick Kleberg's wife, came from a ranching background on her mother's side, and her father was an attorney and judge in Brenham, Texas. She spent much of her childhood on her cousins' ranches across South Texas.[49] Mamie appears in childhood photos wearing a hat and boots. Helen Campbell Kleberg, Bob's wife, was raised as the daughter of a US congressman from Kansas and lived in both Kansas and Arlington, Virginia. She was an accomplished equestrienne in the English style of riding when she arrived at King Ranch, having participated in foxhunts and played polo.[50] Like Mamie Searcy, Helen Campbell was very comfortable outdoors.

Every man and woman on the ranch had his or her own hat shape, whether from constant wear or from intentional forming. Many men wore short-brimmed felt hats with three indentions on the crown, now known as a "cattleman" crease. The creases changed due to constant handling, and hats on King Ranch were literally worn out. Short brims were less likely to catch the breezes blowing off of the gulf. Frissell's photographs show at least two Kleberg women, Helen C. Kleberg and Henrietta Kleberg Larkin Armstrong, wearing very wide-brimmed hats with flat tops. The hats gave the women more protection from the unrelenting sun, and both women had noticeable hatbands. Helen had a silver concho made from a coin on her hatband and a "stampede string" under her chin to prevent the hat from blowing off. Her sister-in-law Henrietta wore a similar hat with a large turkey feather.

While everyone wore boots on the ranch, the styles varied widely. Dick and Bob often wore high-topped cowboy boots with khaki pants tucked in; other times, their pants were over their boot tops. Helen Campbell Kleberg brought a new style to the ranch—English riding boots and English field boots. Helen wore both while riding at the ranch and was photographed riding a Mexican saddle wearing knee-high boots and her usual flat-topped hat. Almost everyone, children included, wore short, canvas brush jackets, which are still worn throughout Texas today.

Changes in management and relationships on and off the ranch occurred while Bob Kleberg was the manager and with Dick Kleberg's entry into national politics. The two brothers and their families traveled around the world representing King Ranch, its business, and the culture. They sometimes changed their respective styles of dress to acknowledge customs and cultures that were different from those back at the ranching empire they called home, but they also always carried some semblance of the King Ranch style with them.

As the ranch holdings spread to Australia, South America, and North Africa, King's descendants became familiar with the cultures of those places. Foreign guests to the ranch brought with them a series of diverse needs and customs, often different from those of the family. Bob Kleberg's wardrobe, like the rest of the family living on the ranch, had plenty of clothing for work, and all family members owned custom-made cowboy boots. Likewise, they also owned proper attire for formal events in Washington, DC, with Dick. They also kept a portion of their wardrobes stocked with appropriate garments for trips to various foreign countries. There were tailcoats for formal events, Argentine button pants for trips to the ranch there, and a monogrammed blue cotton bathrobe for Bob's lounging at home.

The women wore the latest styles, but for more casual social events, they wore blended styles reflecting Mexico and the American Southwest. Calf-length dresses were often embroidered with Mexican designs and made to order in Mexico or Arizona. Mamie wore western-cut gabardine outfits, while Helen wore Mexican-style embroidered dresses.

Hunting became even more important in the twentieth century than it had been in earlier generations, and visitors came to the ranch to socialize and hunt. To accommodate the sporting crowd, a specialized hunting vehicle was created for driving through the South Texas brush and carrying people and their gear. The original prototype for the modern hunting car was a custom-designed Buick Roadmaster convertible modified for Congressman Richard M. Kleberg Sr. in 1949. There were sleeves for rifles or shotguns on the front fenders, a seat on the passenger side front fender above the headlight (with a seat belt), a winch system, grab bars throughout, cabinets for bar decanters with glasses and supplies, and extensive structural and mechanical modifications.[51]

Other hunting vehicles followed for use at King Ranch, but none like the original Buick. Within a few years, South Texas ranches of any size began using specially made hunting vehicles. By the 1960s, it was difficult to discern which vehicles had been custom made for King Ranch and which had been made for other ranches.[52] Modified hunting vehicles are driven throughout the United States today, but they all trace back to the King Ranch Buick.

## Into the Future

King Ranch is a complex ongoing business, not a frozen historical heritage moment. Like the cattle trade that started it, the business follows the changes and demands of the world. Details from events that happened 150 years ago can be studied in the King Ranch Archives and Museum and through the literature and art of the place. The ranch has been operating for 167 years in 2020 under the guidance and ownership of the descendants of Richard and Henrietta King. The ranch, the family, and the employees have experienced drought, hurricanes, heat and cold, sadness and happiness, but continue to endure and celebrate their part in the heritage South Texas.

The art and style of King Ranch continue to reflect work and life on the ranch. Growing from South Texas ranching roots and influenced by international operations, the King Ranch style reflects the individual nature of a place and its people. Today Noe Perez adds his interpretation to the ongoing story of King Ranch. A native son, trained engineer, and accomplished landscape painter, his artwork depicts the twenty-first century King Ranch—the people, places, and legacies of one of the world's greatest ranching operations.

## Notes

1. Harwood P. Hinton, "Wool, John Ellis," *Handbook of Texas Online*, accessed September 5, 2019, http://www.tshaonline.org/handbook/online/articles/fwo48.

2. Tom Lea, *The King Ranch*, 2 vols. (Boston: Little, Brown and Company, 1957), vol. 1, 435n4.

3. Caleb Coker (ed.), *The News from Brownsville: Helen Chapman's Letters from the Texas Military Frontier, 1848–1852* (Austin: Texas State Historical Association for the Barker Texas History Center, 1992), 85.

4. Coker, *News from Brownsville*, 144.

5. Lea, *King Ranch*, 119.

6. Lea, *King Ranch*, 516.

7. Jane Clements Monday and Frances Brannen Vick (eds.), *Letters to Alice: Birth of the Kleberg-King Dynasty* (College Station: Texas A&M University Press, 2012), 10–11.

8. Santa Gertrudis was named the Patroness of the West Indies by King Phillip IV of Spain. Gertrude the Great (Saint Gertrude of Helfta) was a religious mystic scholar in the Benedictine order of nuns in the thirteenth century. Gertrude Casanova, "St. Gertrude the Great," *The Catholic Encyclopedia*, vol. 6 (New York: Robert Appleton Company, 1909), accessed August 18, 2019, http://www.newadvent.org/cathen/06534a.htm.

9. Lea, *King Ranch*, 322.

10. Lea, *King Ranch*, 147.

11. Lea, *King Ranch*, 197.

12. Lea, *King Ranch*, 216–18.

13. Bruce S. Cheeseman, "King, Richard," *Handbook of Texas Online*, accessed September 10, 2019, http://www.tshaonline.org/handbook/online/articles/fki19.

14. Cheeseman, "King, Richard," 516.

15. Lea, *King Ranch*, 481.

16. Lea, *King Ranch*, 569.

17. Edgar Guest, a syndicated poet and journalist from Detroit, was often referred to as the "poet of the people." See "Edgar Guest," Poets.org, accessed August 20, 2019, https://poets.org/poet/edgar-guest.

18. Lea, *King Ranch*, 571.

19. Lea, *King Ranch*, 571.

20. *The Architectural Record*, vol. 40, no. 1, July 1916, serial no. 214, p. 96. King Ranch Archives.

21. Lea, *King Ranch*, 571.

22. Mr. C. E. Conover (Tiffany Studios Madison Avenue, New York) to Mr. R. J. Kleberg, November 14, 1914, King Ranch Archives.

23. In a letter from the King Ranch Archives, C. E. Conover indicates he has been to Tiffany Studios in New York to check the status of the windows during production. Conover states, "Mr. Tiffany figures that they are the handsomest windows of this character he has turned out." Mr. C. E. Conover (Tiffany Studios, Chicago) to Mr. R. J. Kleberg, January 31, 1914, King Ranch Archives.

24. The first three-piece folding fire screen design was rejected by the family, and a subsequent one-piece fire screen was designed by Tiffany Studios and submitted for approval. Hugh White (Tiffany Studios) to Mrs. H. M. King (Kingsville, Texas), October 4, 1913, King Ranch Archives.

25. Two of these floor rugs still exists. One has been conserved and is on the floor in the main entry of the house at this time. The other is currently stored for protection. King Ranch Archives.

26. Edgar P. Sneed, "King, Henrietta Chamberlain," *Handbook of Texas Online*, accessed July 12, 2019, http://www.tshaonline.org/handbook/online/articles/fki16.

27. Lea, *King Ranch*, 355–56.

28. Saloman specialized in portraits of prominent Texans, especially in the ranching world. The portrait of Mrs. King is considered one of his finest paintings. Cecilia Steinfeldt, *Art for History's Sake: The Texas Collection of the Witte Museum* (Texas State Historical Association for the Witte Museum, Austin, 1993), 236–37.

29. "Officers and Men of the Texas Republican Army," accessed August 22, 2019, https://www.sonsofdewittcolony.org/sanjvets.htm.

30. "J. Louis Lundean, Noted Artist, Dies at Blowing Rock," *Durham Morning Herald*, October 26, 1961, accessed August 28, 2019, https://www.findagrave.com/memorial/59494024/james-louis-lundean.

31. J. Louis Lundean papers, 1924–56, Archives of American Art, Smithsonian Institution, accessed August 28, 2019, https://www.aaa.si.edu/collections/j-louis-lundean-papers-7927#overview.

32. Peter E. Palmquist and Thomas R. Kailbourn, *Pioneer Photographers from the Mississippi to the Continental Divide: A Biographical Dictionary, 1839–1865* (Palo Alto: Stanford University Press, 2005), 201.

33. Lawrence T. Jones III Texas Photographs, Digital collections, DeGolyer Library, Southern Methodist University, accessed August 22, 2019, https://www.smu.edu/libraries/digitalcollections/jtx. This online collection contains photographs made by de Planque in Texas.

34. Kendall Curlee, "McGregor, John Frederick," *Handbook of Texas Online,* accessed August 5, 2019, http://www.tshaonline.org/handbook/online/articles/fmaca.

35. Lawrence A. Landis, "Dodd, James Andrew," *Handbook of Texas Online,* accessed November 2, 2019, http://www.tshaonline.org/handbook/online/articles/fdo37.

36. Toni Frissell, *The King Ranch 1939–1944: A Photographic Essay,* with introduction and captions by Holland McCombs (Dobbs Ferry, NY: Morgan and Morgan for the Amon Carter Museum, 1975).

37. See Marisa C. Sanchéz (ed.), *Two Women Look West: Photographs of King Ranch by Helen C. Kleberg and Toni Frissell* (Houston: Museum of Fine Arts, Houston, 2006). This book was published in conjunction with an exhibition of the same name, shown at the Museum of Fine Arts, Houston. The statement by Helen K. Groves can be found on page iv.

38. *Two Women Look West,* exhibition catalog, Museum of Fine Arts, Houston; Helen Kleberg Groves, *Bob and Helen Kleberg of King Ranch* (Albany, TX: Bright Sky Press, 2004).

39. Skip Hollandsworth, "When We Were Kings," *Texas Monthly,* July 31, 1998, accessed August 21, 2019, https://www.texasmonthly.com/articles/when-we-were-kings/.

40. Janell Kleberg, *Waiting for Daylight* (Ketchum, ID: Stoecklein, 2003), 11–12.

41. Robert Moorman Denhardt, *The King Ranch Quarter Horses: And Something of the Ranch and the Men That Bred Them* (Norman: University of Oklahoma Press, 1970), 37.

42. John Ashton and Edgar P. Sneed, with Bob Kinnan, "King Ranch," *Handbook of Texas Online,* accessed June 26, 2019, http://www.tshaonline.org/handbook/online/articles/apk01.

43. King Ranch and Ford teamed up in 2000 to produce King Ranch model trucks. See King Ranch, Inc., "Licensing/Partnership, King Ranch Ford F-Series Trucks," accessed June 26, 2019, https://king-ranch.com/operations/partnerships/.

44. Lisa A. Neely, "History of John B. Ragland Mercantile Building," *King Ranch Wellspring* 29, no. 2 (Summer 2017), n.p.

45. Kurt House, *Hand Forged for Texas Cowboys* (San Antonio: Three Rivers Publishing, 2001). This book is an excellent source on Bianchi and his work in Victoria, Texas.

46. Frissell, *The King Ranch 1939–1944,* plate no. 100.

47. Lea, *King Ranch,* 612.

48. Helen Kleberg Groves, *Bob and Helen Kleberg of King Ranch* (Albany, TX: Bright Sky Press, 2004), 21. Helen "Helenita" Grove's publication shows many personal photographs of the family, both formal and casual. Many were made by family members and clearly show the styles of dress of various eras on the ranch from the nineteenth century well into the twentieth century.

49. Bruce M. Shackelford, *The Wests of Texas: Cattle Ranching Entrepreneurs* (Austin: Texas State Historical Association, 2015), 105.

50. Groves, *Bob and Helen Kleberg,* 56–57.

51. Craig Fitzgerald, "The First 'King Ranch' Branded Vehicle Was a Buick," accessed September 1, 2019, http://www.bestride.com/news/entertainment/the-first-king-ranch-branded-vehicle-was-a-buick.

52. The author has seen two early 1960s four-door Oldsmobiles made into hunting cars. The doors were removed for rapid exit, and modifications included gun sleeves and racks throughout. All were professionally modified but not necessarily by the Oldsmobile factory.

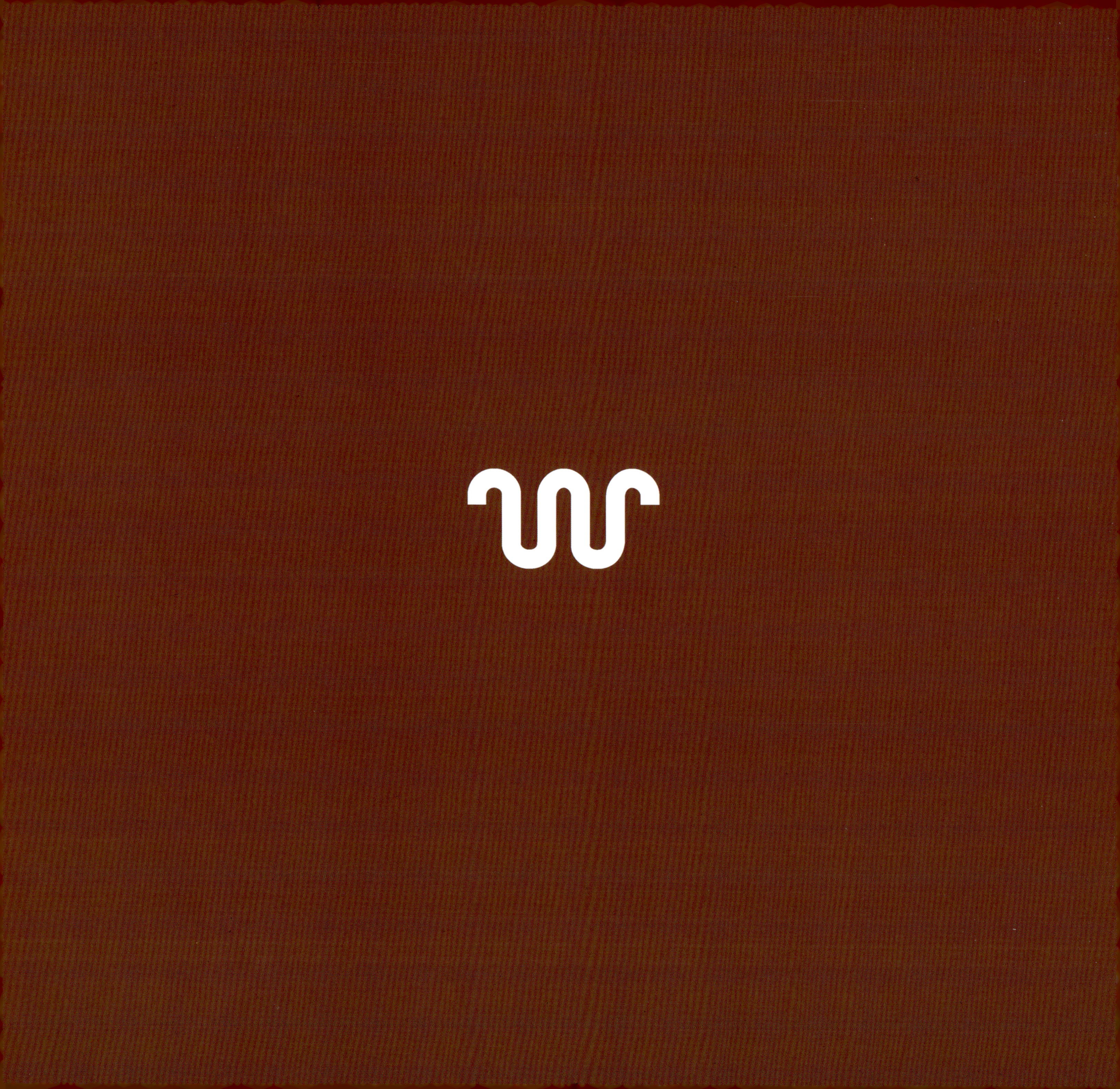

# Noe Perez and the Texas Landscape Tradition

Ron Tyler

Crossing the mustang, or wild horse desert, either from the Nueces or the bay, the country is almost as level as the ocean: which it strikingly resembles; when clothed with the tall grass, which is ever fan[n]ed by the bland southern breeze, Excepting a motte or small chaparral of them [thin?] bushes at long intervals, it is destitute of timber. No running water is found in this region, unless it may be for a few days during the rainy season. A miserable substitute for this inestimable element is found in holes and ponds. But these "are few and far between." Around these "water holes" thousands of wild horses, deer, Antelope, Wolves, leopards, cats, cougars, rattle snakes, horned frogs, with other numberless reptiles and fowls, congregate. Countless herds of wild cattle once roamed over these extensive plains. They have been destroyed or driven off by the Indians and Texans. The latter have stocked their country with them from the Trinity to the Nueces, few are now met with south of the latter. When time, industry, and increase of population have made all Texas north of the Nueces an agricultural country; necessity may make that portion lying south of it a grazing district.

—William A. McClintock, 1846[1]

---

Ron Tyler is the retired director of the Amon Carter Museum of American Art in Fort Worth and Professor of History at the University of Texas at Austin. His most recent publications are *Western Art, Western History: Collected Essays* and (as editor) *The Art of Texas: 250 Years*.

Noe Perez is a quiet-spoken Texas A&I University (now Texas A&M–Kingsville) educated engineer, who as a boy fell in love with the cactus-studded prairies around his native Falfurrias, in the middle of what early on was called the Wild Horse Desert. He spends his days overseeing and managing plans, budgets, and project teams related to the refining industry in Corpus Christi, but most of his evenings are reserved for painting scenes of the natural beauty of his native South Texas landscape in his comfortable, well-kept studio. There is an easel in the center of the room, a computer displaying photographic references to the left, and a couple of chairs back about eight or ten feet so that he can step back and compare the developing painting with his sketches, whether they be a small canvas painted quickly on location or a photograph. "I think it is very pretty here," he confesses. "I know that comes from my growing up here and seeing the different things that happen, the color changes, and I try to capture that, especially in the spring when things are blooming. South Texas is not known for its beautiful landscapes and colorful vistas, but I want to reveal to the viewer the unique beauty that is to be found here, which is all too often overlooked."

Today, many people drive through the heart of the Wild Horse Desert on US 77 or 281 and see nothing but flat land and scrubby mesquites, all the while wondering how long it will take them to get to Raymondville or Edinburg. But Noe has spent a lifetime acquainting himself with the beguiling features of the region and appreciates its subtle attractions. It was home to numerous prehistoric peoples, thanks to hundreds of those "holes and ponds"—wind-deflated depressions that are, in fact, the ephemeral wetlands first described by Álvar Núñez Cabeza de Vaca, the shipwrecked Spaniard who beached on Follet's Island (on the Texas coast southwest of Galveston Island) in 1528. Passing through the region as he made his way into northern Mexico, he observed "vast and handsome pastures, with good grass for cattle, and . . . soil [that] would be very fertile were the country inhabited and improved by reasonable people."[2] More than three centuries later, however, Richard S. Hunt (1812–69) and Jesse F. Randel (n.d.), in their 1839 *Map of Texas*, noted that "very little is known" of this part of the country, surmising that because neither the Nueces nor the Rio Grande had "considerable tributaries, it is inferred that it is mostly a dry elevated prairie."[3] British diplomat and journalist William Kennedy (1799–1871) agreed, calling it a "barren sandy ridge . . . which extends nearly one hundred miles inland [that] . . . is so utterly arid and sterile that it is unfrequented even by reptiles and insects, and the traveler rarely encounters a living thing in traversing its desolate surface."[4] A few years later, in 1848, a member of a mounted company of Texas volunteers on his way to war in Mexico passed through the same area, describing it as "indeed a curiosity —grand gloomy—and interesting," naively speculating on its origin: "The sand was . . . supposed by some to be produced by the receding of the flood or the effect of a whirlwind—others by a volcanic eruption—and some of the work of ant or gofers—in all human probability it was a fort of antique structure."[5] Today's visitor might ponder the same question.

Environmental scientists have designated the region as the South Texas Sand Sheet, which covers most of Kenedy and Brooks counties, including the Norias and Encino Divisions of King Ranch, along with much of the adjacent counties.[6] The patchwork of dunes is steadily moving inland, into the live oak and mesquite woodlands, propelled at a rate of eight to ten feet a year by the prevailing winds and the absence of stabilizing vegetation. During a drought, it becomes loose and impassable. A few miles south of the "sandy ridge," Kennedy noted the presence of two large salt lakes, La Sal Vieja and La Sal del Rey, which have supplied salt to the region's residents for centuries. To the north, he found the "best range for cattle in Texas, being free

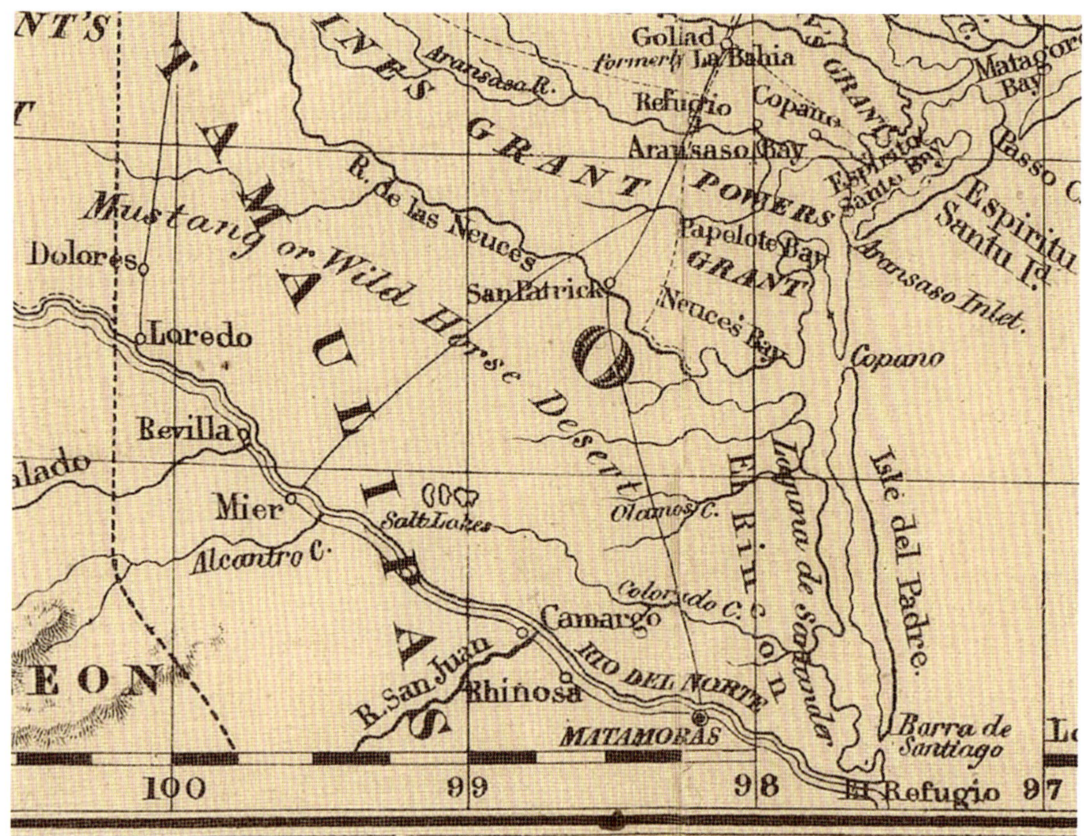


Detail from John Arrowsmith, *Map of Texas, Compiled from Surveys Recorded in the Land Office of Texas, and Other Official Surveys*, April 17, 1841. From William Kennedy, *Texas: The Rise, Progress, and Prospects of the Republic of Texas*, 2 vols. (London: R. Hastings, 1841), vol. 1, following p. 336. Courtesy of the Texas State Library and Archives, Map #01594. Arrowsmith labeled the territory between the Nueces and the Rio Grande the "Mustang or Wild Horse Desert." Notice that it is considered a part of the Mexican state of Tamaulipas.

from troublesome insects, and its musquit [*sic*] prairies supplying the best pasture." Stephen F. Austin had noted on his 1830 map of Texas that there were "Droves of Wild Horses" between the Nueces and the Rio Grande, and Kennedy echoed the claim: "It is not uncommon to see a drove of from 1,500 to 2,000 wild horses, some of which are remarkable for symmetry and speed, bounding over these prairies."[7]

A few years later, in 1852, John Russell Bartlett (1805–86), a former New York City bookseller and publisher now serving as commissioner of the US and Mexican Boundary Survey, crossed the Wild Horse Desert. "The rolling prairie continued without trees or shrubbery, save here and there a little *mot* or group," he wrote. His party marveled at the "herds of mustangs, going at full speed" across the prairie, "presenting a beautiful spectacle as they stretched for a mile or more, with their long bushy tails streaming in the wind." The following day, Bartlett noticed that "the prairie near the horizon seemed to be moving, with long undulations, like the waves of the ocean." Surveying the area through his telescope, he "discovered the whole prairie towards the horizon alive with mustangs." Then the herd turned toward Bartlett's wagon train, frightening the mules, "who dashed off at full speed after and among the wild horses." The runaways were finally calmed, but one of their most valuable horses had escaped and joined "his wild brethren and disappeared on the prairie, with his saddle, bridle, and trappings." That afternoon, Bartlett came upon the reason for the stampede—a large prairie fire extending for miles across the horizon. Only when they found a break in the line of fire could Bartlett and the train make their way safely through to "another chain of lagunas, or small ponds, known as *Santa Gertrude*,"

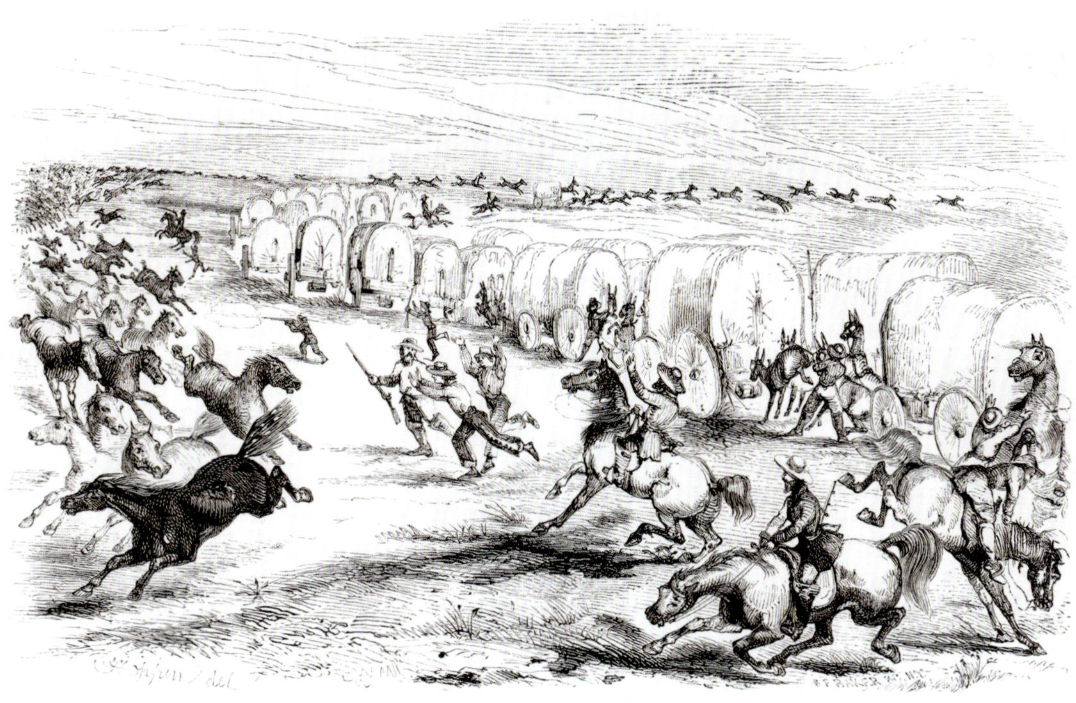


August Hoppin after John Russell Bartlett, *Stampede of the Train by Wild Horses,* engraving, 3¾ × 5⅝ inches. From John Russell Bartlett, *Personal Narrative of Explorations and Incidents in Texas, New Mexico, California, Sonora, and Chihuahua,* 2 vols. (New York: D. Appleton & Company, 1854), vol. 2, opp. 522. Courtesy of the Amon Carter Museum of American Art Library, Fort Worth. The wild horse herd, stampeded by a prairie fire, overruns Bartlett's party, startling the train's horses and mules.

John Russell Bartlett, *Prairie on Fire—From the Rio Grande to Corpus Christi, Texas,* December 31, 1852, pencil and sepia wash on paper, 10 × 12⅔ inches. Courtesy of the John Carter Brown Library, Providence, Rhode Island. The South Texas Coastal Plain was ablaze, and Bartlett's wagon train dashed through a gap in the wall of fire. Note the flank-high grass, probably on what had just become King's Rancho.

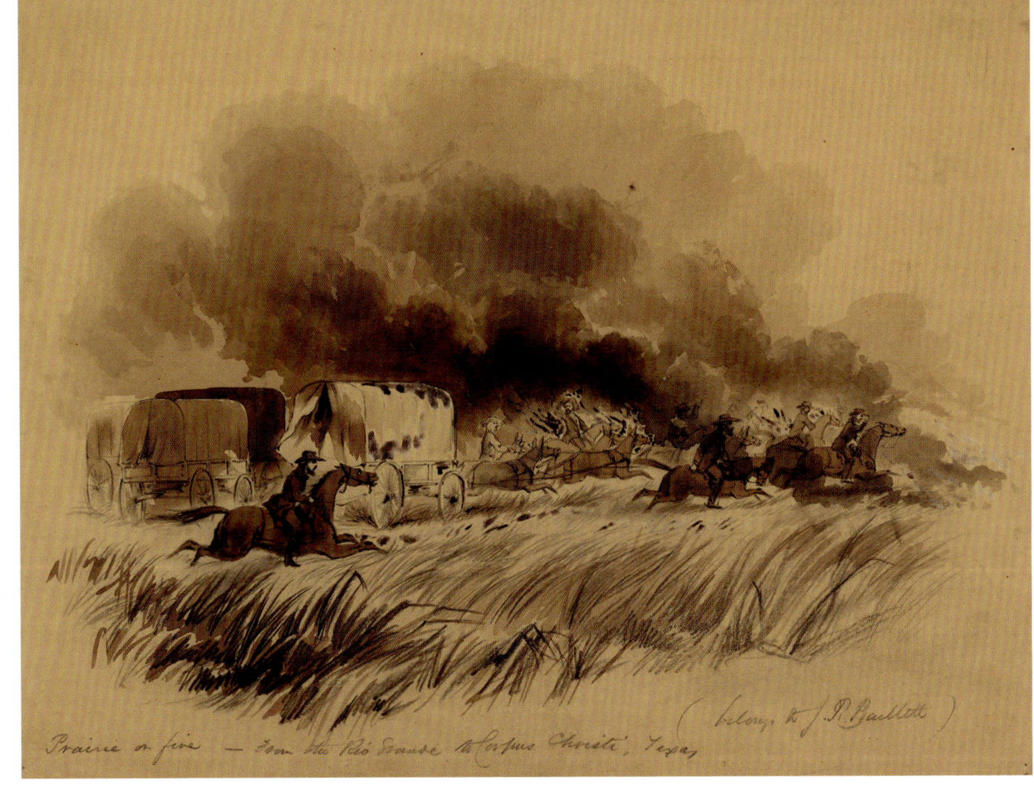

where they paused to refresh themselves.[8] This is the land that had just become part of King's Rancho and that Noe Perez has been painting for decades.

The herds of wild horses that caught Austin's and Kennedy's attention, and almost stampeded Bartlett's train, originated with the arrival of the first Spanish explorers in Texas—Francisco Vázquez de Coronado in 1541 and Luis de Moscoso Alvarado in 1542—and their offspring were soon running free because the Spaniards found no precious metals or great cities in Texas and largely ignored the region for the next century and a half or so. French explorer René-Robert Cavelier, Sieur de La Salle's inadvertent landing at Matagorda Bay in 1685 compelled the Spaniards to defend their territorial claims, leading to the establishment of missions in East Texas in 1690 and San Antonio in 1718, followed by the importation of a number of Canary Islanders in 1731, putting the village of San Antonio on course to become the region's first civilian, self-governing community.

In 1746, hoping to settle a territory that had been the home of "*indios bárbaros*, pagans, and apostates" for more than two centuries, the viceroy appointed José de Escandón y Elguera (1700–70) as governor of the newly created province of Nuevo Santander (comprising the Mexican state of Tamaulipas and much of South Texas below San Antonio).[9] Escandón established peaceful relations with the various Indian tribes living along the coast and the Rio Grande and founded towns up the river as far as Laredo, along with missions to minister both to the Indians and the colonists. By 1755, he had

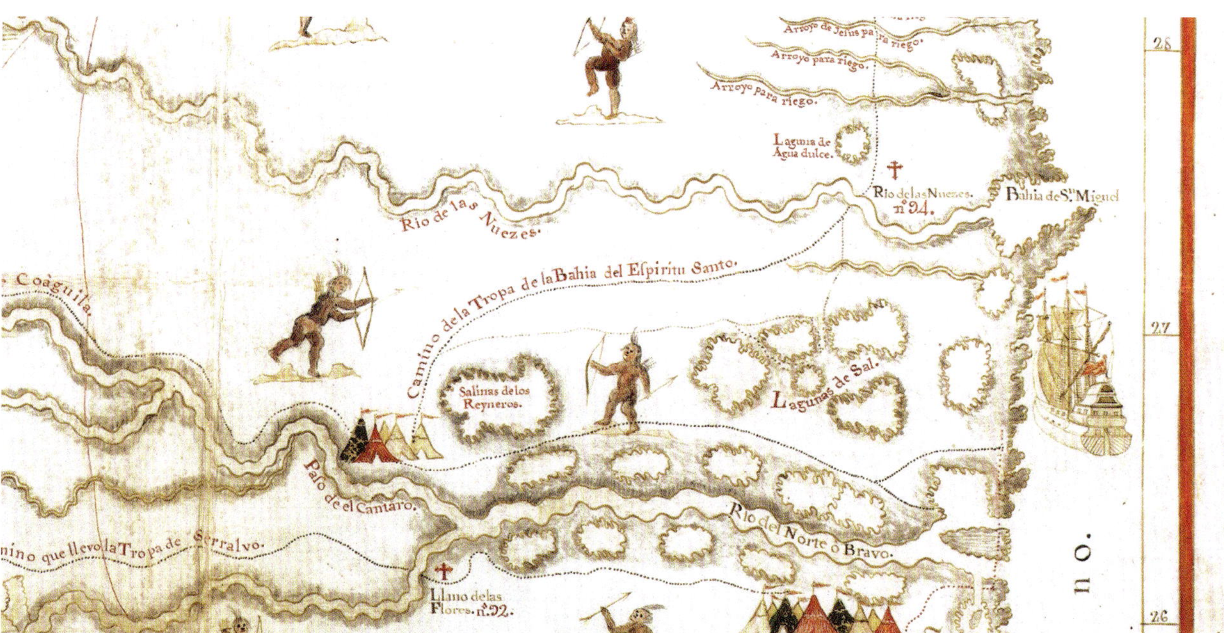


Detail from José de Escandón, *Mapa de la Sierra Gorda y Costa de el Seno Mexicano, desde la Ciudad de Querétaro, que se halla situada cerca de los veinte y un grados, hasta los veinte y ocho y medio en que esta la Bahía de el Espiritu Santo, sus Rios, Ensenadas, y Fronteras,* circa 1747. Archivo General de Indias, Seville, Spain. Copy donated to the General Land Office of Texas by Dr. Andrés Tijerina (see https://medium.com/save-texas-history/colonizing-cartography-josé-de-escandóns-mapa-de-la-sierra-gorda-y-costa-del-seno-mexicano-3d7e7edeb531). Escandón pictures Indians and teepees that he encountered between the Rio de las Nuezes and the Rio del Norte o Bravo.

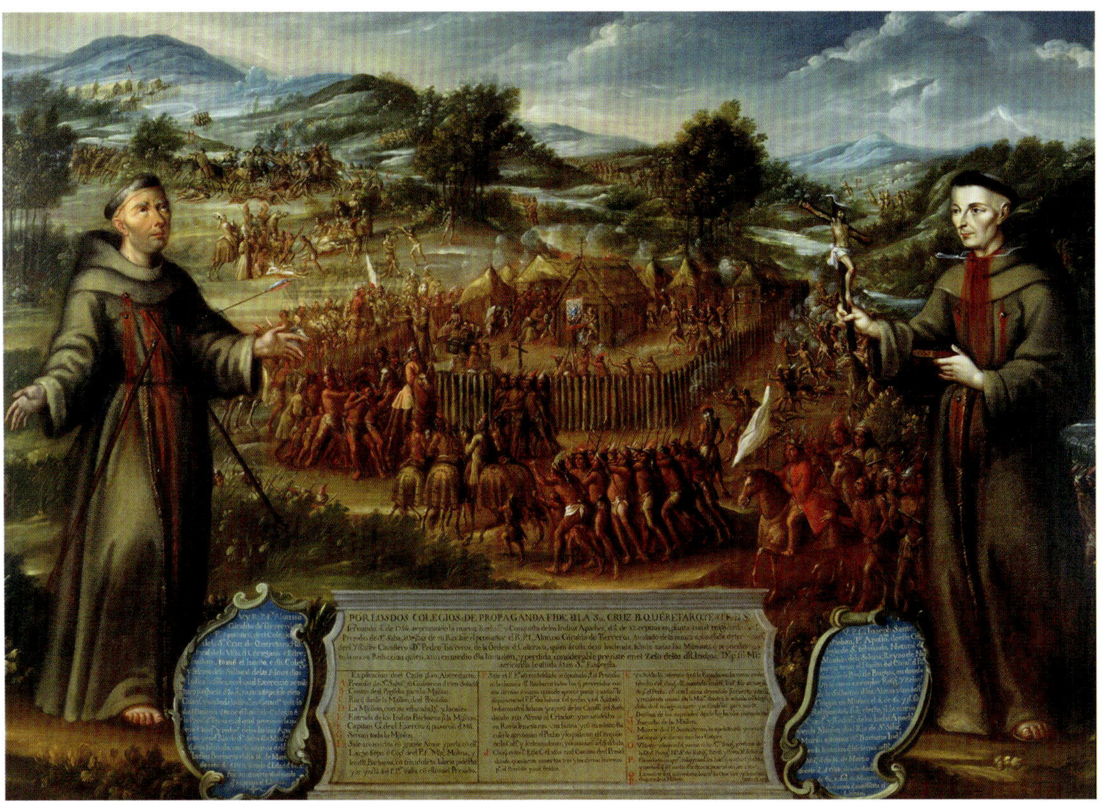

José de Páez (attrib.), *Destruction of Mission San Sabá in the Province of Texas and Martyrdom of the Fathers Alonso Giraldo de Terreros and José Santiesteban*, circa 1763, oil on canvas, 83 × 115 inches. Copyright © D. R. Museo Nacional de Arte / Instituto Nacional de Bellas Artes y Literatura 2019, Mexico City.

established twenty-three settlements with a population of 6,384 persons, and, although hostile natives and a lack of reliable sources of water hampered further settlement of the Wild Horse Desert, the Spanish crown made numerous land grants throughout South Texas.[10] The Spanish push northward was blunted in 1758 when Taovayas, Comanches, and a number of other northern tribes looted and burned Mission Santa Cruz de San Sabá, near present-day Menard, killing two priests and four soldiers.[11] Despite continued indigenous resistance and near-desert conditions in arid seasons, these early stock-raising operations slowly spread northward and became the progenitors of the famous Texas ranches of later decades.[12]

South Texas was relatively tranquil during the tumultuous decade after 1810 as Mexico struggled for its independence from Spain, finally succeeding in 1821. But when residents of Texas declared and won their independence from Mexico in 1836, the land of the Wild Horse Desert became the subject of conflicting claims. Following a near-miraculous victory over Mexican troops at the battle of San Jacinto, the Texans entered into a secret treaty with Gen. Antonio López de Santa Anna, granting that the southern boundary of Texas would be the Rio Grande, rather than the Nueces River, the historical southern boundary. When Texas became the twenty-eighth state in the Union in 1846, Pres. James K. Polk took up the state's claim, quickly engaging in a war against Mexico, with the first two battles occurring in the southern tip of the disputed territory, only a few miles north of the Rio Grande. It was in 1852, four years after the close of the war, that Capt. Richard King first saw the "handsome pastures" and "good grass for cattle" that Cabeza de Vaca had

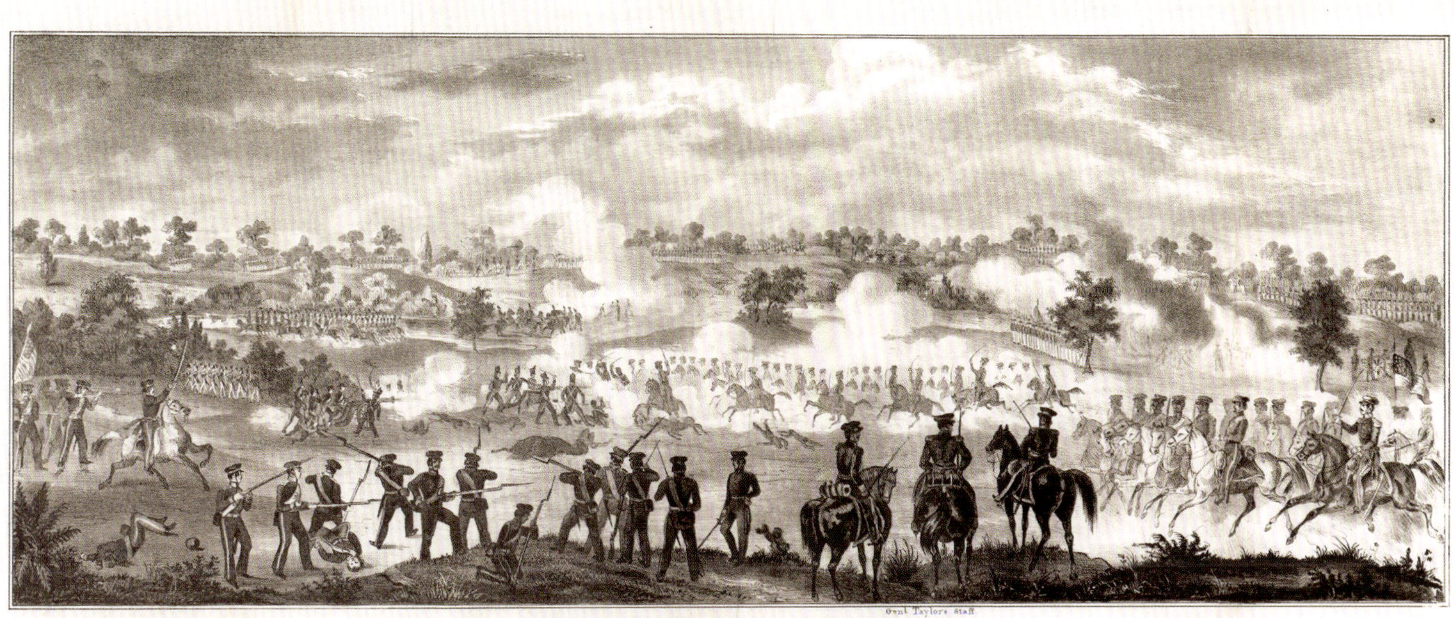


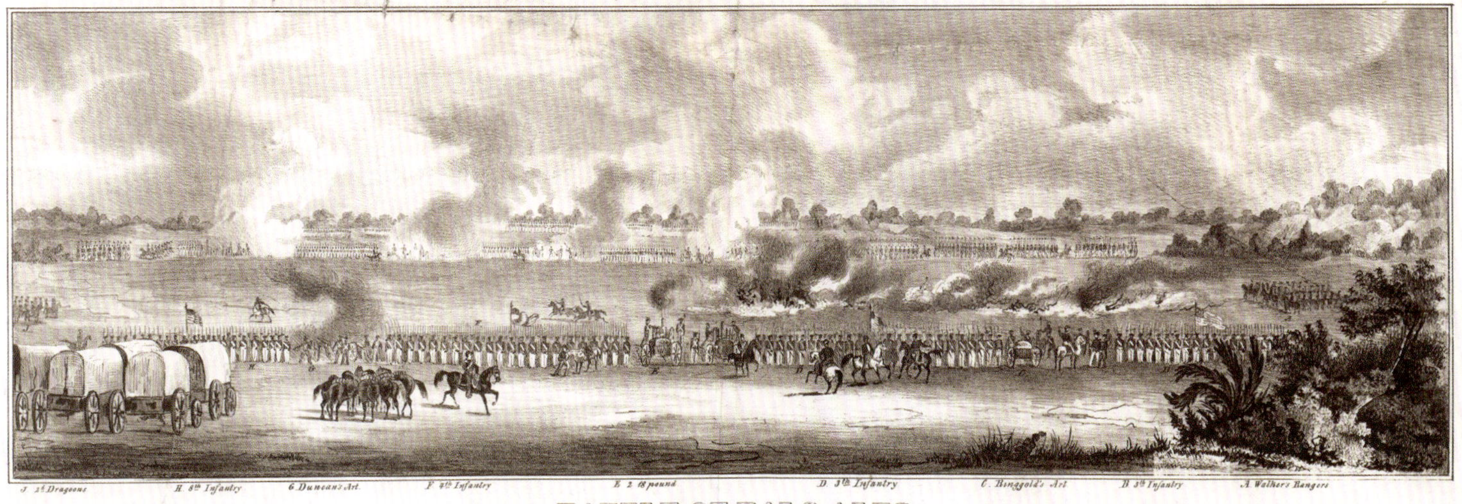


Emil Klauprecht after Angelo Paldi, *Battle of Resaca de la Palma, May 9, 1846. Battle of Palo Alto, May 8, 1846,* 1847, lithograph, 14⅞ × 19¼ inches, by Klauprecht & Menzel. Courtesy of the Prints and Photographs Division, Library of Congress, Washington, DC. Angelo Paldi was an Italian-born musician in the Fifth US Infantry Regiment who witnessed the first two battles of the war and sketched them on the spot. Sometime in August 1847, Emil Klauprecht, editor of the Cincinnati-based German literary journal *Fliegende Blätter,* and his partner, Adolphus Menzel, reproduced Paldi's sketches as a lithograph in their journal. Wm. Wiswell issued the print separately.

described and, accompanied by his partner Gideon "Legs" K. Lewis, he purchased land on Santa Gertrudis Creek for his rancho.

Noe's father was a South Texas vaquero: "When anyone had cowboying work to do, they would call my dad," he recalled during an interview in his studio, "and, beginning about age six or seven, I would tag along. Dad was a teacher. He liked to show us stuff and would point things out—'That's not how that should happen,' or 'When you do this, here is the kind of knot you should use.' Or he would say, 'This time of the year (or this time of the day), the light is so pretty.' He loved horses and worked with a lot of horses and cattle. He would tell me, 'Be careful—don't touch him there, don't touch him here.' He was very in tune with the animals and the land, and I spent a lot of time out there. Looking back, I think that sunk in more than I realized. My appreciation for these things—the land, the cattle—probably started right there." Today, his father's quirt and chaps occupy a prominent spot in Noe's studio.

It was also around that time when Noe started drawing. "I used to draw as a kid, but I stayed at it. I didn't grow out of it," Noe continued. At age twelve or thirteen, he began taking art lessons from a teacher in Falfurrias who worked at the school but also was a fairly accomplished artist in her own right and sold her paintings. "She taught me how to stretch a canvas, how to use underpaint so that a certain color comes through, which brush to use with which paint." Noe's mother did not encourage him to pursue his art because the family did not know anyone who made their living as an artist, so he did not study art in college. Because he was good at math, he got an engineering degree.

But he continued painting after taking his first job in Houston, and he continued to look. While driving through Refugio one Sunday afternoon, he noticed a little landscape painting in the window of a small gallery known as GeoGina. He stopped and carefully examined the painting, concluding that it looked like a landscape by Porfirio Salinas Jr. (1910–73), a San Antonio artist whose work he admired. The gallery was closed, but he talked with the dealer the next day and purchased the painting on monthly installments. Learning that Noe was also an artist, the dealer invited him to show some of his work in the gallery and sold several of his paintings right away. Encouraged, Noe continued to paint in his spare time, sometimes copying work that intrigued him—paintings by western artists Charles M. Russell (1864–1926) or Frank Tenny Johnson (1874–1939) that he saw in galleries in Houston or San Antonio, for example—and lamenting that he had missed working with more sophisticated teachers while he was in college. He later remedied that shortcoming by participating in workshops with contemporary western artists Howard Terpning (b. 1927) and Ken Riley (b. 1947) at the Museum of Western Art in Kerrville.

Although Noe had not formally studied art history, he was aware of the many Texas landscape artists who had painted South Texas and the Hill Country in the nineteenth century—Theodore Gentilz (1819–1906), who emigrated from France to Castroville, about thirty miles west of San Antonio, in 1844 and painted the people and landscape of South Texas and Mexico for the remainder of his life; Hermann Lungkwitz (1813–91), a Düsseldorf-trained landscape artist who settled in Fredericksburg in 1851 and introduced German romantic landscape painting to Texas; Thomas Allen (1849–1924), who also trained at the Royal Academy in Düsseldorf and painted several San Antonio and South Texas scenes during his 1878–79 residency in Texas; and even William Henry Huddle (1847–92), better known as a painter of historical Texas revolutionary scenes but also capable of charming and quiet landscapes, such as his *Marble Falls* (1885, oil on canvas, 10½ × 16½ inches;

Dallas Museum of Art, The Karl and Ester Hoblitzelle Collection, gift of the Hoblitzelle Foundation).

But Noe was attracted to the work of the French impressionists and their followers, such as Anders Zorn (1860–1920) of Sweden and Spanish master Joaquín Sorolla y Bastida (1863–1923). This led him to draw inspiration from American impressionists such as William Merritt Chase (1849–1916) and John Singer Sargent (1856–1925). Only then did he discover the Texas impressionists, and today he views himself in the tradition of famous predecessors such as Julian Onderdonk (1882–1917), José Arpa y Perea (1858–1952), Dawson Dawson-Watson (1864–1939), and Salinas, all of whom produced South Texas and Hill Country landscapes.

Born in 1882, Robert Julian Onderdonk grew up in a family of artists in San Antonio. He received his earliest lessons from his father, Robert Jenkins Onderdonk (1852–1917), a painter who had trained at the National Academy of Design and the Art Students' League in New York, including study with William Merritt Chase, then one of the more accomplished artists and teachers in the country. When it became apparent that Julian's talent would benefit from further development, he also enrolled in the Art Students' League and studied with Chase. He returned to San Antonio in 1909, and his impressionistic landscapes of the Texas Hill Country, particularly depicting scenes bathed in bluebonnets, quickly became his "calling card" and eventually inspired so many copycats that the sobriquet "bluebonnet painter" had become a cliché, even during his own short life.[13]

José Arpa was an accomplished artist by the time he arrived in San Antonio. A Spanish painter who had won prizes in Europe and spent several years in Mexico, he first visited San Antonio in 1899 and over the years became an influential and popular member of the local art scene. Moving there in 1923, he established his own art school and soon offered classes *en plein air* at Bandera,

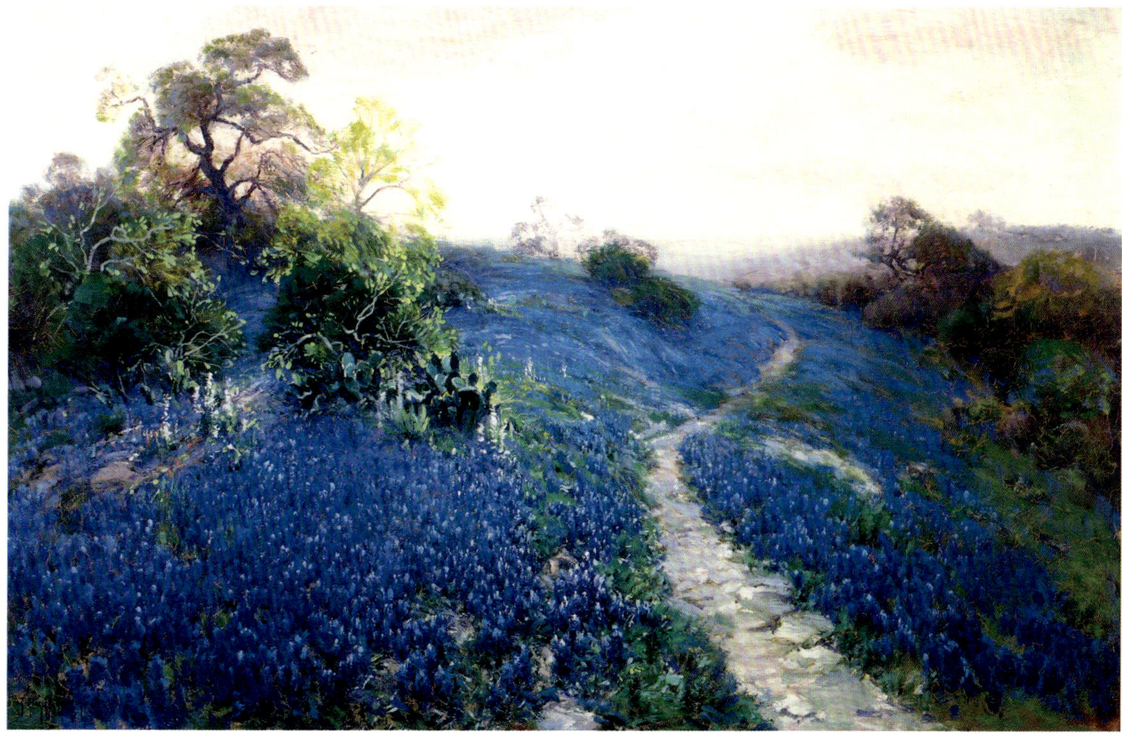

Julian Onderdonk, *Bluebonnet Field,* 1912, oil on canvas, 20 × 30 inches. Gift of the Estate of Grace Irving Gosling. Witte Museum, San Antonio, Texas.

in the Texas Hill Country. Arpa came out of the same Spanish tradition as Sorolla, whose brilliant whites and vigorous pinks and greens enlivened his dazzling canvases. Where Onderdonk seemed to focus on the bluebonnets and luminous flashes of limestone along the Hill Country creeks and cliffs, Arpa, according to art historian Cecilia Steinfeldt (1915–2013), was drawn to the Texas sunlight, imbuing the lambent atmospheres of his landscapes with exuberant colors.[14]

An artistic family also nurtured the fledgling talents of a young Dawson Dawson-Watson, who was born in London in 1864 and studied in Paris before emigrating to New York in 1893. He was one of several artists, including Emma Richardson Cherry (1859–1954), who brought the influence of French impressionism to America. Dawson-Watson earned his living by selling paintings, teaching, and serving as an arts administrator in St. Louis. He began to spend time in San Antonio in 1915 and moved there in 1926 to enter the first Edgar B. Davis Texas Wildflower Competition. Dawson-Watson completed seventy different canvases of cacti before painting *Glory of the Morning*, which won the first prize of $5,000 the following year, and colorful prickly pear cacti (*Opuntia*) became as characteristic of his work as the bluebonnets did of Onderdonk's. Dawson-Watson enjoyed a long career in the Alamo City, painting murals during the Depression and exhibiting frequently at the Witte Museum until his death in 1939.[15]

Like Onderdonk, Porfirio Salinas Jr. was a native of Texas. Born in Bastrop in 1910, he attended San Antonio public schools and learned his craft by watching Arpa paint in and around San Antonio and by working for the painter Robert Wood (1889–1979), another well-traveled Englishman who had studied

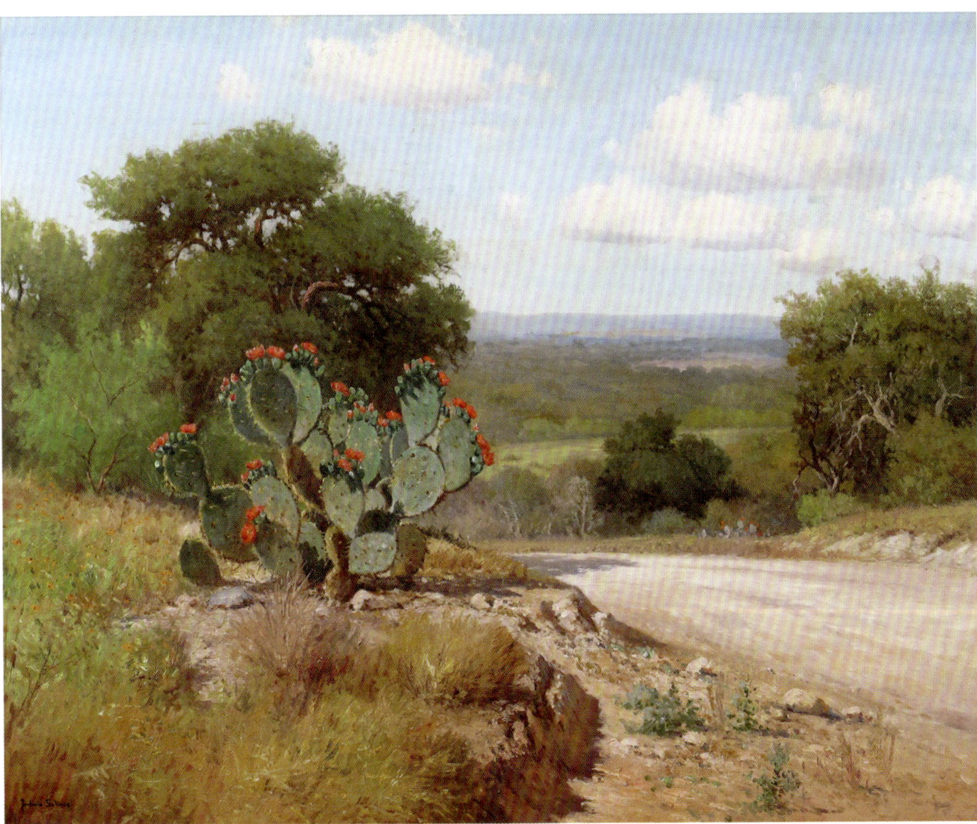

Porfirio Salinas, *Road to Hondo*, 1940, oil on canvas, 30 × 36 inches. The John L. Nau III Collection of Texas Art.

with Arpa and reportedly paid Salinas five dollars per picture to paint the bluebonnets on his canvases, which Wood found tedious. Salinas's picturesque landscapes of Central Texas soon found a following, especially among well-known politicians such as Congressman and Speaker of the House Sam Rayburn (1882–1961), Gov. John Connally (1917–93), and Pres. Lyndon B. Johnson (1908–73), who began to collect his work in the 1940s.[16]

And these individuals weren't the only impressionist artists working in Texas during the first half of the twentieth century. The 1893 Columbian Exposition in Chicago marked the coming of age of impressionism in the United States and spurred cultural aspirations throughout the West and Midwest. The great French impressionist Pierre-Auguste Renoir (1841–1919) wrote, "What seems most significant to me about our movement is that we have freed painting from the importance of the subject."[17] But many Americans disagreed. Trained in the principles of nineteenth-century landscape painting, which highly valued place, many American artists felt that scenes of treasured locales inspired and enhanced a sense of national identity. The following year, three midwestern critics, writer Hamlin Garland (1860–1940), his brother-in-law and sculptor Lorado Taft (1860–1936), and painter Charles Francis Browne (1859–1920), produced an essay arguing that "American art must be developed by the artists in happy sympathy with American surroundings and supported by a public loving the home things more than imported foreign sentiment." Frank Reaugh (1860–1945), a Dallas artist who had two paintings in the Chicago exhibition, no doubt agreed.[18] Robert Henri (1865–1929) later added that the "only one reason for the development of art in America . . . is that the people of America learn the means of expressing themselves in their own time and in their own land."[19]

Emma Richardson Cherry, a New York and Paris trained artist who moved to her new home in Houston in 1893, is generally credited with exhibiting the first impressionist paintings in the state. The Texas Coast Fair in Dickinson in 1896 included work by Reaugh, his

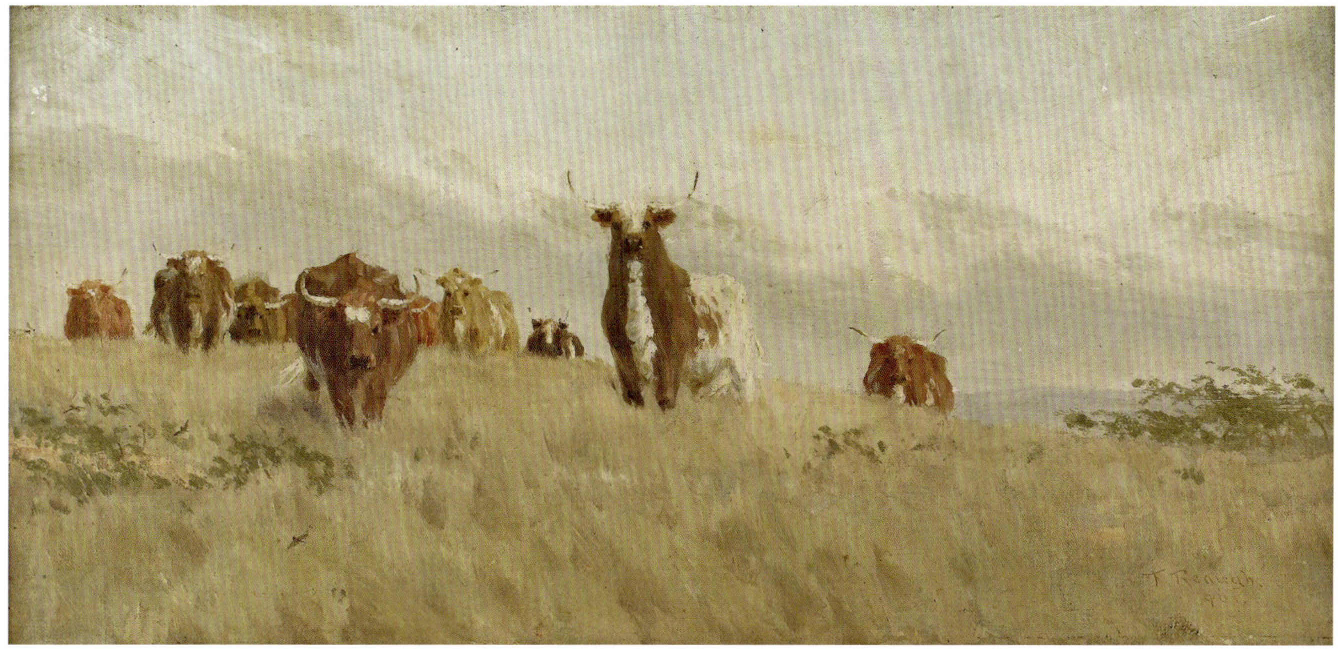

Frank Reaugh, *Breezy Morning*, 1896, oil on canvas, 12 × 24 inches. Albritton Collection.

student Edward G. Eisenlohr (1872–1961), and Dawson-Watson, as well as Cherry.[20] Reaugh was, perhaps, the artist who best connected impressionism to his "own land," with his West Texas landscapes and portraits of Texas Longhorns, but Eisenlohr and others also painted the local landscape. In reviewing the exhibition, Cherry's sister wrote that Reaugh's *Breezy Morning* (1896) was "one of the best exhibits from the State," showing "truthfulness and earnestness, and promise for the future."[21] With Reaugh embarking on his long career in Dallas and Cherry teaching and painting in Houston, impressionism was firmly fixed in Texas by the time Julian Onderdonk returned home in 1909. Noe clearly had talented artists to look to as he continued to develop his own style.

In truth, some critics sounded the death knell for impressionism in America just as it seemed to be gaining popularity in Texas.[22] But, with the founding of women's clubs, libraries, art societies, and various cultural organizations, followed shortly by the establishment of the first art museums, all determined to improve the cultural life of the state, impressionism grew in popularity. In addition to Onderdonk, Cherry, and Reaugh, artists like Louis Oscar Griffith (1875–1956) and Lloyd Goff (1908–82) (two of Reaugh's many students), Grace Spaulding John (1890–1972), Frederic Browne (1851–1941), John Eliot Jenkins (1868–1937), Frank Klepper (1890–1952), Adele Brunet (1871–1965), Samuel P. Ziegler (1882–1967), Murray P. Bewley (1884–1964), and many others kept impressionism relevant in Texas by exhibiting and selling their work. As art historian and curator Rebecca Lawton has pointed out, impressionism has remained popular in Texas largely because the artists heeded the tenets laid down by the Chicago triumvirate of Garland, Taft, and Browne—in this case, Texas artists painting familiar Texas scenes in an attractive and morally uplifting manner for a public that preferred appealing, engaging, and recognizable scenes of their own state.[23] As author and Nobel laureate John Steinbeck (1902–68) observed in 1962, "Texas is a state of mind . . . a mystique closely approximating a religion," so it is no surprise that there is an ongoing demand among Texas collectors for scenes of their state.[24] Noe Perez is one of several artists in Texas today who paint impressionistic landscapes, but he stands out as one of the very few who paint the Wild Horse Desert, leading his audience to recognize and appreciate the beauty that he sees all around him.

Onderdonk loved to paint *en plein air*, but Noe has found the typical South Texas wind to be such a hindrance that he limits such instances to sketching on small, six-by-eight or ten-by-twelve canvases and taking photographs. "I just like being out and trying to capture what is out there, especially in the spring. I can go out somewhere and things are blooming, and things are happening. I get excited. I am in a hurry because I am going to miss out on something if I'm not out there. That is the feeling I am trying to capture on canvas." Artist Rockwell Kent's description of Chase's technique seems also to inform Noe's process: "He went to nature, stood before nature, and painted it as his eyes beheld it . . . more interested in 'impressions' of the subject than in the deeper and more labored probing."[25]

When Noe finds a scene that he wants to paint and he knows how he wants it to be arranged, he simply begins painting. But if there are other elements that he needs to work out—such as architecture, figures, and/or animals—he takes a more studied approach. He may sketch the scene first, perhaps via a small pencil drawing or charcoal on canvas. "I am a structural engineer working up and down refinery row," he explains, "and there is a 'construction' aspect to painting: You have to know your materials, underpainting, colors, which colors will show through, what does this and what does that, what will crack in fifty years. To me, a painting is no more than a problem that you are trying to solve. There are rules about composition, color, edges, values—all those things that you need to keep in mind while you are putting it together. It is really like a puzzle that you need to solve." He continues: "I have gone through various stages in my painting. I would say that one of the biggest changes is in the values that I use now—with 'value' meaning relative darkness. All my paintings used to be high key, bright, flatter, and more colorful. Now I like colors that are grayer—Sorolla used a lot of gray in his paintings, and then when he added color, it really popped."

For his King Ranch project, Noe set out to visualize one of the iconic Texas legends—the ranch itself. "I was absolutely thrilled but a bit apprehensive about the commission," he recalled. "Thrilled because, ever since I can remember, King Ranch has always represented the pinnacle of Texas ranching tradition, especially in South Texas, and to be afforded the chance to portray in paint my vision of that tradition is hard to explain. We live life as a series of challenges," he continued. "You don't consciously try to capture 'what I am going through' or 'what I am feeling' in a painting, but your state of mind has a real impact on it. Ultimately, I feel that I am uniquely qualified for this assignment because I have been here all of my life, and when I was growing up, I spent a lot of time on South Texas ranches with my dad."

Of course, Noe isn't the first artist to paint King Ranch. The first, after John Russell Bartlett, was probably Thomas Allen, a Missouri-born, Düsseldorf-trained painter who spent the winters of 1877–78 and 1878–79 in the Galveston and San Antonio areas. Allen was a member of a wealthy St. Louis family. His father was a railroad magnate and congressman, and his mother was a member of the locally prominent Russell family. In addition, his younger second cousin

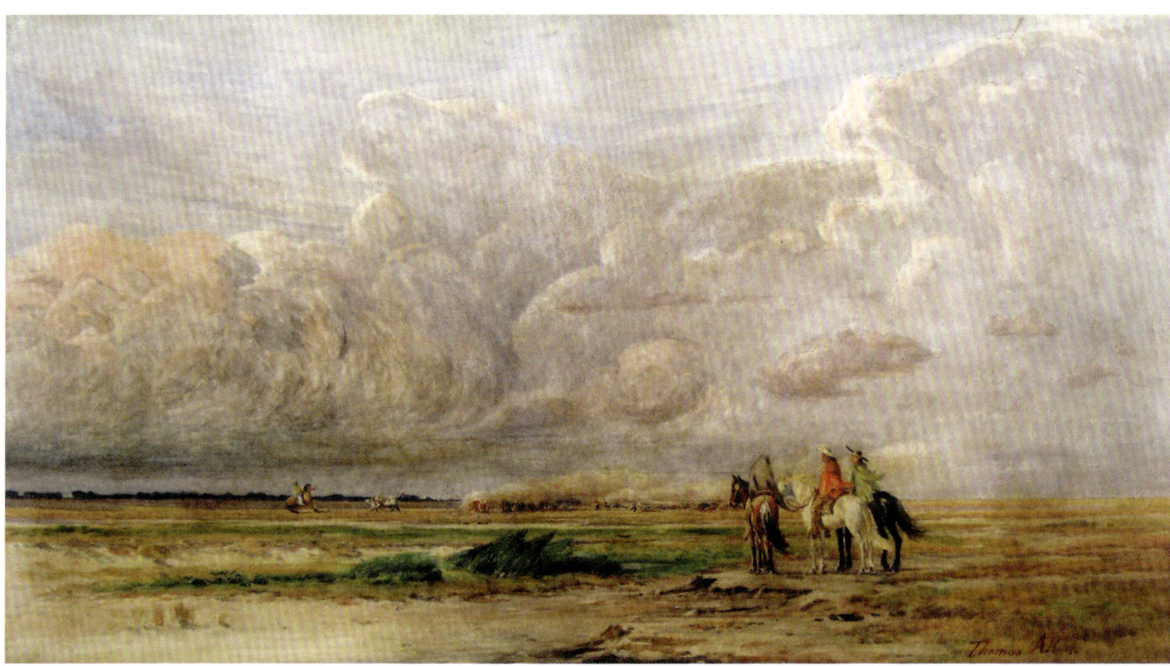

Thomas Allen, *Texas Roundup with Three Cowboy Observers*, circa 1878, watercolor on paper, 15 × 26¾ inches. The John L. Nau III Collection of Texas Art.

was the famous western artist Charles M. Russell, who also grew up in St. Louis. In the winter of 1877, Allen arrived in San Antonio via the recently completed railroad from Galveston, sketching and painting along the route. He ultimately produced several major paintings between San Antonio and the coast, including one made while visiting King Ranch, *Texas Roundup with Three Cowboy Observers,* which features a trio of riders in the right-center and a herd of wild horses shrouded in a cloud of dust in a typical Wild Horse Desert landscape. He later settled in Boston and pursued various business interests, continuing to paint in his leisure time. Allen was a member of the American Society of Artists and served on the board of judges for the World's Columbian Exposition in Chicago in 1893 and as president of the board of trustees of the Museum of Fine Arts, Boston.[26]

A few years later, in 1887, James F. McCan (1869–1925), a native of Ireland who had studied at the National Art Training Schools of South Kensington, London, emigrated to the United States. He worked for several years as a banker in Omaha, Nebraska, and

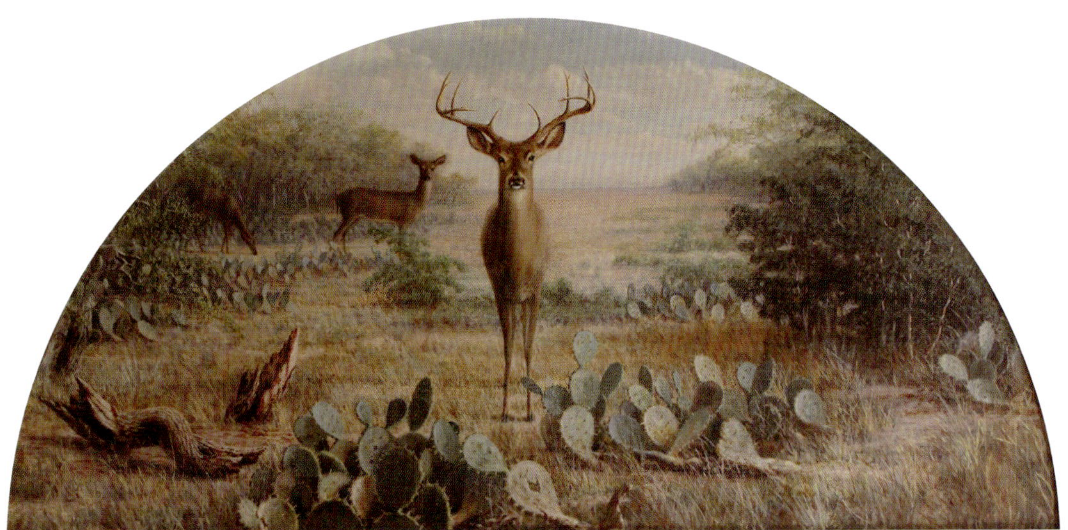

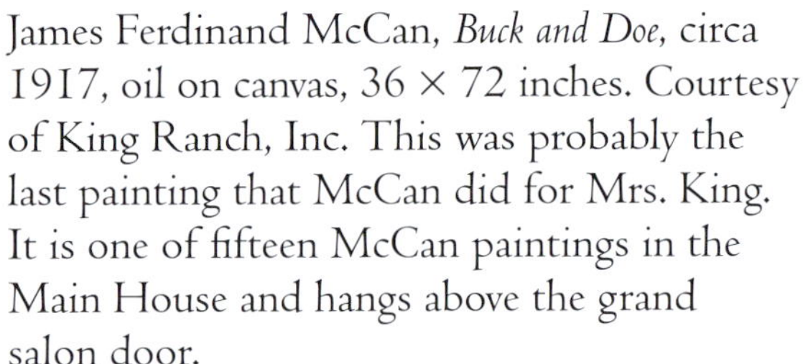

James Ferdinand McCan, *Buck and Doe,* circa 1917, oil on canvas, 36 × 72 inches. Courtesy of King Ranch, Inc. This was probably the last painting that McCan did for Mrs. King. It is one of fifteen McCan paintings in the Main House and hangs above the grand salon door.

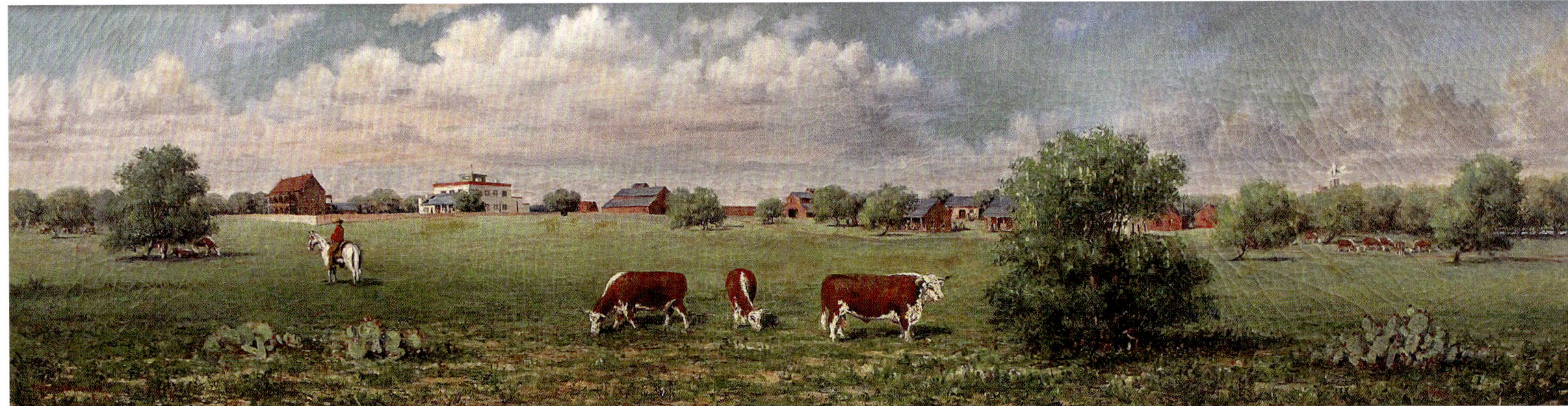

Tom Brown, *Santa Gertrudis Headquarters,* circa 1905, oil on canvas, 17 × 60 inches. Courtesy of Cecilia J. Hager and King Ranch, Inc.

then returned to Ireland in 1893 to continue his art studies, before establishing a studio in San Antonio two years later. There an exhibition brought him to the attention of Mrs. Henrietta King and Robert Kleberg Sr., who invited him to come and paint on the ranch. He spent much of 1895–97 at the ranch and in Corpus Christi, painting family portraits, landscapes, and ranch scenes, which established his statewide reputation.[27] Fortunately, Mrs. King kept a number of his paintings in her house in Corpus Christi, so they survived the catastrophic fire that destroyed the old ranch house in 1912.[28] McCan remained close to the family over the years and made many trips to the ranch.

Robert Kleberg Sr. paid close attention to the paintings that he commissioned for the house, even requiring that Tiffany Studios repaint a pastoral scene of Hereford cattle grazing in a pasture—the artist had not included a bull in the scene. But even after that correction, he did not like the picture and eventually had it removed from the library.[29] Among the pictures that McCan painted was a scene of the ranch headquarters, with the Main House in the left-center and Durham cattle in the foreground. By that time, Kleberg had imported Hereford cattle, and he commissioned Tom Brown (1859–1916), a well-known San Antonio businessman (a jeweler) and self-taught artist to repaint the scene with Hereford cattle prominent in the foreground. Brown also added a horseman on the left. A native of Providence, Rhode Island, Brown was a charter member of the San Antonio Art League.[30]

J. Louis Lundean (1894–1961) arrived at the ranch in 1933 to create illustrations for a *Fortune* magazine story. Born in Iowa in 1894, Lundean grew up in Wyoming, where he drove a six-horse hitch to a stagecoach as a

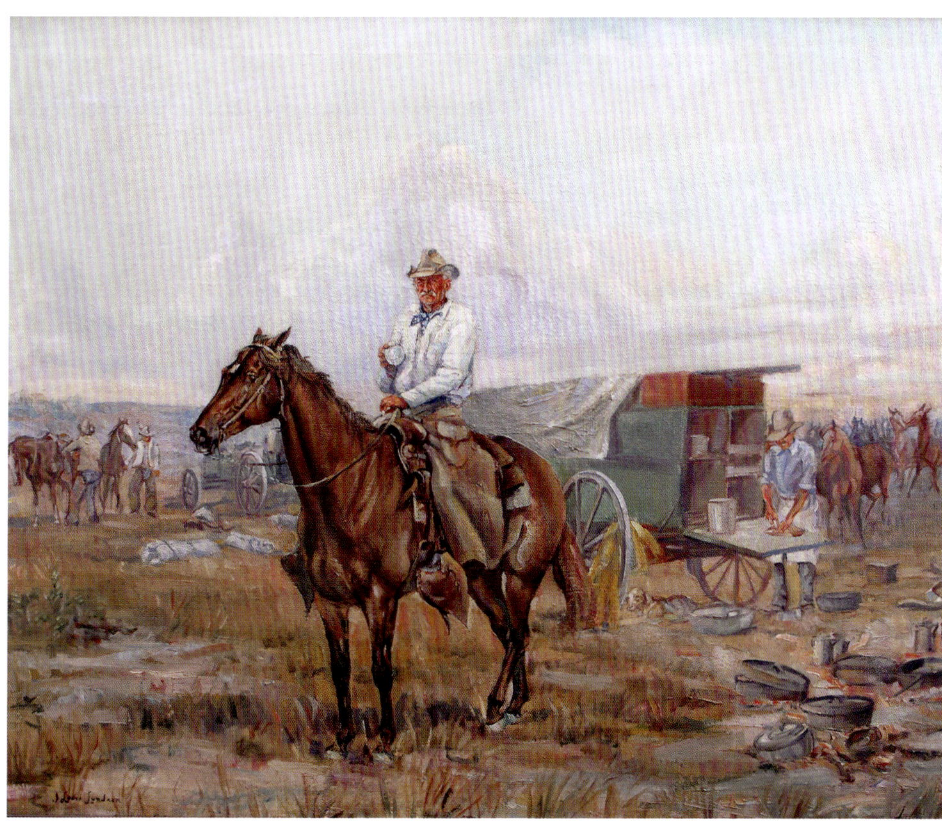

J. Louis Lundean, *Augustine Quintanilla Drinks His Morning Coffee*, circa 1933, oil on canvas, 24 × 30 inches. Courtesy of King Ranch, Inc. Augustine was a King Ranch *caporal* of historic reputation. Lundean described him as “one of the three cowmen or supreme commanders on the ranch. He is very old, very hot-tempered, and all-wise in the ways of cattle.” He is mounted on his favorite horse, Frentone.

youth and, no doubt, became familiar with the work of the "cowboy artist" of Montana, Charles M. Russell. He went east with the 101 Ranch Wild West Show but soon began to focus on his own art career. By the time he arrived in Texas, he was one of the country's noted horsemen artists.[31] He spent a significant amount of time on the ranch with the Klebergs and the vaqueros, working corridas and painting prominent Kineños and horses and cattle, which were illustrated in *Fortune* in December 1933. Lundean's *Augustine Quintanilla Drinks His Morning Coffee* bears a resemblance to Russell's work, with its vague hint of some hills on the horizon. In addition, there are also some distinctly un-Wild Horse Desert landscapes in the backgrounds of his other paintings. Lundean passed away in 1961.[32]

The most famous artist to work on the ranch, of course, was Tom Lea (1907–2001) of El Paso, who wrote the centennial history of the ranch, published in 1957. Lea became well acquainted with the ranch and its residents over the course of his three years working on the book and provided forty-three illustrations for the two-volume history, many of which designer Carl Hertzog (1902–84) gracefully worked into its chapter titles.[33]

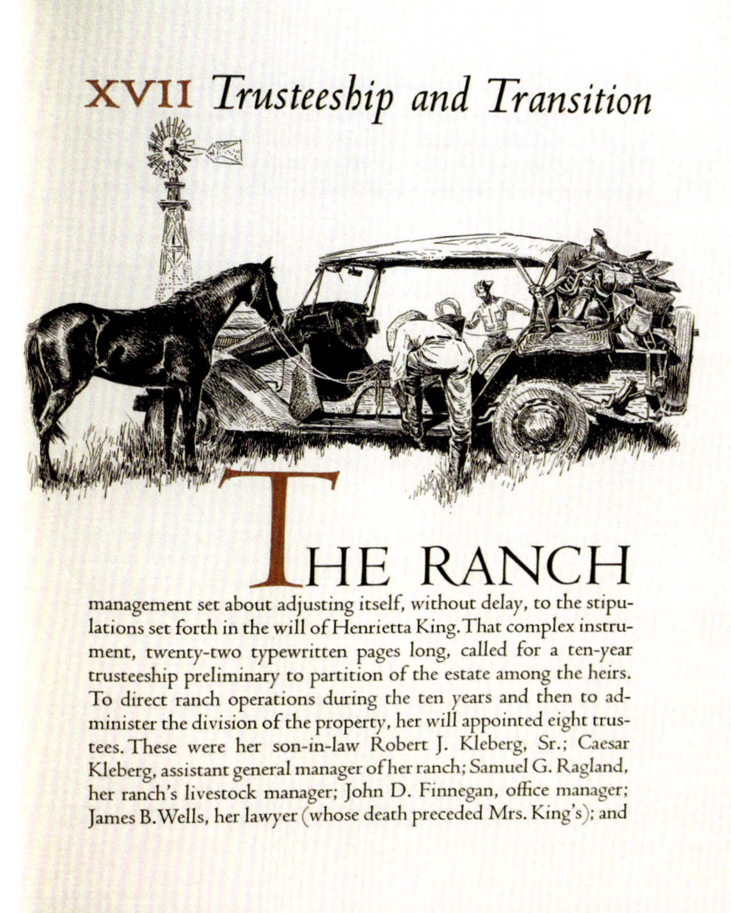

XVII *Trusteeship and Transition*

THE RANCH management set about adjusting itself, without delay, to the stipulations set forth in the will of Henrietta King. That complex instrument, twenty-two typewritten pages long, called for a ten-year trusteeship preliminary to partition of the estate among the heirs. To direct ranch operations during the ten years and then to administer the division of the property, her will appointed eight trustees. These were her son-in-law Robert J. Kleberg, Sr.; Caesar Kleberg, assistant general manager of her ranch; Samuel G. Ragland, her ranch's livestock manager; John D. Finnegan, office manager; James B. Wells, her lawyer (whose death preceded Mrs. King's); and

Book designer Carl Hertzog, also of El Paso, gracefully worked Tom Lea's drawings into chapter headings for book commemorating the centennial history of the ranch. From Tom Lea, *The King Ranch*, 2 vols. (Boston: Little, Brown and Company, 1957), vol. 2, p. 605. Courtesy of King Ranch, Inc.

Yet none of the previous artists who painted King Ranch exhibited Noe's sensitivity and passion for the landscape. Noe has produced a collection of images that reveal scenes to viewers as if they were touring the ranch, with the Main House probably being the most recognizable feature (see image 1, in chapter 4). Designed by San Antonio architects Carl and Carlton Adams, an uncle and nephew team, the Mexican hacienda-style *casa grande* replaced the Victorian pile that fell victim to an arsonist in 1912. Tiffany Studios of New York designed the interior. Among the historical details that Noe has painted are the "key hole" (the entrance to the east porch), one of the Tiffany gates, quarter horses grazing within sight of the Main House's Moorish-style three-story tower, Mrs. King's nearby carriage house, and the carriage house breezeway (see images 2–7).

The Kineños are an important element of the King Ranch story, with a legacy that is almost as old as the ranch itself. When Captain King visited northern Mexico to purchase stock during a severe drought in 1853 and 1854, he came upon the Tamaulipas village of Cruillas and purchased all the villagers' cattle. Realizing that he might have deprived the villagers of their livelihood, he offered them a proposition: he would provide them with food, shelter, and wages if they would come to live and work on his rancho. A number of them accepted his offer, and more than one hundred men, women, children, and assorted beasts, with all their possessions, joined King on his return to Santa Gertrudis. These experienced stockmen and horsemen became known as *los Kineños,* King's people or King's men, and generations of them have served the ranch in its more than a century and a half of operation (see images 11–15). Of course, conditions on the ranch have changed today, with mechanization and the like, but a proud remnant still serves.

Characteristic ranch scenes include a *manada* of King Ranch–bred quarter horses grazing under a stupendous sky of blotchy, feathery clouds, much like Chase might have painted (see image 19), and the famous Santa Gertrudis cattle (see image 23). The ranch still keeps Texas Longhorns to remind everyone of how things all started (see image 26). And anyone who has been to the ranch will recall the classic windmills and treacherous drive-through or bump gates, with Noe combining both landmarks in a painting of the Caldwell Windmill, featuring one of the quirky gates on the Santa Gertrudis Division that requires some getting used to before you can pass through without risking a dent in the side of your truck (see image 27).

Noe also wanted to depict scenes from the different parts of the ranch. The Norias Division, the southernmost section, is located in southern Kenedy County and the northwestern corner of Willacy County, reaching all the way to the coast (see images 28–30 and 32–34). It is home to coastal brush, sand dunes, and an oak motte that covers an area of about 70,000 acres—tall, spindly oaks, all natural growth, that provide a welcome canopy on a hot day (see images 35–38). This is quite different from Santa Gertrudis, where there are historical, architectural structures such as the Main House, the carriage house, the distinctive stable, the barn near the headquarters (see image 10). The Laureles Division also goes all the way to the coast, occupying the eastern half of Kleberg County and bordering on Cayo del Grullo and Alazán and Baffin Bays (see images 39–42). Some of this division is devoted to cotton and milo, and it also contains a huge lake, Laguna Larga. The Encino Division, south of Falfurrias, is a cattle operation that offers hunting rentals, suggesting just how significant hunting is for many of these South Texas ranches. Several camp houses were built on the division (as well as the others) to house the men when they were working cattle; these are used by hunters today. Venada Camp is an example (see image 49).

Noe's scenes accurately capture the brilliant South Texas light. Appreciating this same beauty, artist Julian Onderdonk was anxious to return home to Texas after his years of study in New York because he remembered scenes from his childhood that he wanted to paint. But they were not as he remembered. "It was like stepping into another world, the wonders of which had been read of, never seen," he recalled. His days on Long Island had caused him to forget the intensity of the South Texas light, something that Noe knows well and has captured in bright, colorful landscapes such as *Summer Clouds (Norias)* and *Spring Flowers at Encino* (see images 50–51). In *Spring Flowers at Encino,* he dampens the colors a bit so that the yellow of the summer flowers and the green of the mesquite trees seem more vibrant, while the sky is still a muted but lucent blue. And, perhaps because of the relentlessness of the Wild Horse Desert sun, Noe's colorful *Lauro's Field Prickly Pear (Santa Gertrudis)* seems brighter than the similar renderings of Dawson-Watson (see image 52).

Noe's choice of subject for his paintings differs from most contemporary landscape artists, who depict the Big Bend, the Big Thicket, the Hill Country, Texas rivers, and/or the High Plains. Nor does it conform to

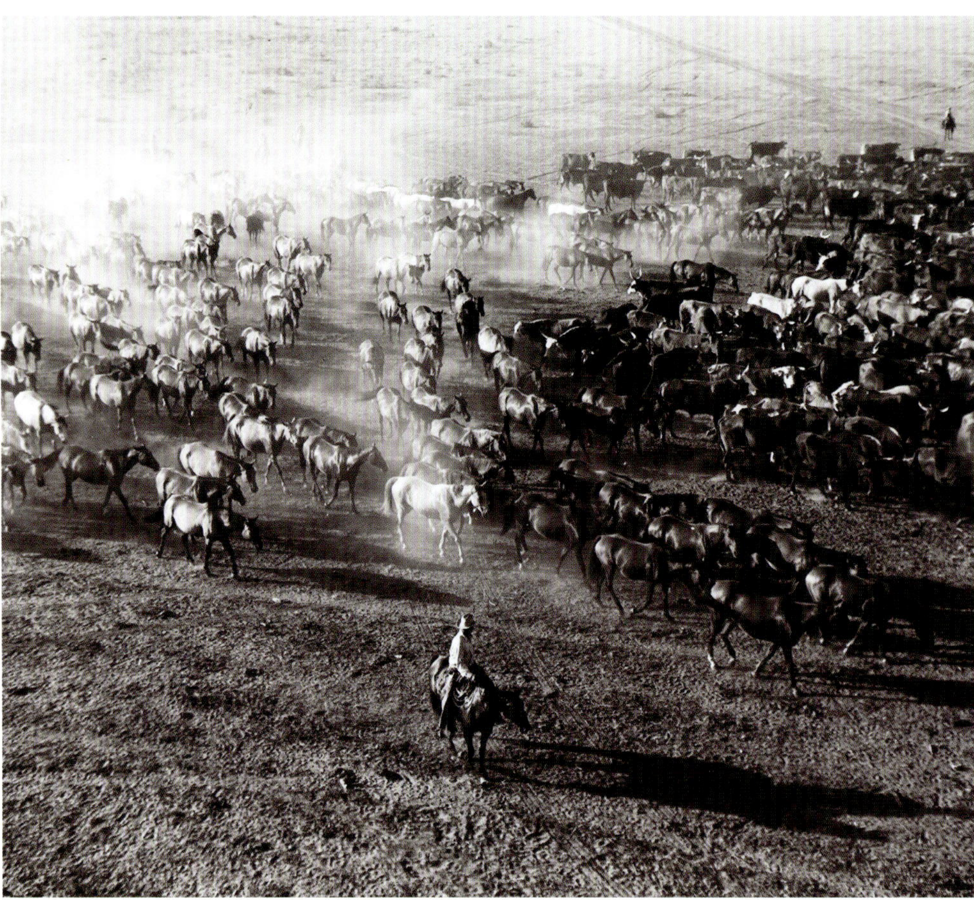

Toni Frissell climbed a windmill to get this photograph of vaqueros moving a mixed herd of horses and cattle in 1940. Toni Frissell Collection, Library of Congress Prints and Photographs Division, Washington, DC. Courtesy of King Ranch, Inc.

the state's mythology as seen in popular culture—the western movies, the Alamo, big oil, big ranch. Gifted fashion photographer Toni Frissell captured that vision of the ranch during multiple visits between 1939 and 1944: Kineños relaxing around the stable, their children watching from a distance or roping calves; vaqueros saddling up for the day's work, roping horses and calves, branding calves, herding cattle; the camp cook preparing breakfast on the range; the chuck wagon and water wagon moving from one location to another—but no landscapes.[34]

Noe also focuses on the big ranch—indeed, the ranch that inspired the classic Hollywood film *Giant* (1956)—but his quiet, calm, vast, serene, humble, boundless, and picturesque landscapes defy the stereotype (see images 54–60). His insight is in understanding that the land that others believe only to be a blistering wilderness is, ultimately, captivating and seductive. There is hardly a vaquero in sight in his modestly presented scenes, but he depicts a South Texas that he knows well. His art reflects his passion for and knowledge of place.

## Notes

1. William A. McClintock, "Journal of a Trip through Texas and Northern Mexico in 1846–1847, III," *Southwestern Historical Quarterly* 34 (January 1931): 237–38.

2. Juan L. González, Russell K. Skowronek, and Bobbie Lovett, "Deflation Troughs, Water, and Prehistoric Occupation on the Margins of the South Texas Sand Sheet," *Journal of Texas Archeology and History* 1 (2014): 70–93; Álvar Núñez Cabeza de

Vaca, *The Journey of Alvar Nuñez Cabeza de Vaca and His Companions from Florida to the Pacific, 1528–1536*, trans. Fanny Bandelier (New York: A. S. Barnes & Company, 1905), 97.

3. Richard S. Hunt and Jesse F. Randel, *Map of Texas, Compiled from Surveys on Record in the General Land Office of the Republic, to the Year 1839* (New York: J. H. Colton, 1839).

4. William Kennedy, *Texas: The Rise, Progress, and Prospects of the Republic of Texas*, 2 vols. (London: R. Hastings, 1841), 1: 178–79.

5. James K. Holland, "Diary of a Texan Volunteer to the Mexican War," *Southwestern Historical Quarterly* 30 (July 1926): 10.

6. John Cypher, who for years acted as assistant to the president of King Ranch, estimated that more than half of the ranch is sandy land. See John Cypher, *Bob Kleberg and the King Ranch: A Worldwide Sea of Grass* (Austin: University of Texas Press, 1995), 15.

7. Kennedy, *Texas*, 1: 178–79.

8. John Russell Bartlett, *Personal Narrative of Explorations and Incidents in Texas, New Mexico, California, Sonora, and Chihuahua*, 2 vols. (New York: D. Appleton & Company, 1854), 2: 521–25. See also Robert V. Hine, *Bartlett's West: Drawing the Mexican Boundary* (New Haven: Yale University Press, 1968), 79.

9. Robert S. Weddle, *The French Thorn: Rival Explorers in the Spanish Sea, 1682–1762* (College Station: Texas A&M University Press, 1991), 260.

10. Robert S. Weddle, "Nuevo Santander," *Handbook of Texas Online*, accessed August 3, 2019, http://www.tshaonline.org/handbook/online/articles/usnue (quotation); Brian Robertson, *Wild Horse Desert: The Heritage of South Texas* (Edinburg: Hidalgo County Historical Museum and New Santander Press, 1985), 1–32.

11. For more information on Mission San Sabá, see Robert S. Weddle, *The San Sabá Mission: Spanish Pivot in Texas* (Austin: University of Texas Press, 1964), and *After the Massacre: The Violent Legacy of the San Sabá Mission* (Lubbock: Texas Tech University Press, 2007).

12. Jesús F. de la Teja, Ron Tyler, and Nancy Beck Young, *Texas: Crossroads of North America*, 2nd ed. (Boston: Cengage Learning, 2016), 58.

13. Julian died at the age of forty in 1922. See Harry A. Halff and Elizabeth Halff, *Julian Onderdonk: A Catalogue Raisonné*, featuring an essay by Emily Ballew Neff (Houston: Museum of Fine Arts, Houston, 2016), 65; William Rudolph, *Julian Onderdonk, American Impressionist* (New Haven: Yale University Press for the Dallas Museum of Art, 2008); and Cecilia Steinfeldt, *The Onderdonks: A Family of Texas Painters* (San Antonio: Trinity University Press for the San Antonio Museum Association, 1976).

14. Cecilia Steinfeldt, *Art for History's Sake: The Texas Collection of the Witte Museum* (Austin: Texas State Historical Association for the Witte Museum, 1993), 9–13; and Michael R. Grauer, *José Arpa: A Spanish Painter in Texas* (Canyon, TX: Panhandle-Plains Historical Museum, 2016).

15. Steinfeldt, *Art for History's Sake*, 38–42.

16. Jacinto Quirarte, "Salinas, Porfirio, Jr.," *Handbook of Texas Online*, accessed September 11, 2019, http://www.tshaonline.org/handbook/online/articles/fsa11; Nan Robertson, "White House Gets a Touch of Texas," *New York Times*, December 10, 1963, 37; Porfirio Salinas, *Bluebonnets and Cactus: An Album of Southwestern Paintings by Porfirio Salinas* (Austin: Pemberton Press, 1967); and Ruth Goddard, *Porfirio Salinas* (Austin: Rock House, 1975).

17. Jean Renoir, *Renoir, My Father*, trans. Randolph and Dorothy Weaver (New York: New York Review Books, 2001), 174.

18. The locations of his two paintings *Landscape with Cattle* and *February in Texas* (known only through a small sketch in the Panhandle-Plains Historical Museum collection in Canyon) are unknown. Michael R. Grauer, *Rounded Up in Glory: Frank Reaugh, Texas Renaissance Man* (Denton: University of North Texas Press, 2016), 93–94

19. Charles Francis Browne, Hamlin Garland, and Lorado Taft, *Impressions on Impressionism; Being a Discussion of the American Art Exhibition at the Art Institute, Chicago, by a Critical Triumvirate* (Chicago: n.p., 1894), 23 (quotation); H. Barbara Weinberg, Doreen Bolger, and David Park Curry, *American Impressionism and Realism: The Painting of Modern Life, 1885–1915* (New York: Metropolitan Museum of Art, 1994), 15 (quotation).

20. Michael R. Grauer, *Texas Impressionism: Branding with Brushstroke and Color, 1885–1935* (Canyon, TX: Panhandle-Plains Historical Museum, 2012), 16.

21. Grauer, *Texas Impressionism*, 16.

22. See Rebecca Lawton, "Texas Impressionism," in Ron Tyler (ed.), *The Art of Texas: 250 Years* (Fort Worth: Center for Texas Studies at Texas Christian University and Texas Christian University Press, 2019), 186.

23. Lawton, "Texas Impressionism," 207.

24. John Steinbeck, *Travels with Charley in Search of America* (New York: Viking Press, 1962), 203.

25. Ronald G. Pisano, *The Students of William Merritt Chase* (Huntington, NY: Hecksher Museum, 1973), 7.

26. Heather Elizabeth White, "Thomas Allen's Sketches and Paintings of Texas, 1877–1879," in *American Material Culture and*

*the Texas Experience: Itinerant and Immigrant Artists and Artisans in 19th Century Texas* (Houston: David B. Warren Symposium, 4, 2014), 120–49.

27. "Texas Visitors at Omaha," *San Antonio Express*, August 25, 1912, p. 6, col. 4; and "J. Ferdinand McCan, Renowned as Artist, Dies in San Antonio," *Victoria Advocate* (August 31, 1925), 1, cols. 1–4. McCan married Emily D. McFadden, the daughter of a local rancher, James A. McFadden, and became a prominent member of the Victoria community. Emily later divorced him and married artist Royston Nave.

28. Email from Bob Kinnan, September 10, 2019.

29. Email from Bob Kinnan, September 17, 2019.

30. See *The Daily Express* (San Antonio), November 1, 1906, p. 3, col. 5; October 25, 1907, p. 11, col. 6; November 9, 1909, p. 2, col. 5; *San Antonio Express*, March 29, 1914, p. 9, col. 6; November 1, 1914, p. 18, col. 2; and July 16, 1916, p. 5, cols 1–2.

31. "25 Years Ago in Chappaqua," *North Westchester Times* (Mount Kisco, NY), April 14, 1960, p. 6, col. 3; "County Leads U.S. in Rating for Works of Art Projects," *Yonkers* (NY) *Herald Statesman*, accessed October 10, 2020, https://fultonhistory.com/newspaper%2010/Yonkers%20NY%20Herald%20Statesman/Yonkers%20NY%20Herald%20Statesman%201934%20Grayscale/Yonkers%20NY%20Herald%20Statesman%201934%20Grayscale%20-%203763.pdf; Augusta Owen Patterson, "The Decorative Arts," *Town and Country* 84 (October 1, 1929): 55–57, and 86 (October 1, 1931): 48–49.

32. "The World's Biggest Ranch," *Fortune*, 8, no. 6 (December 1933), 48–61, 89–90, 92, 95–96, 98, 103–104, 106, 109; "J. Louis Lundean, 66, Artist and Teacher," *New York Times*, (October 26, 1961): 35.

33. Bruce S. Cheeseman, "Tom Lea and the Writing of *The King Ranch*," 8, and Al Lowman, "Carl Hertzog: The Design and Printing of *The King Ranch*," 4–5, in Bruce S. Cheeseman and Al Lowman (eds.), *The Book of all Christendom: Tom Lea, Carl Hertzog, and the Making of "The King Ranch"* (Kingsville: King Ranch, Inc., 1992).

34. Toni Frissell, *The King Ranch, 1939–1944: A Photographic Essay*, with introduction and captions by Holland McCombs (Dobbs Ferry, NY: Morgan & Morgan for the Amon Carter Museum, 1975).

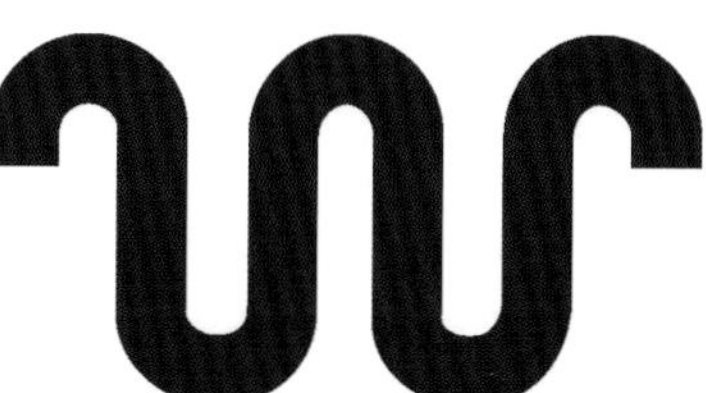

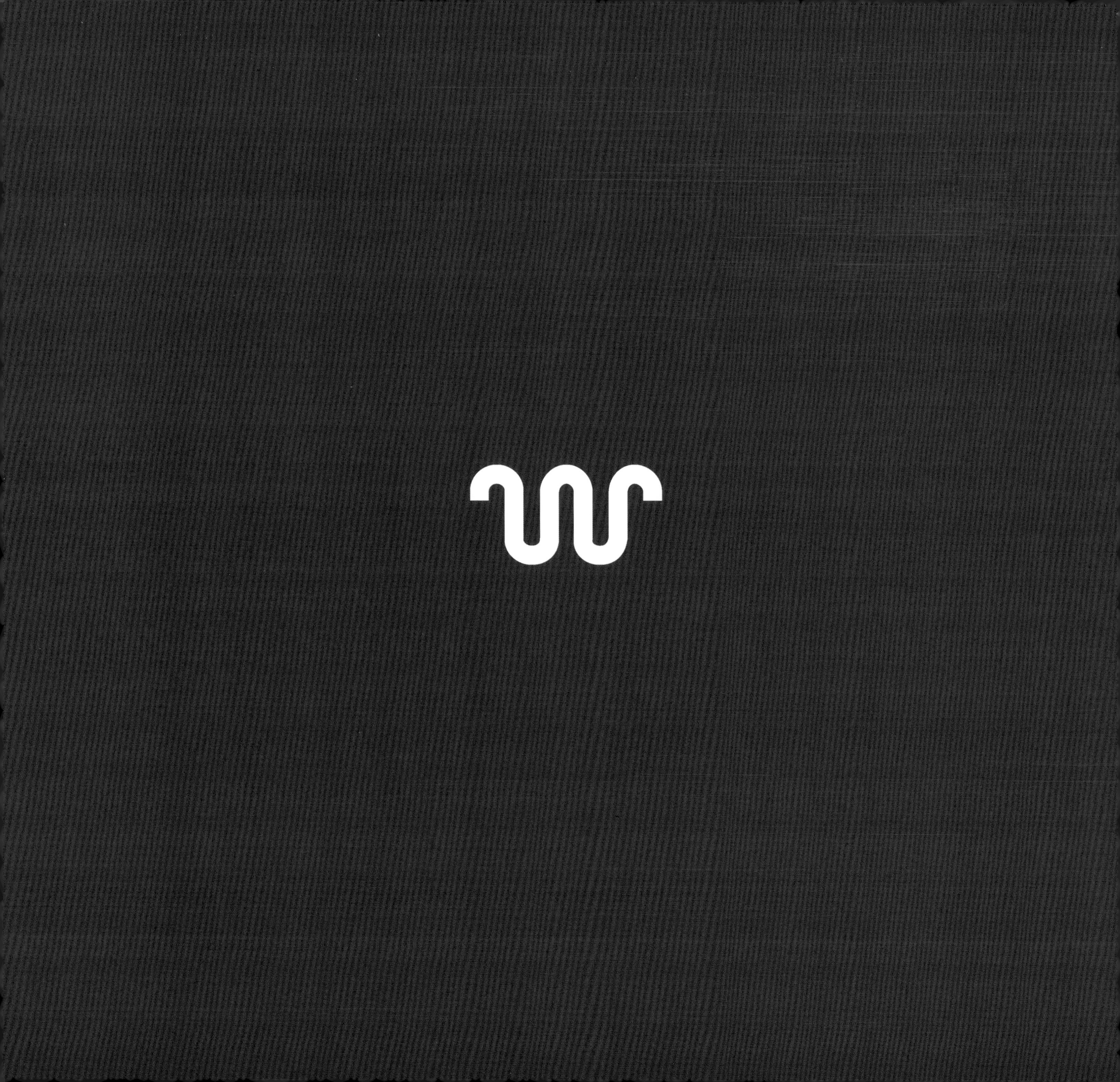

# Interpretations of King Ranch

## *Paintings and Commentary*

Noe Perez

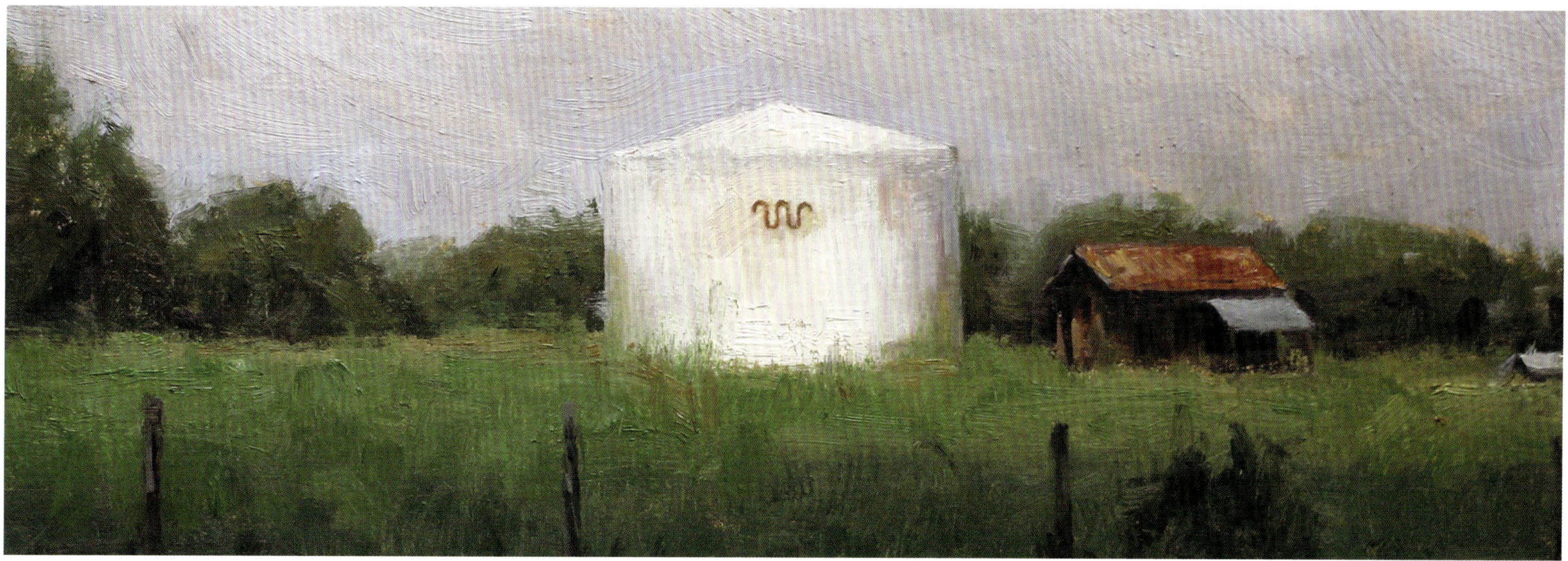

Noe Perez is a contemporary Texas painter living in Corpus Christi. He has painted his native South Texas his entire life. His works have been exhibited in the Witte Museum in San Antonio, the San Angelo Museum of Fine Art, the Nave Museum in Victoria, the Mayborn Museum at Baylor University in Waco, and at the Texas State Capitol Rotunda in Austin. His paintings have been published in *Of Texas Rivers and Texas Art* (Texas A&M University Press, 2017) and *Texas Traditions* (Frensco Fine Arts Publications, 2010). Perez is currently a member of the board of directors of the Center for the Advancement and Study of Early Texas Art (CASETA).

## King Ranch Main House

I was commissioned by King Ranch to do a painting of the Main House in celebration of the hundredth anniversary of the house. Of course, I was thrilled to do it. However, it turned out to be a more challenging undertaking than I had originally thought. The fact that it is a white structure presented compositional issues that were accentuated by the architectural aspects of the building. There are so many nooks and lines and curves throughout the structure that I wondered if I had taken on more than I could handle. I wanted it to be accurate, but I was afraid that it would look like an architectural rendering instead of a work of art. In the end, I was pleased with the outcome.

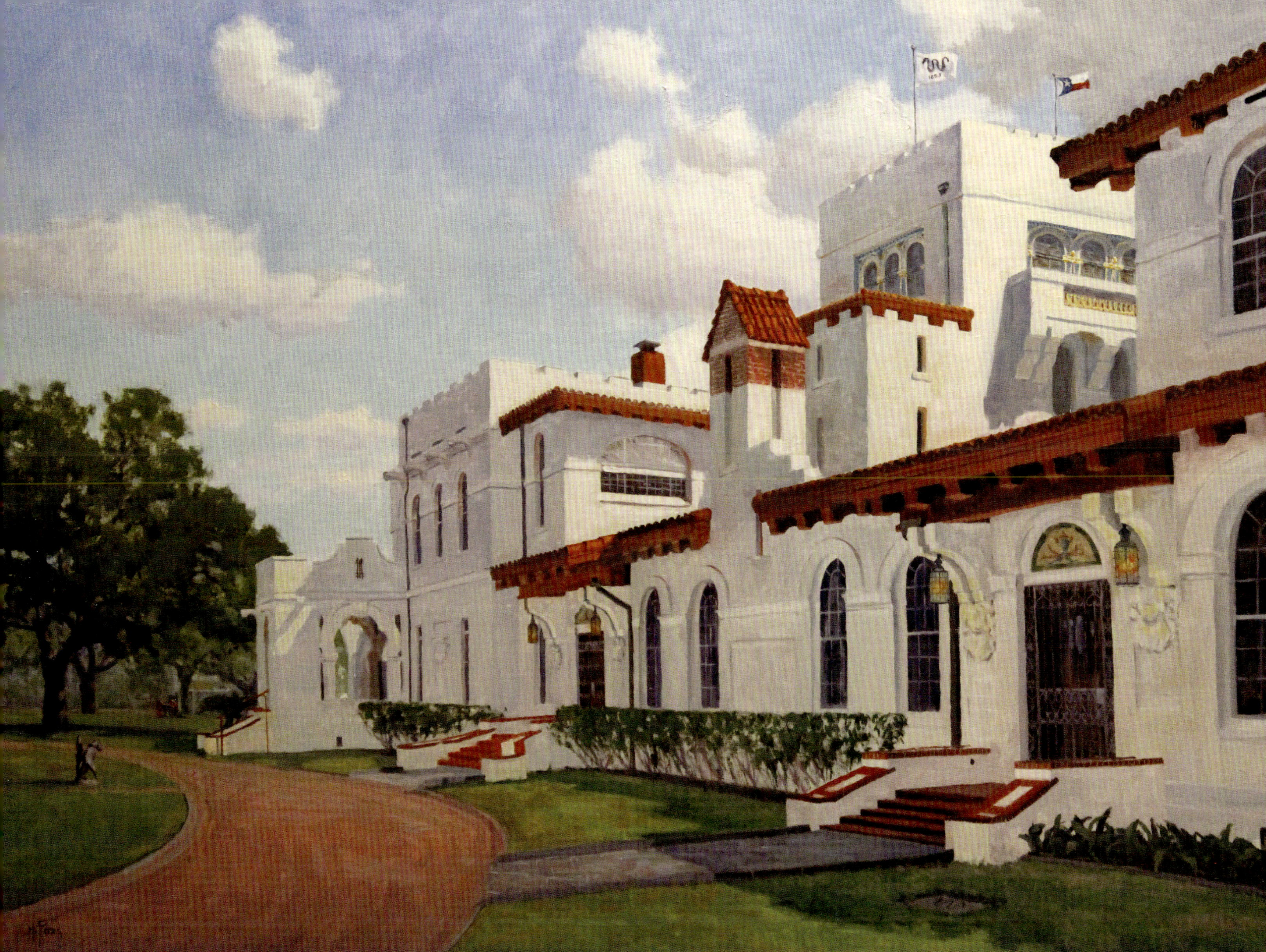

**1**

*King Ranch Main House*, 2015
Oil on canvas, 30 × 40 inches
Collection of King Ranch, Inc.
Courtesy of the artist

## Main House Key Hole

The Main House is embellished with interesting architectural detail of Moorish design. I chose to do this subject with a strong side light, but it was a real challenge to capture the light as it bounced around from white wall to white wall.

**2**

*Main House Key Hole (Santa Gertrudis)*, 2019
Oil on canvas, 20 × 16 inches
Courtesy of the artist

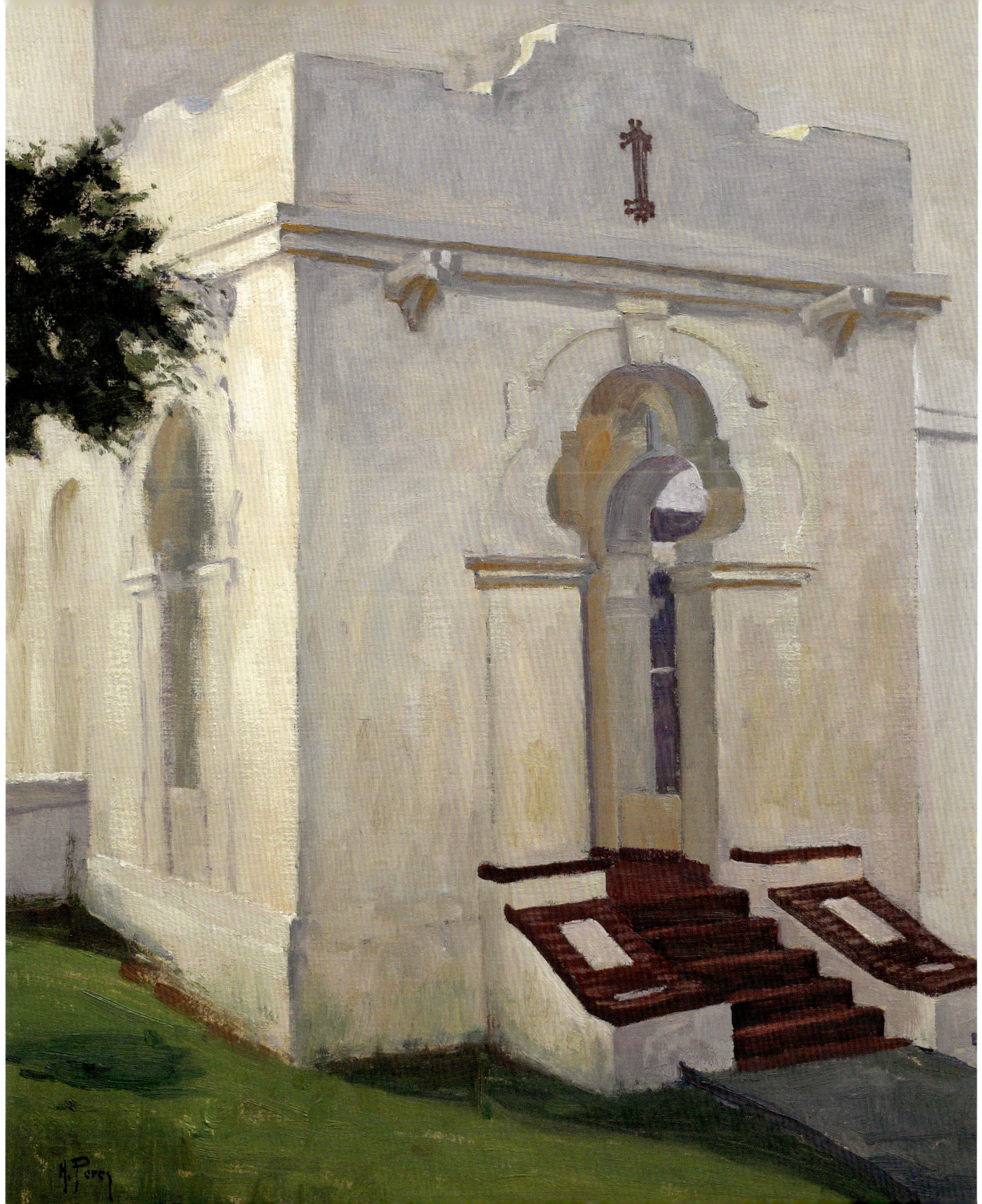
H. Perez

## Tiffany Gate at the Main House

I was immediately drawn to the patterns that appear in the gate and the lunette that is above the gate. This is just one example of five unique iron-gate designs at the Main House.

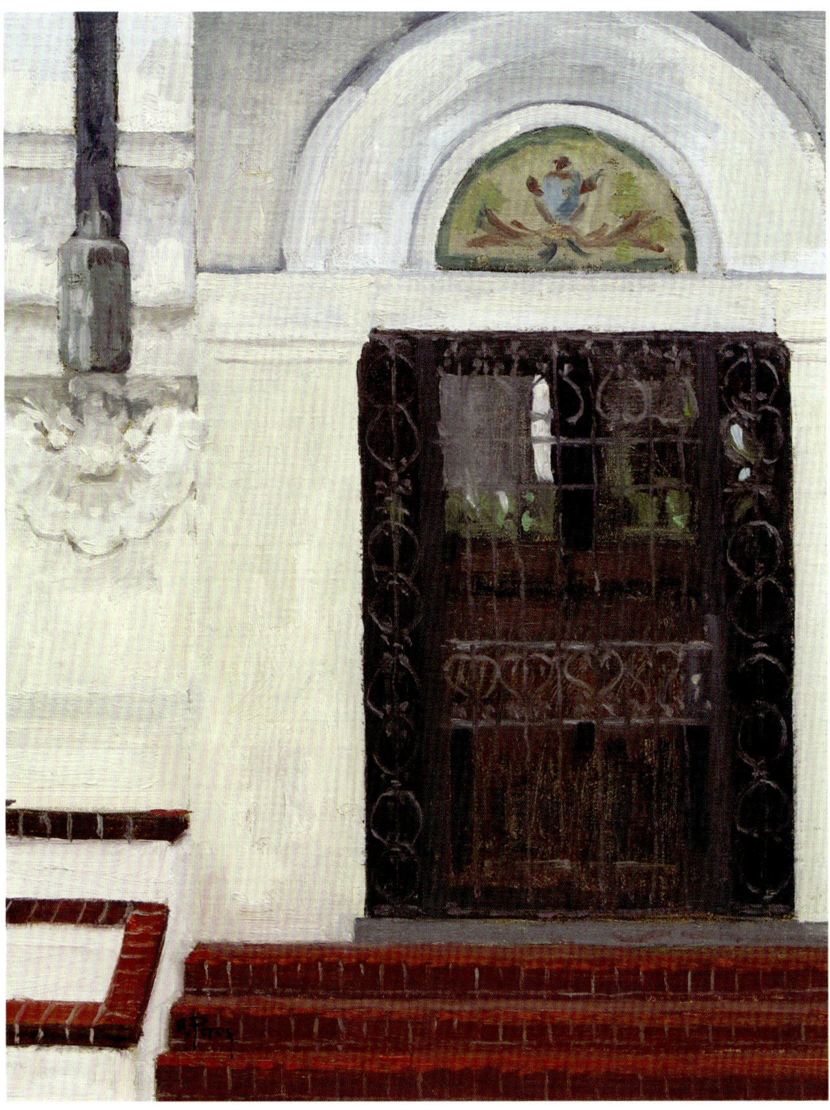

3

Study for *Tiffany Gate at the Main House (Santa Gertrudis)*, 2019
Oil on canvas, 16 × 12 inches
Courtesy of the artist

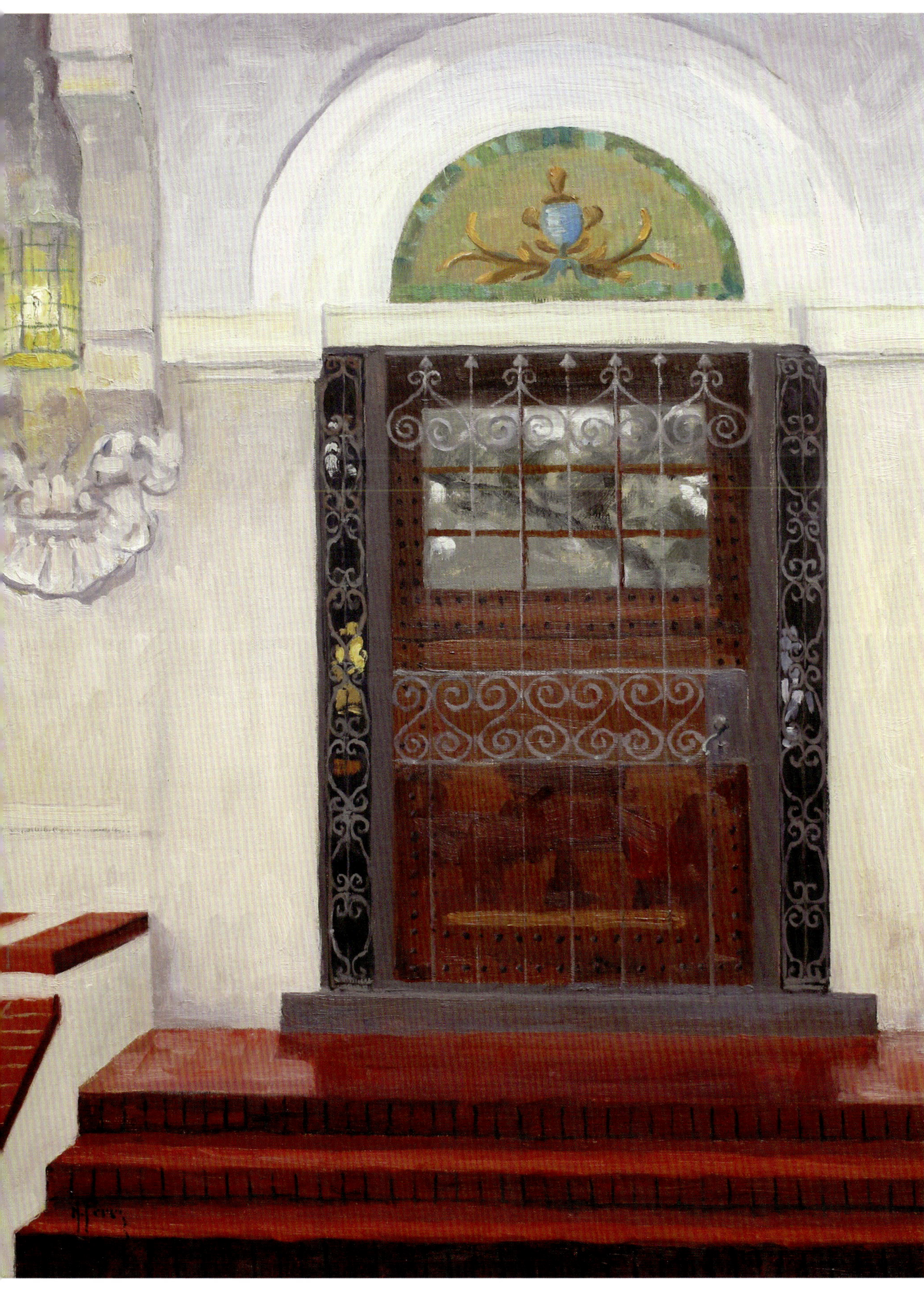

4

*Tiffany Gate at the Main House (Santa Gertrudis)*, 2019
Oil on canvas, 24 × 18 inches
Courtesy of the artist

## Creek Barn Trap Grazers

On this particular journey through King Ranch, I renewed my appreciation for a beautiful horse, especially as a subject worthy of art. They truly are majestic animals. This scene was almost too easy—quarter horses grazing within sight of the Main House.

**5**

*Creek Barn Trap Grazers* (*Santa Gertrudis*), 2019
Oil on canvas, 25 × 30 inches
Courtesy of the artist

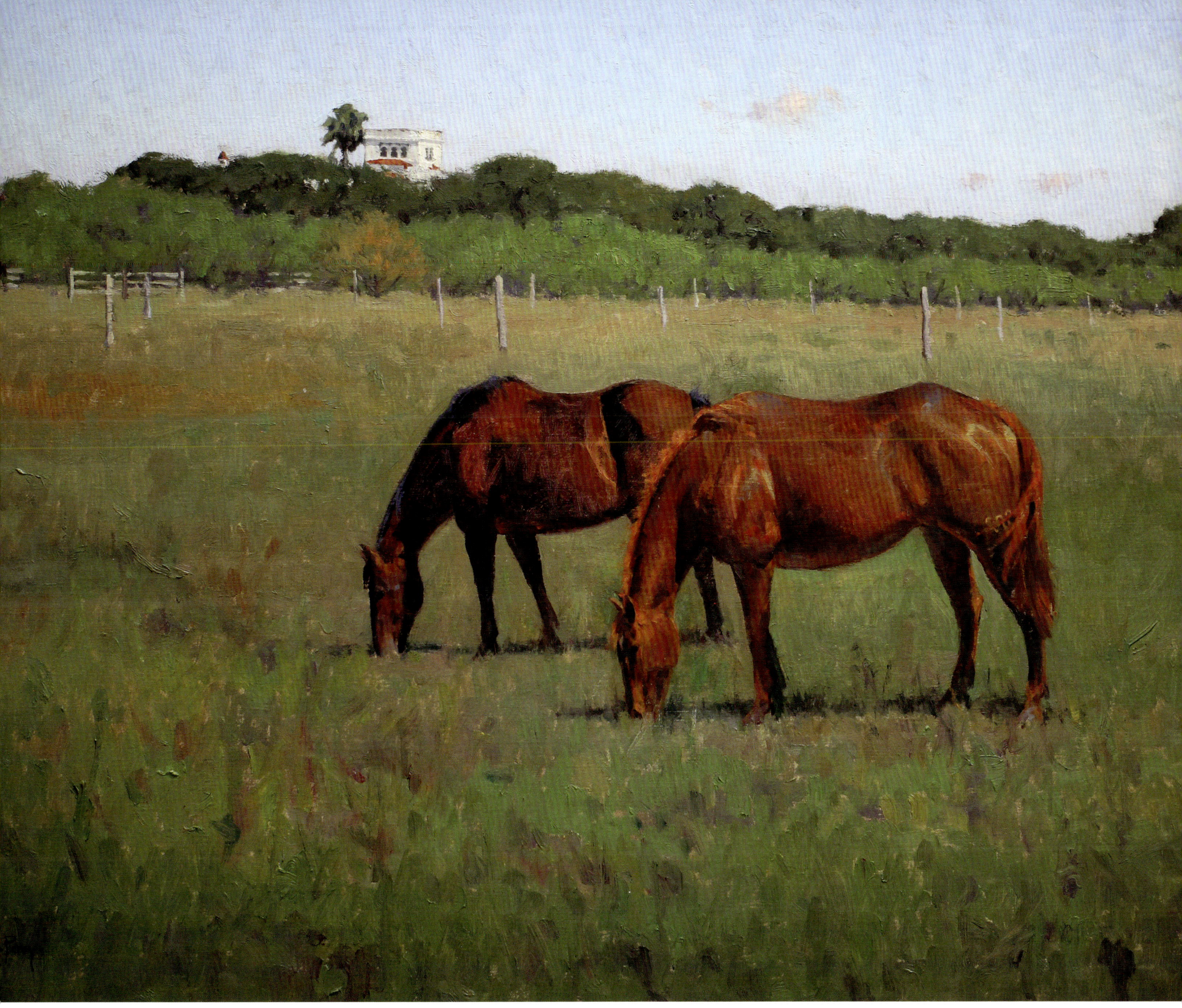

## The Carriage House in Morning Light

Mrs. King's carriage house was built in 1909. It has served as a stable for King Ranch Family horses. I saw this structure on an early trip to the ranch. Clear morning light was hitting the east face of the carriage house, emphasizing its beautiful architecture in the bright morning light.

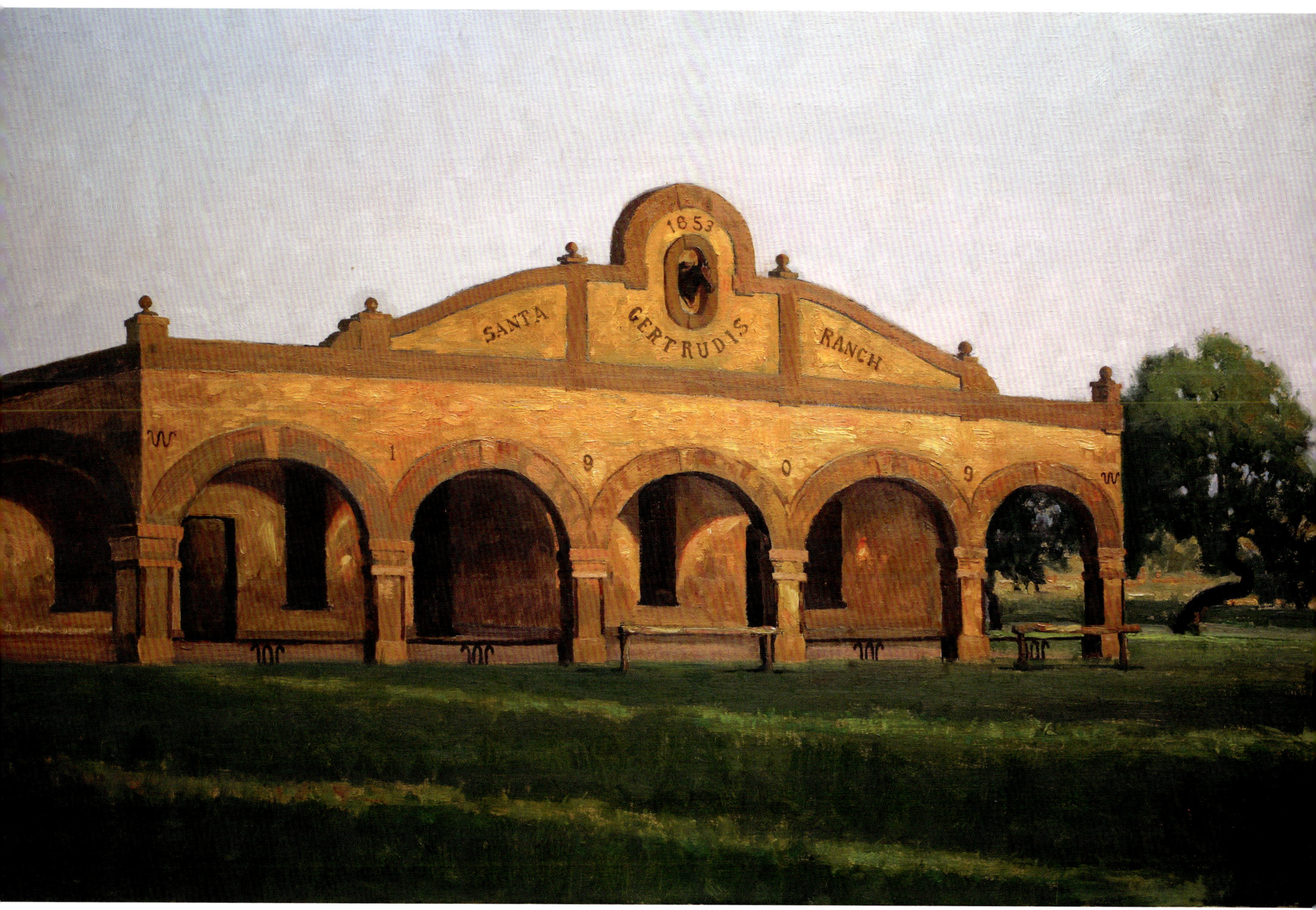


6

*The Carriage House in Morning Light (Santa Gertrudis)*, 2019
Oil on canvas, 24 × 36 inches
Courtesy of the artist

## Breezeway View

I think that most visitors with a camera want to shoot this scene because it captures the view looking through the carriage house to the Running W on Chon's barn beyond. But I love the arches and architectural elements of the carriage house. I had to give this scene a motivated attempt.

**7**

*Breezeway View (Santa Gertrudis)*, 2019
Oil on canvas, 20 × 20 inches
Courtesy of the artist

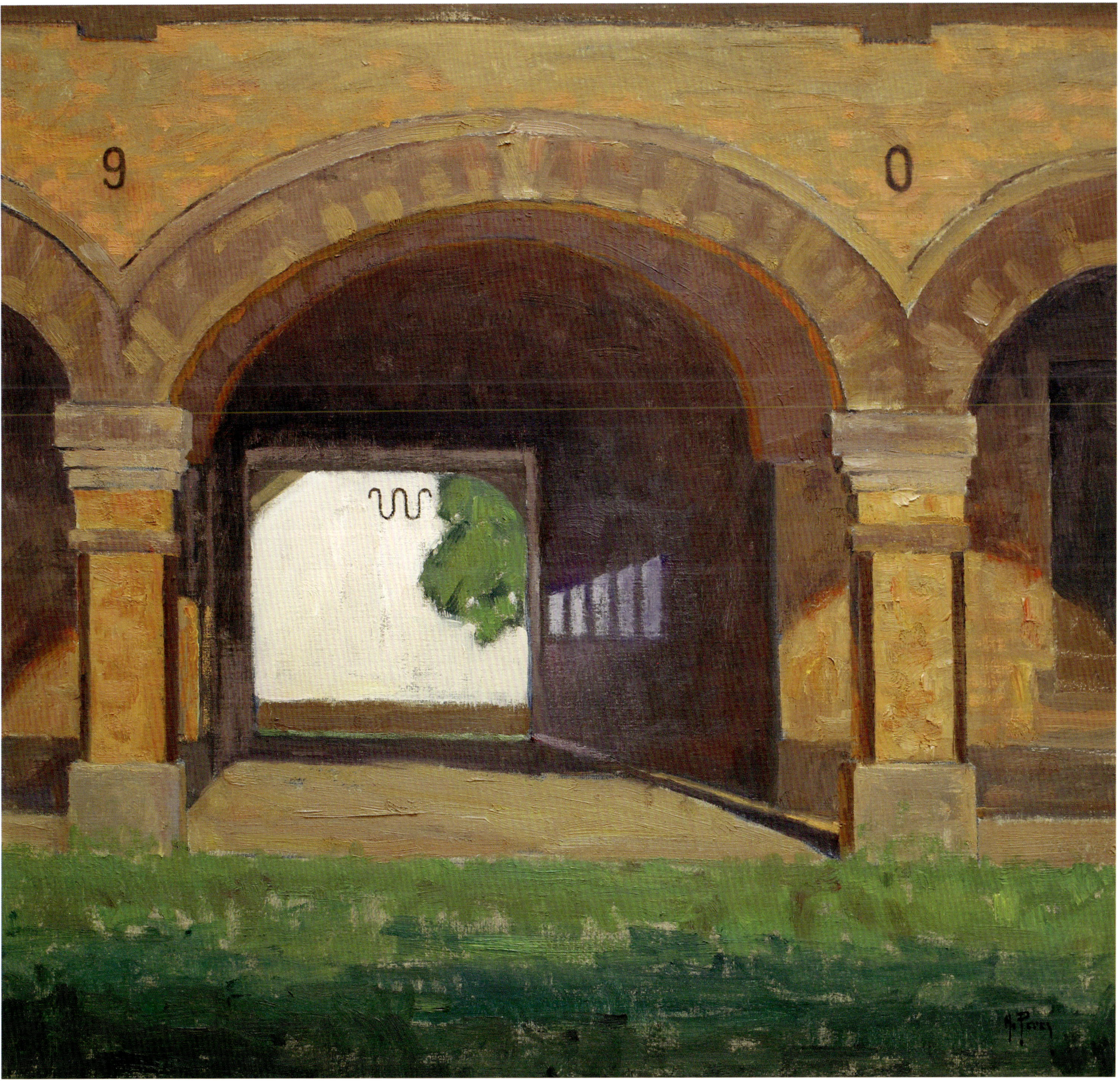
9
0

## Chon's Barn

This beautiful barn is a stone's throw from the Main House, the last remaining barn of this design once located around the Santa Gertrudis headquarters. Its stately structure commands attention and fits well within the ranch landscape.

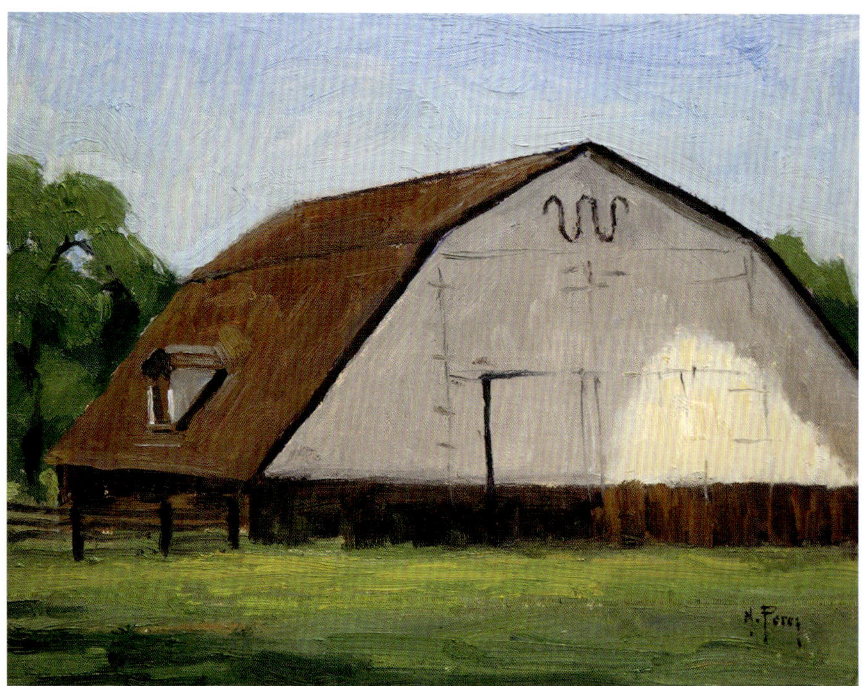

8

*Chon's Barn Plein Air Study (Santa Gertrudis)*, 2019
Oil on canvas, 8 × 10 inches
Courtesy of the artist

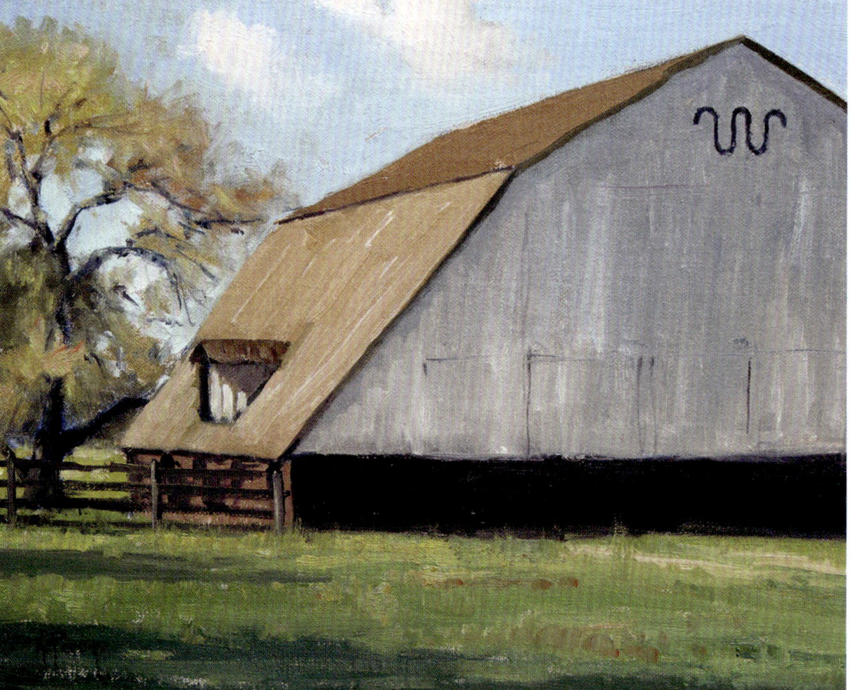

9

Study for *Chon's Barn (Santa Gertrudis)*, 2019
Oil on canvas, 10 × 12 inches
Courtesy of the artist

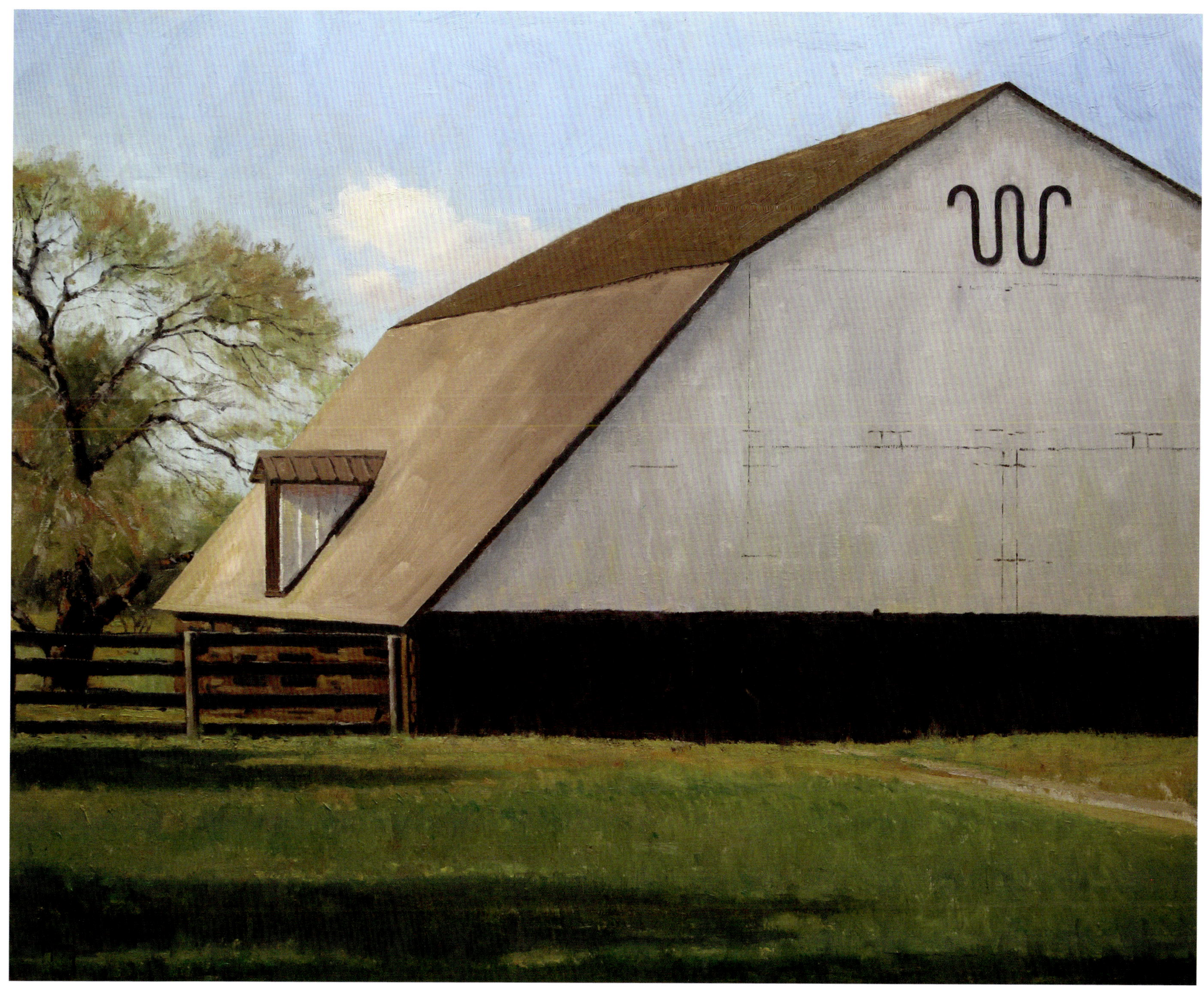

**10**

*Chon's Barn (Santa Gertrudis)*, 2019
Oil on canvas, 30 × 36 inches
Courtesy of the artist

## Kineños (La Corrida)

The original Kineños traveled from their northern Mexico home of Cruillas in 1854 with a promise from Captain King of a home and livelihood on the Santa Gertrudis. The King's people have served King Ranch for seven generations. I've seen many photos depicting this sort of mounted vaquero lineup. I followed that tradition in this painting, hoping to honor the legacy of the South Texas vaquero.

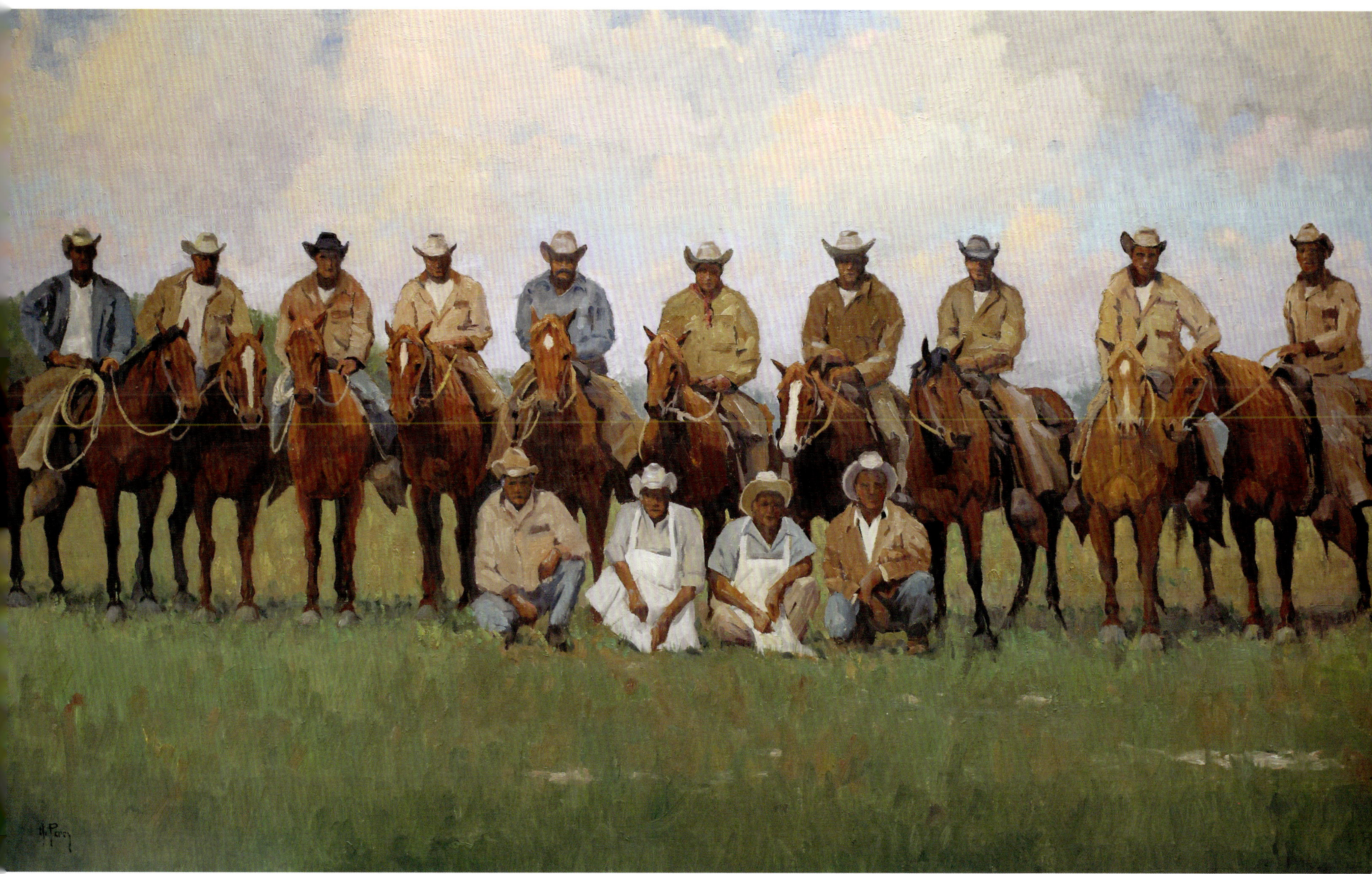

**11**

*Kineños (La Corrida) (Santa Gertrudis)*, 2020
Oil on canvas, 30 × 48 inches
Courtesy of the artist

## Old Ranch Well

The Old Ranch is the location of the original Kineño colony on the Norias Division.

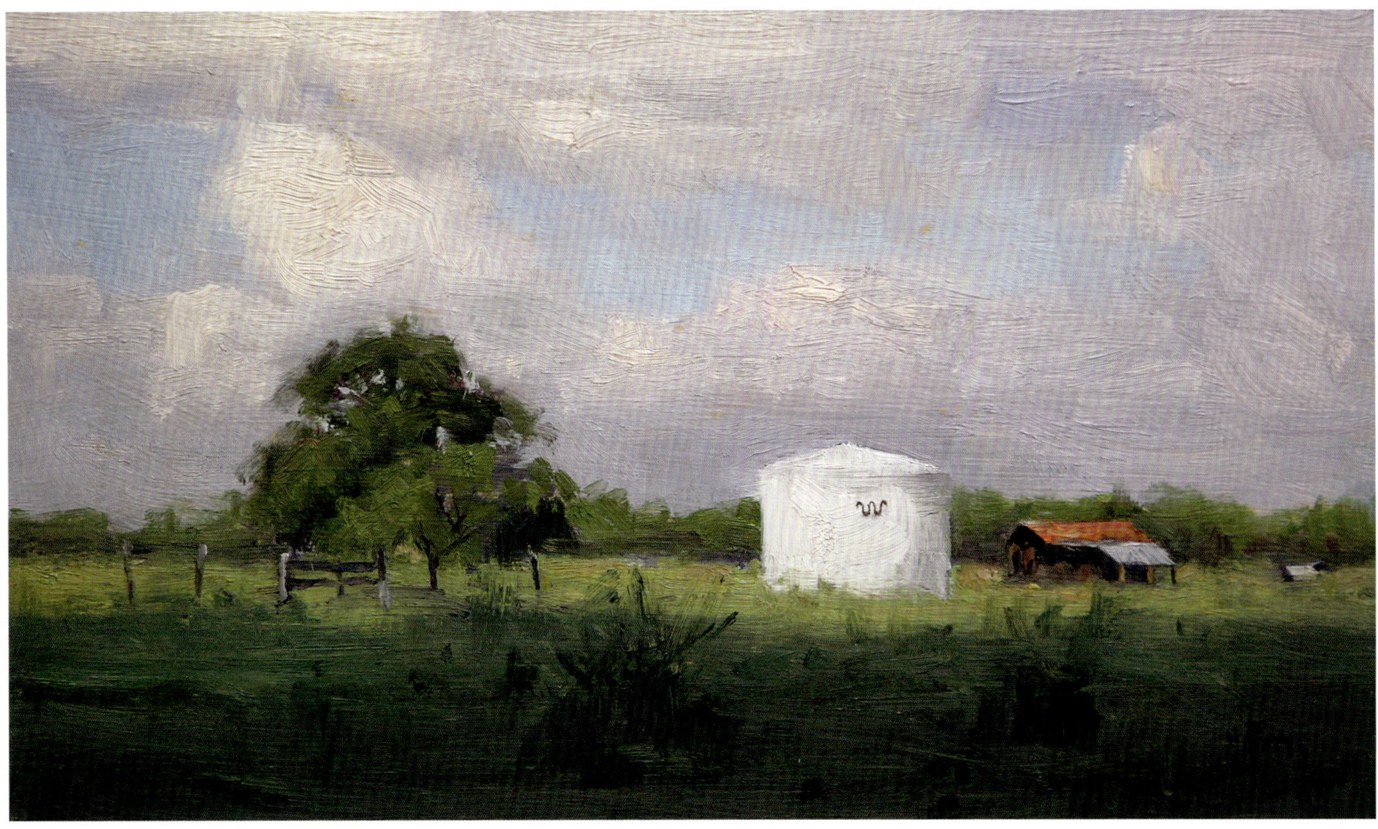

**12**

Study for *Old Ranch Well (Norias)*, 2019
Oil on canvas, 7½ × 12 inches
Courtesy of the artist

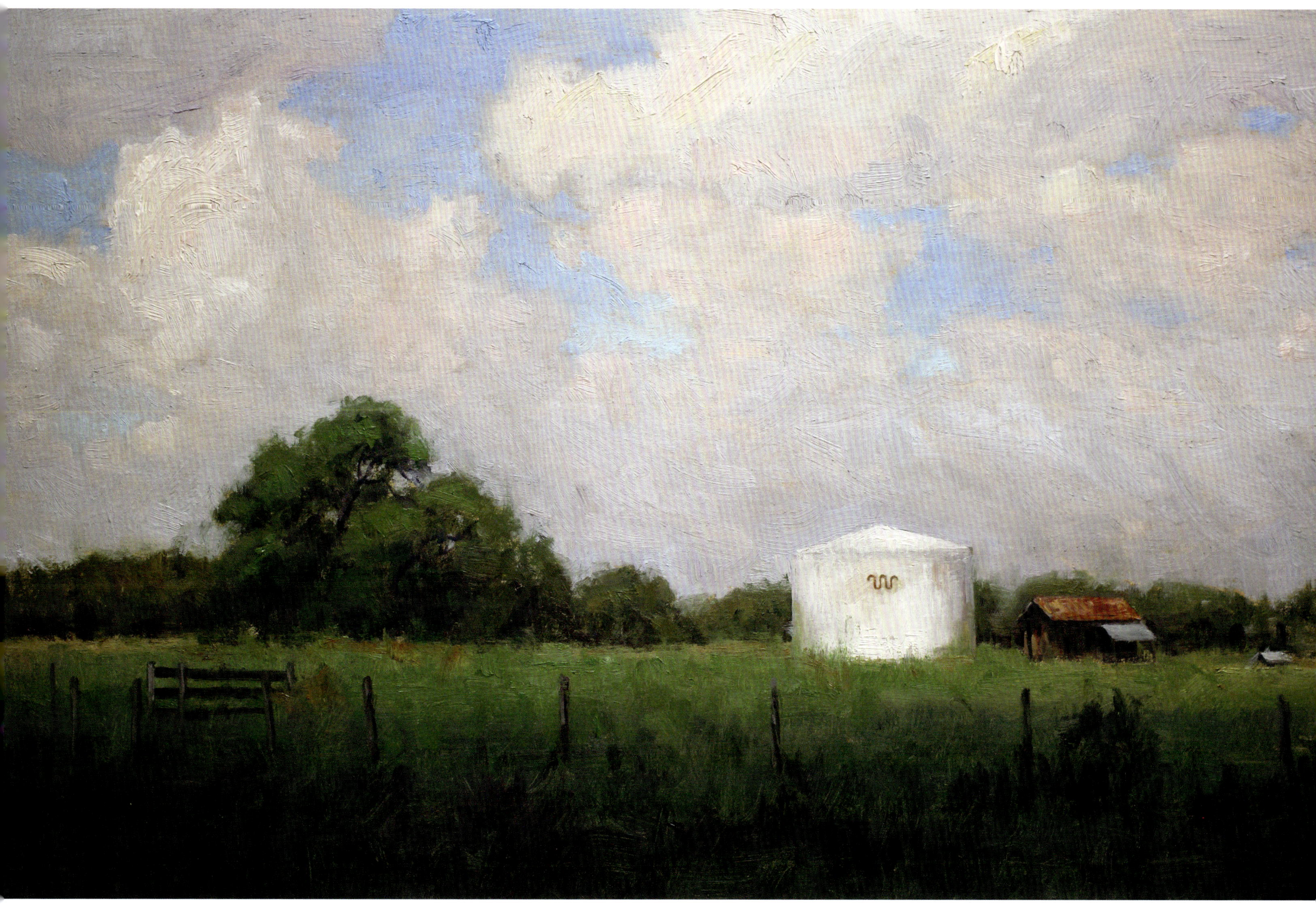

13

*Old Ranch Well (Norias)*, 2019
Oil on canvas, 16 × 24 inches
Courtesy of the artist

## Old Colony Casitas

These are the last of the early Kineño colony casitas on Santa Gertrudis, dating back to the 1850s.

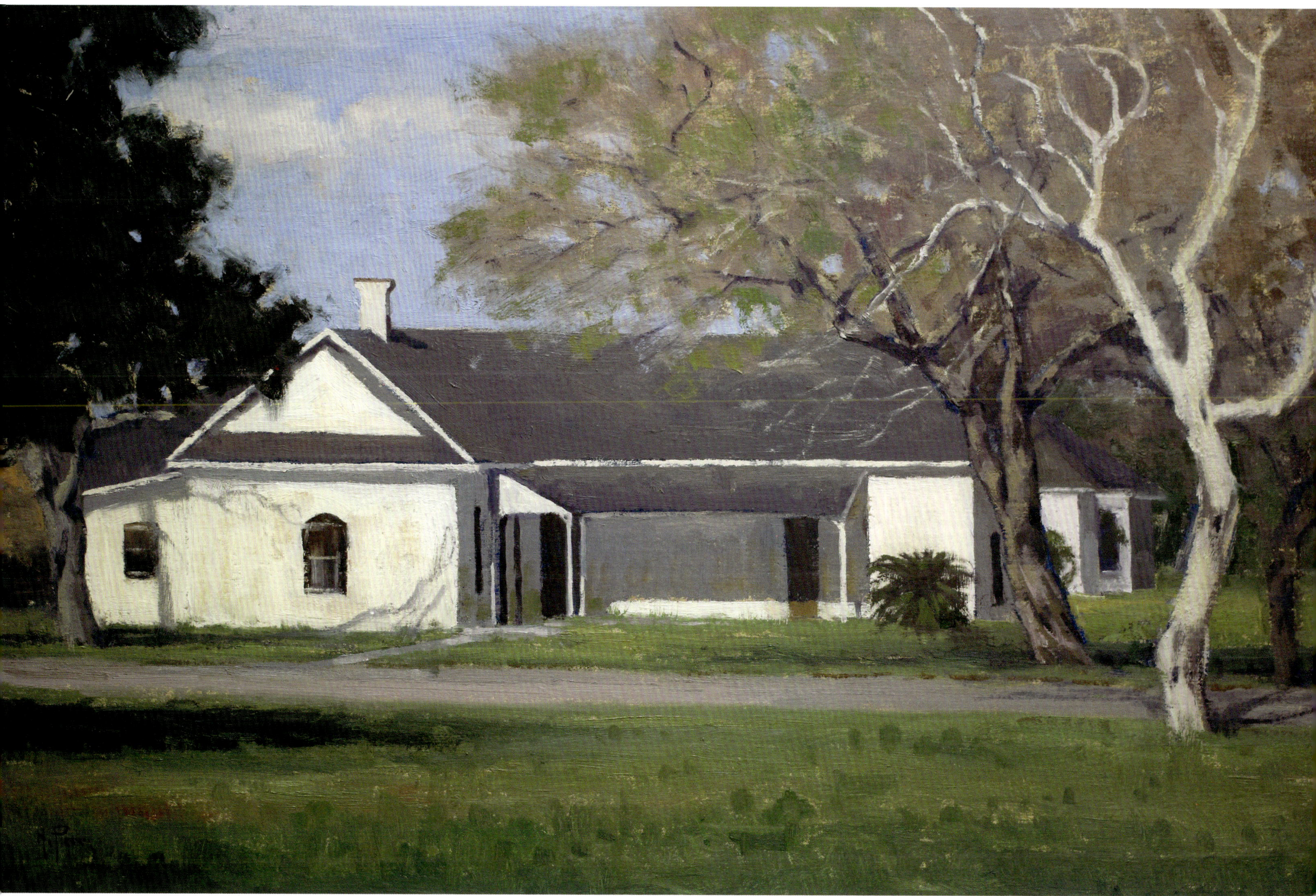

**14**

*Old Colony Casitas* (*Santa Gertrudis*), 2019
Oil on canvas, 16 × 24 inches
Courtesy of the artist

## Campo Santo de los Kineños

This scene shows one of the oldest cemeteries on King Ranch, Laureles Division. Generations of early Kineños are interred here. The place evinced a quiet beauty on a hot summer day.

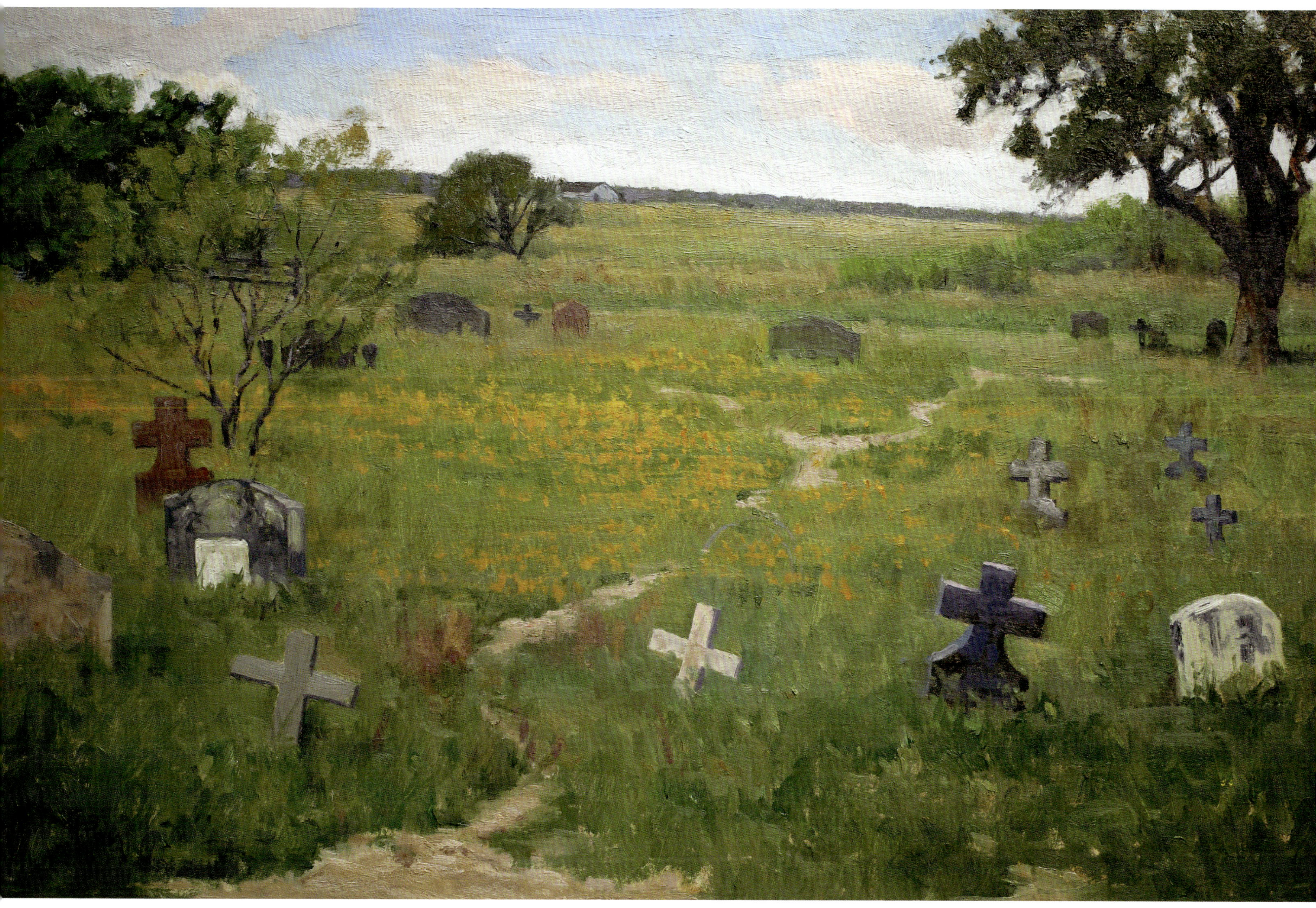

**15**

*Campo Santo de los Kineños (Laureles)*, 2020
Oil on canvas, 16 × 24 inches
Courtesy of the artist

## Picking the Day's Mount

The cowboy and horse have a symbiotic relationship in the ranching culture. Here a King Ranch vaquero and his mount prepare for the day's work. The scene in Study 1 was originally going to be one of the final paintings, but then I decided to expand the idea. The finished painting is the result of Study 2.

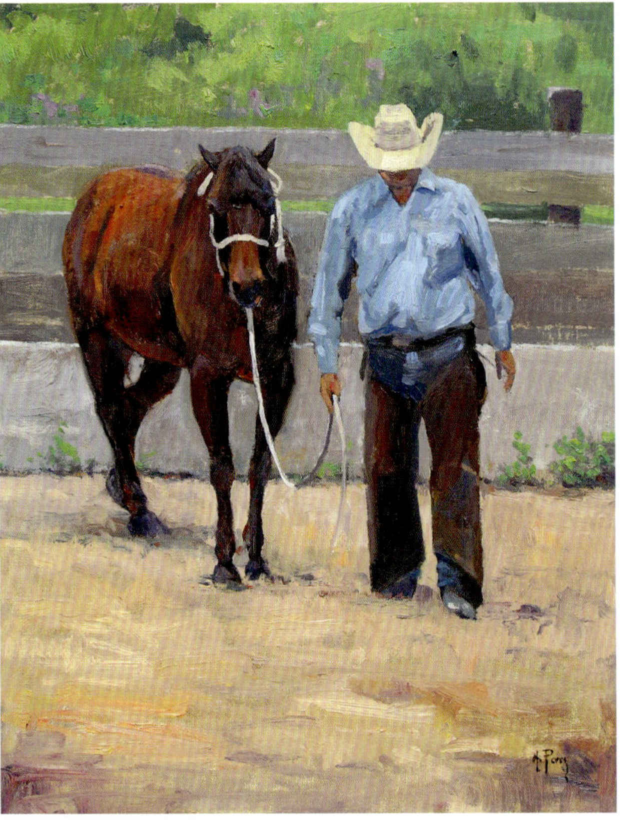

**16**

Study 1 for *Picking the Day's Mount (Laureles)*, 2019
Oil on canvas, 17 × 13 inches
Courtesy of the artist

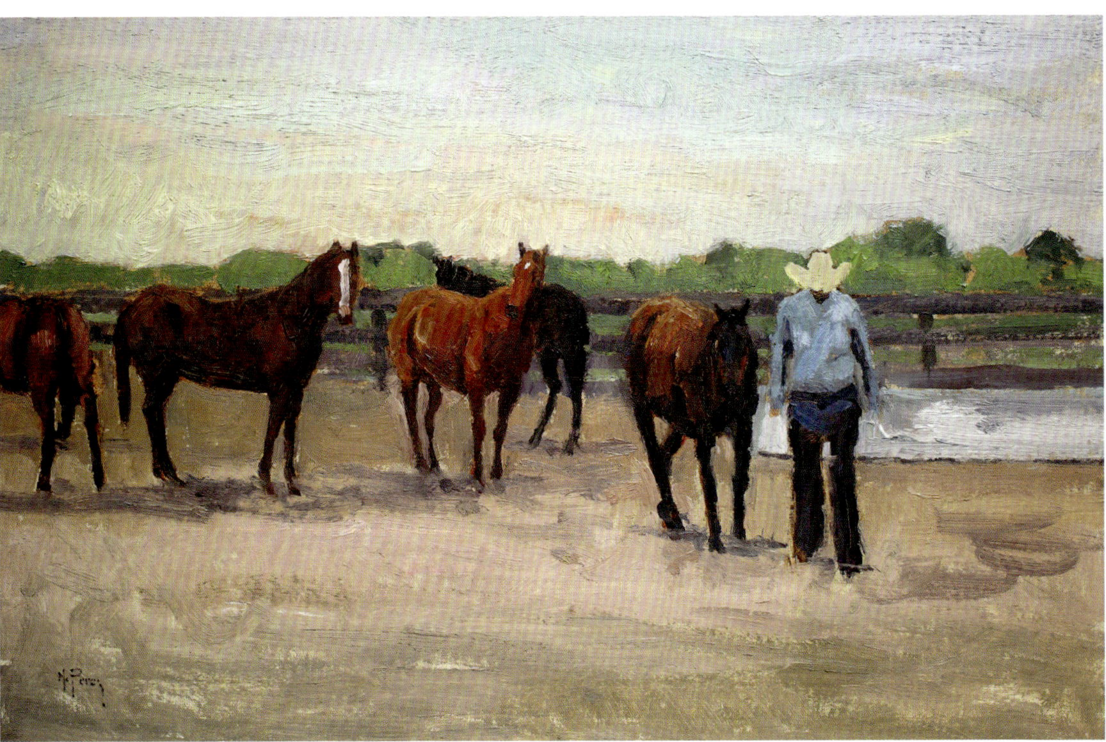

**17**

Study 2 for *Picking the Day's Mount (Laureles)*, 2019
Oil on canvas, 12 × 18 inches
Courtesy of the artist

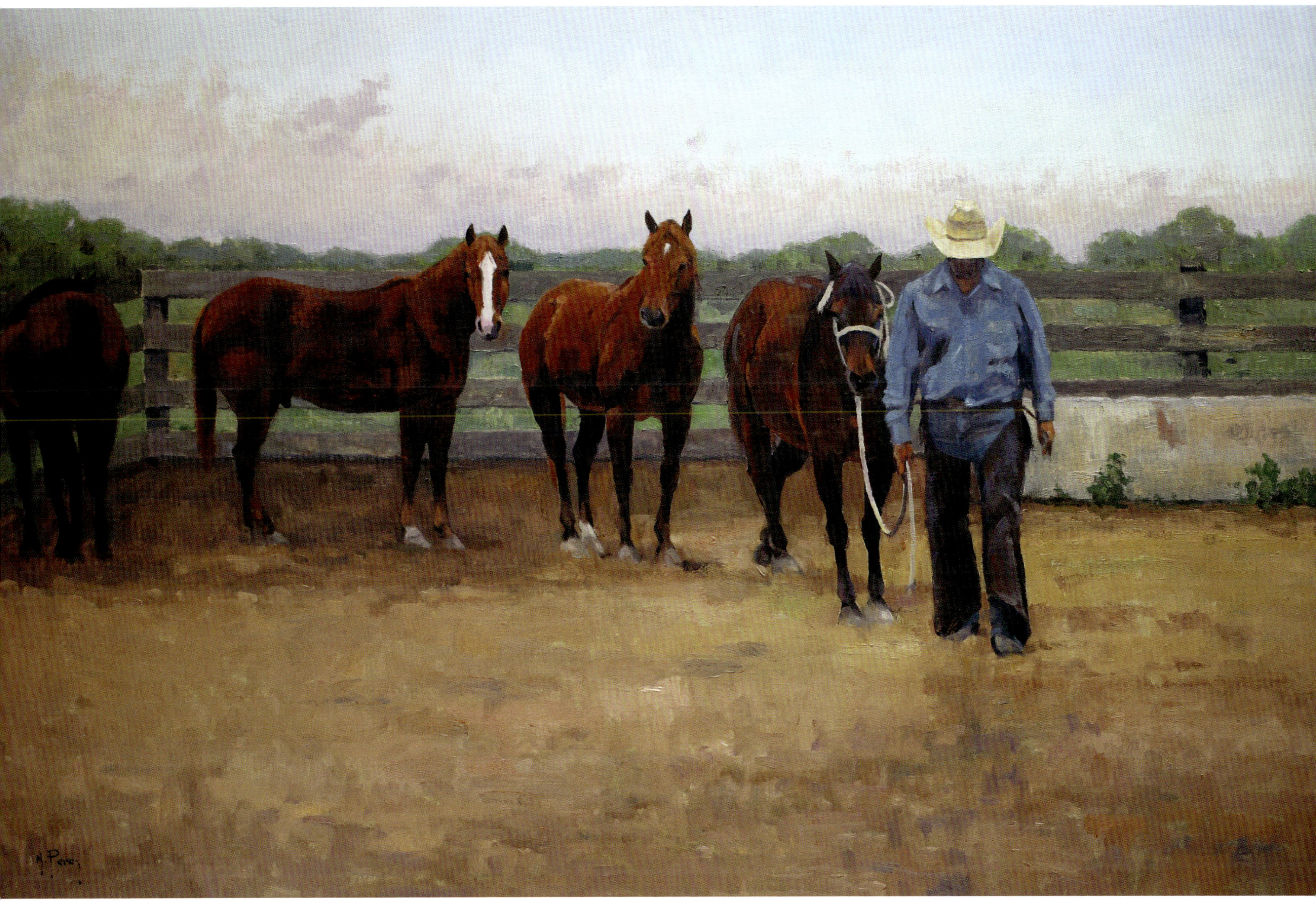

18

*Picking the Day's Mount (Laureles)*, 2020
Oil on canvas, 24 × 36 inches
Courtesy of the artist

## Drifting Manada

This painting started as a cloudscape, and it basically still is. I was going to call it *Drifting*, but with the addition of the small band of mares in the foreground, I thought *Drifting Manada* was appropriate.

**19**

*Drifting Manada (Santa Gertrudis)*, 2018
Oil on canvas, 30 × 24 inches
Courtesy of the artist

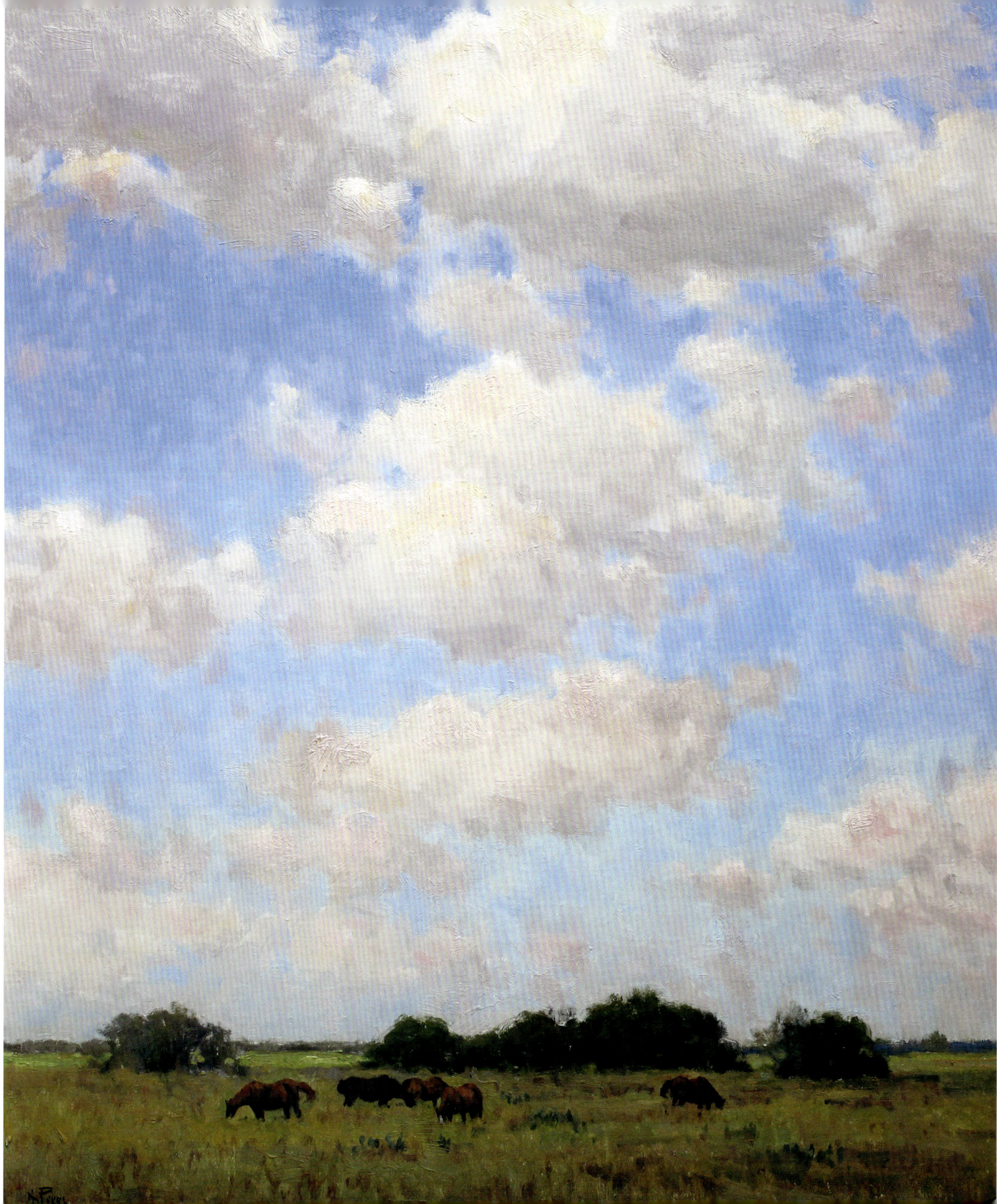

## Morning Shadow

Here I painted one of the ranch's many sorrel quarter horse mares in the morning light.

**20**

*Morning Shadow (Santa Gertrudis)*, 2019
Oil on canvas, 24 × 24 inches
Courtesy of the artist

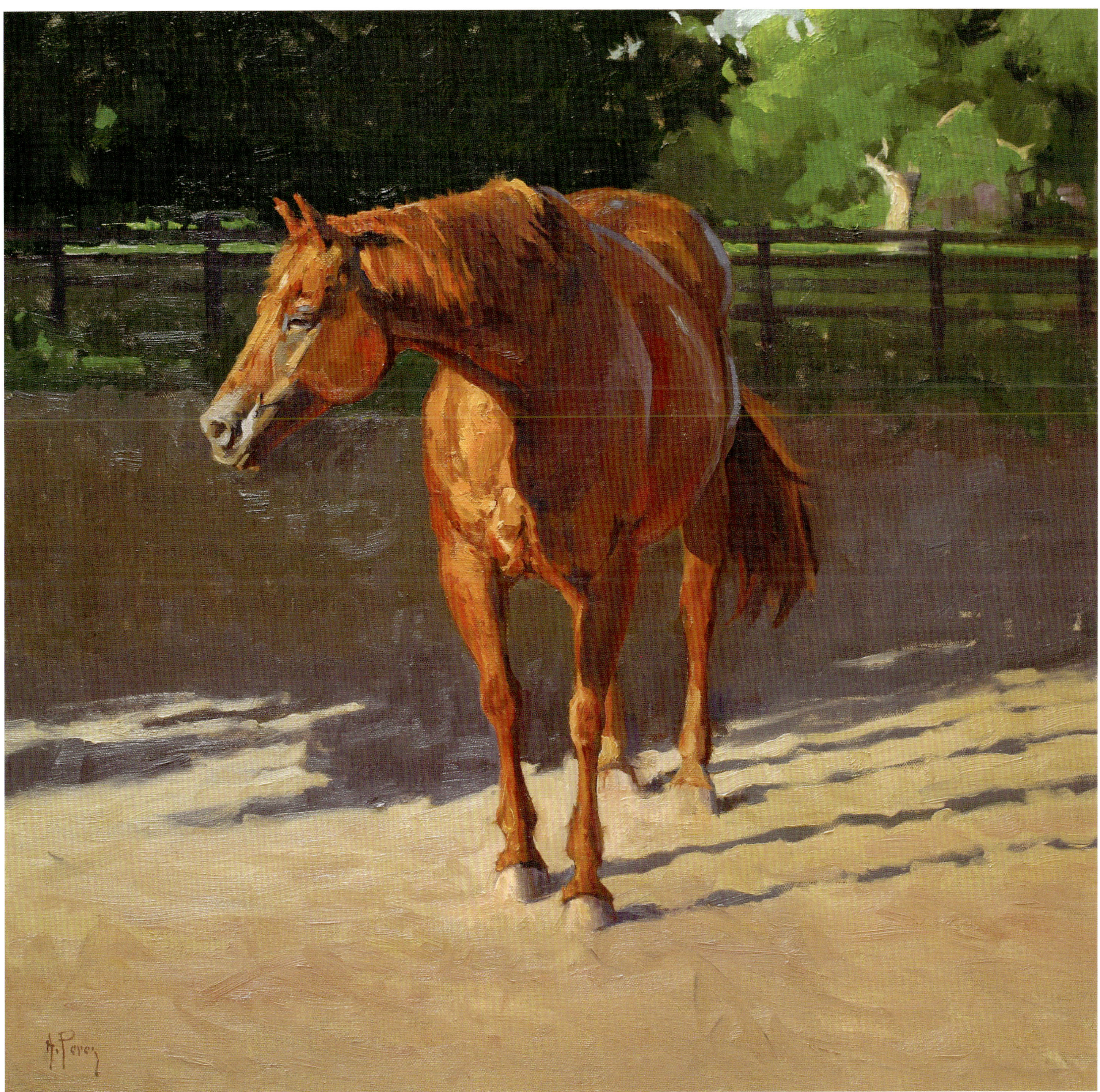

## Dog Pens

These horses were relaxing under a massive oak tree at the Encino headquarters dog pens. It was the middle of the day and really hot. I liked the way the light was bouncing off of the horses' backs. Of course, my focus was the big oak tree—the way the large limbs were lit up by the reflected light off the ground. I was trying to capture the heat that we experienced that day.

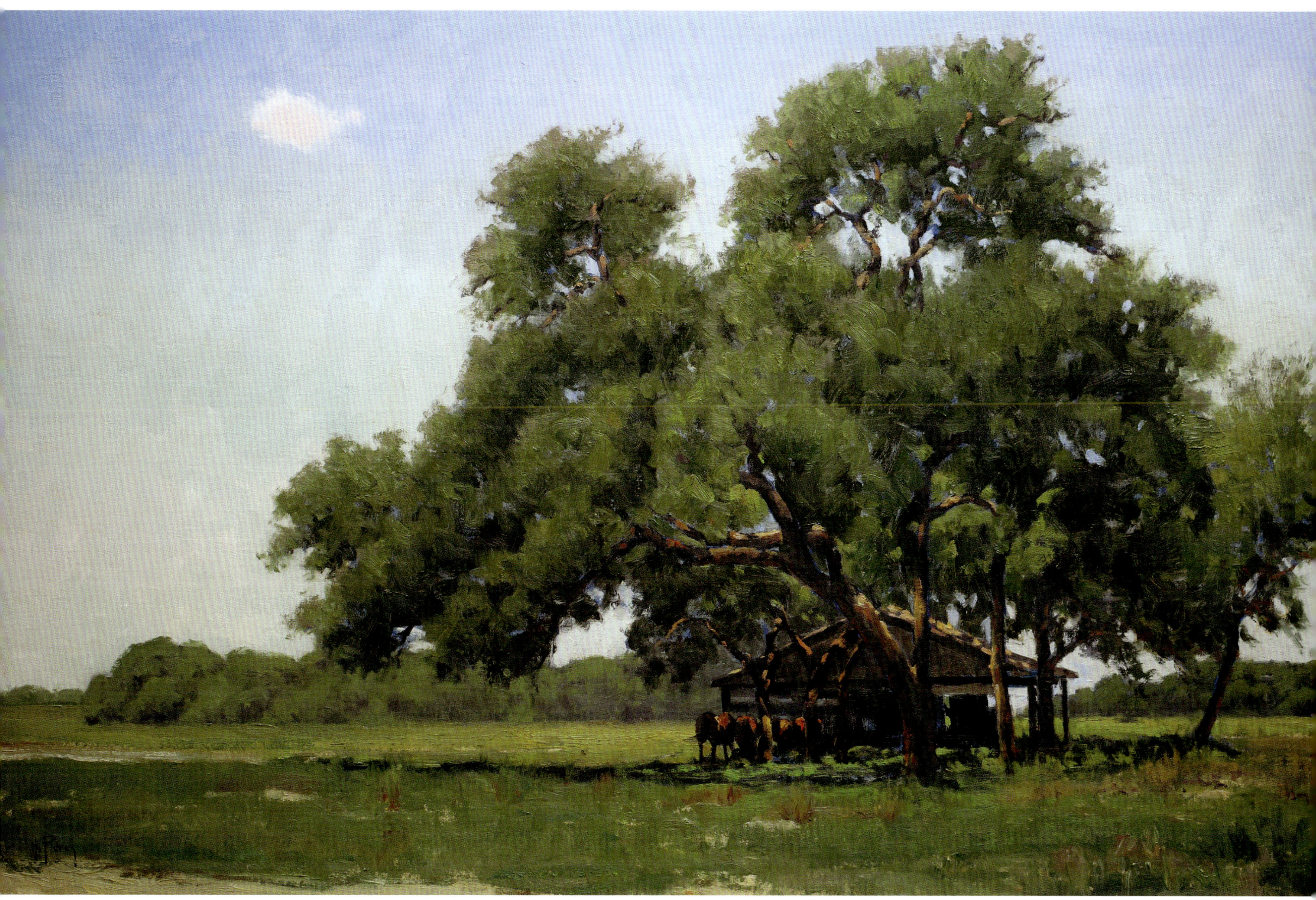

**21**

*Dog Pens (Encino)*, 2019
Oil on canvas, 20 × 30 inches
Courtesy of the artist

## Loafing at D Pens

Quarter horses from the Kineños' remudas are ready to begin the day. The great light magnifies the beauty of these fine animals.

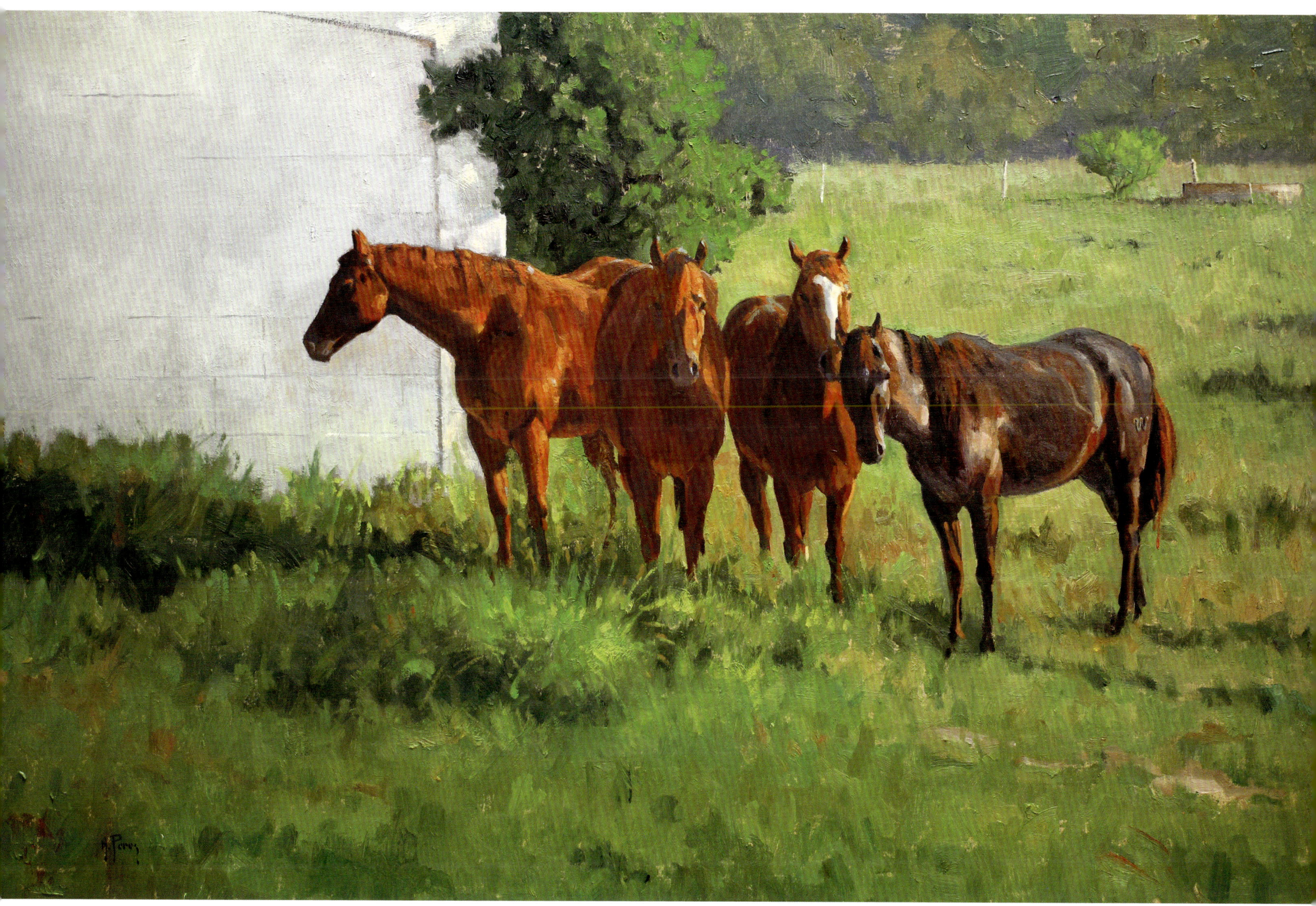

**22**

*Loafing at D Pens (Santa Gertrudis)*, 2019
Oil on canvas, 24 × 36 inches
Courtesy of the artist

## Santa Gertrudis Pair

The Santa Gertrudis breed originated with the birth of the foundation bull, Monkey. The breed was recognized as the first beef breed in the United States in 1940. I felt like this pair was the perfect image of the iconic breed. Also, the emerald water in the tank behind them was hard for me to resist.

**23**

*Santa Gertrudis Pair (Santa Gertrudis)*, 2018
Oil on canvas, 20 × 16 inches
Courtesy of the artist

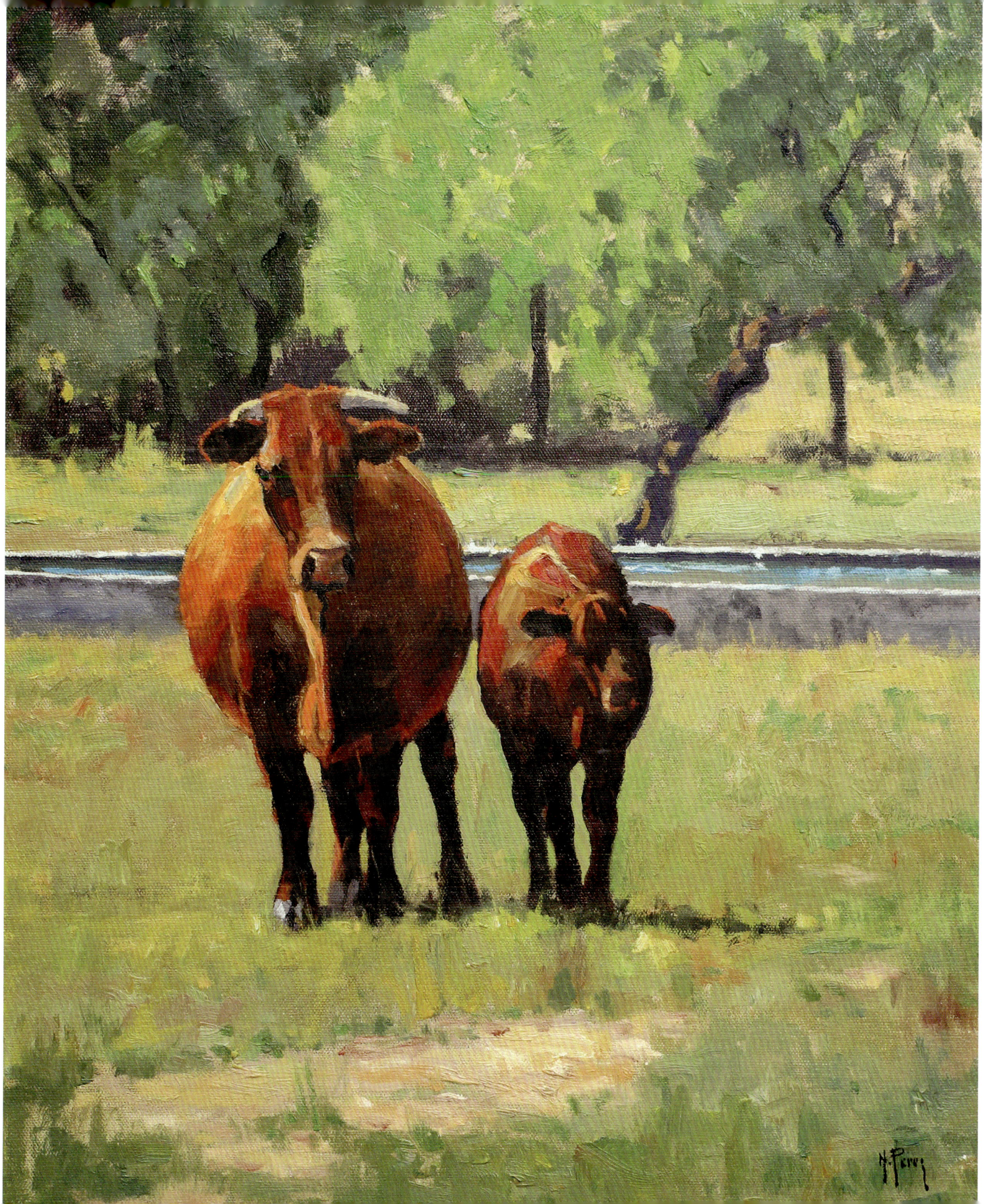

## Ladinas

*Ladina* is a Spanish word meaning "crafty" or "cunning." Growing up, we referred to cattle that wouldn't follow along with the herd as *ladinas* (*una vaca ladina*). When we encountered these cattle, they ran from us like we were chasing them. I thought of *ladinas*.

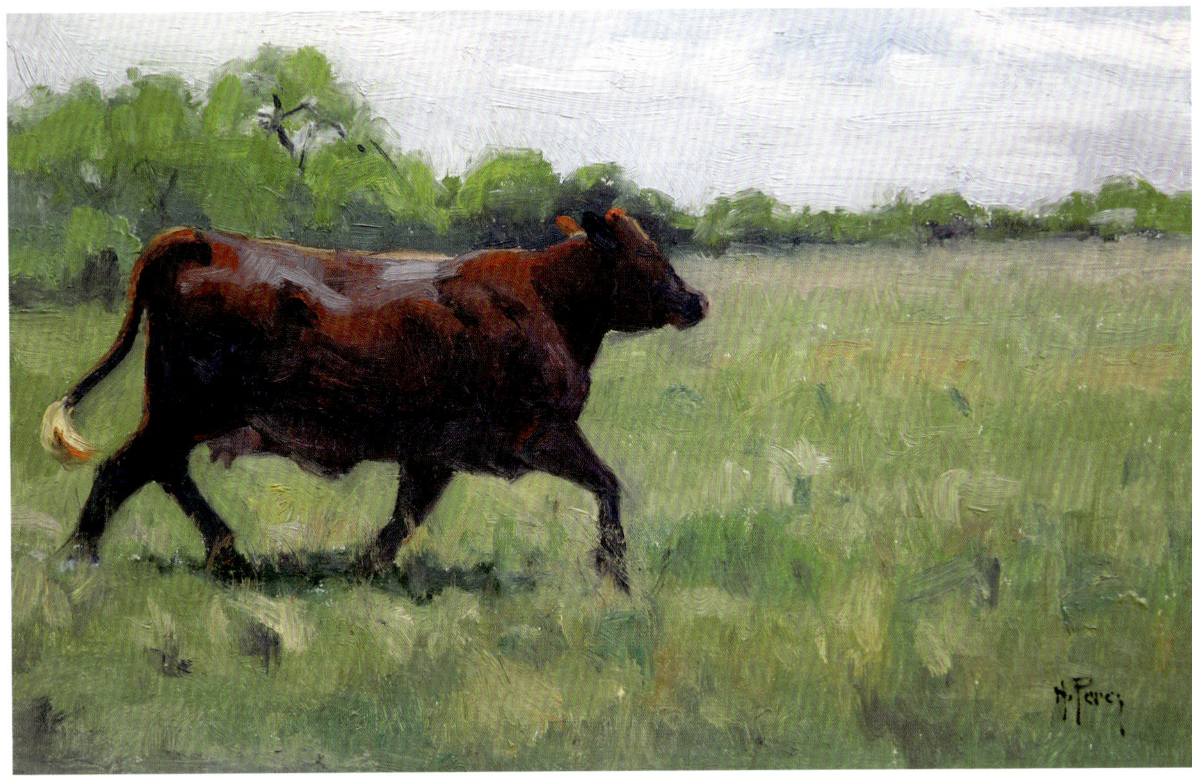

**24**

Study for *Ladinas* (*Norias*), 2018
Oil on canvas, 8 × 12 inches
Courtesy of the artist

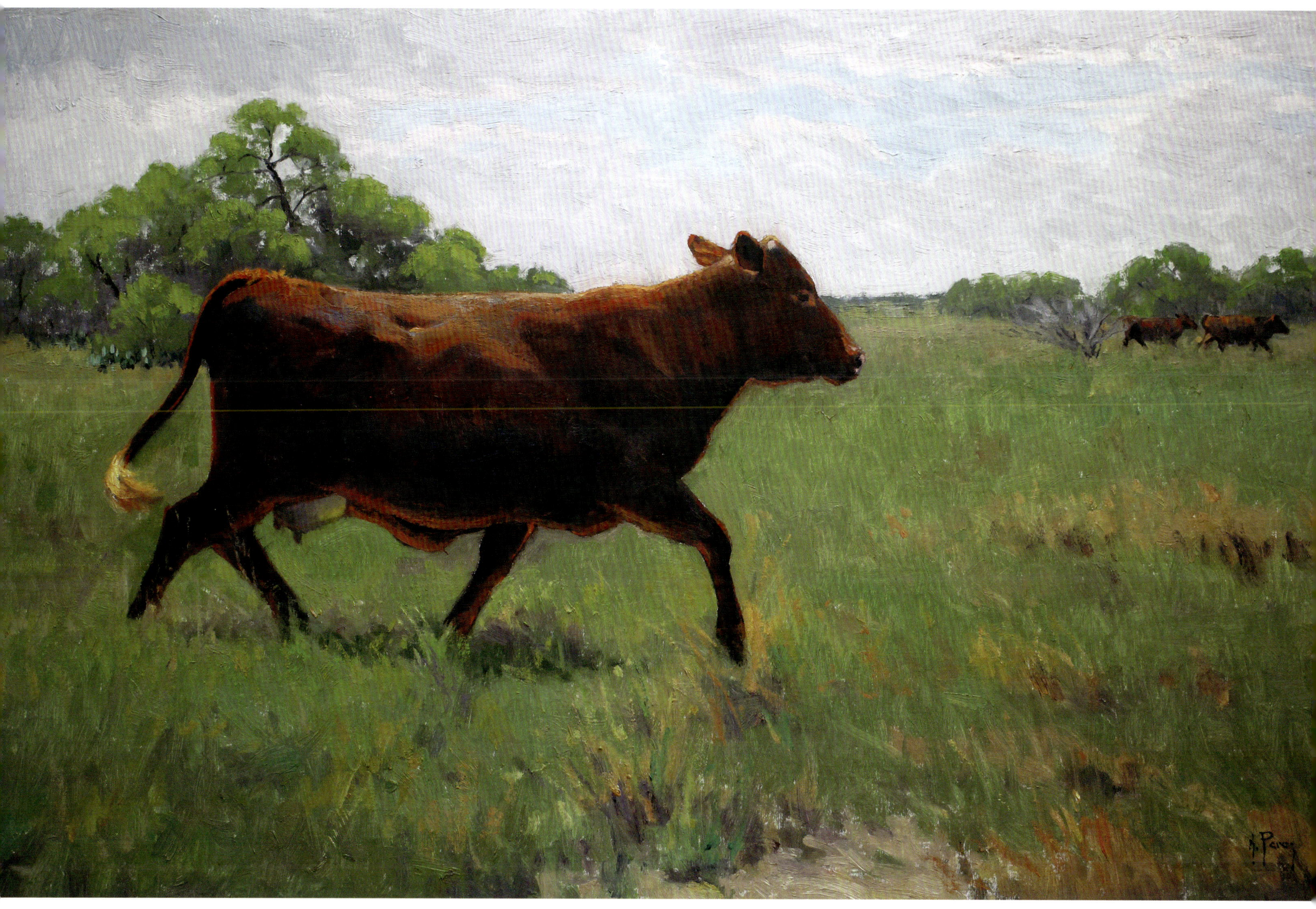

25

*Ladinas (Norias)*, 2019
Oil on canvas, 20 × 30 inches
Courtesy of the artist

## Horns Molded by Thorns

Longhorn cattle were brought back to King Ranch in 1961 when Bob Kleberg traded thirty Santa Gertrudis heifers for these Graves Peeler Longhorns. Peeler is credited with saving Longhorn cattle from extinction and preserving them for future generations.

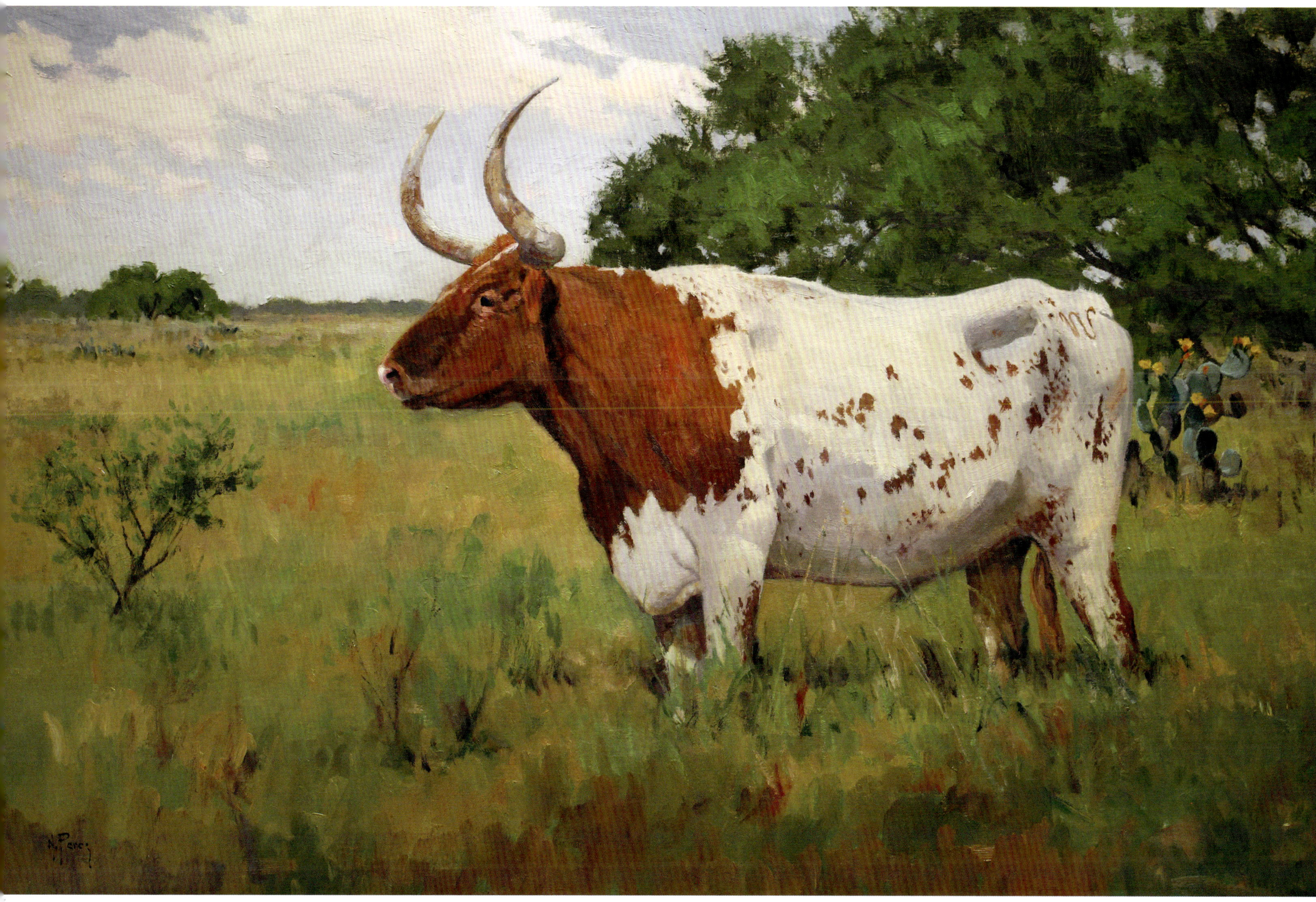

## 26

*Horns Molded by Thorns (Santa Gertrudis)*, 2019
Oil on canvas, 24 × 36 inches
Courtesy of the artist

## Bump Gate at the Caldwell Windmill

This unique "self-opening" gate design was originally used on King Ranch in the 1920s. The modern bump gate was perfected by Bob Kleberg and a Humble Oil engineer for use on all four divisions of the ranch. I especially liked this one, with its proximity to the windmill and tank.

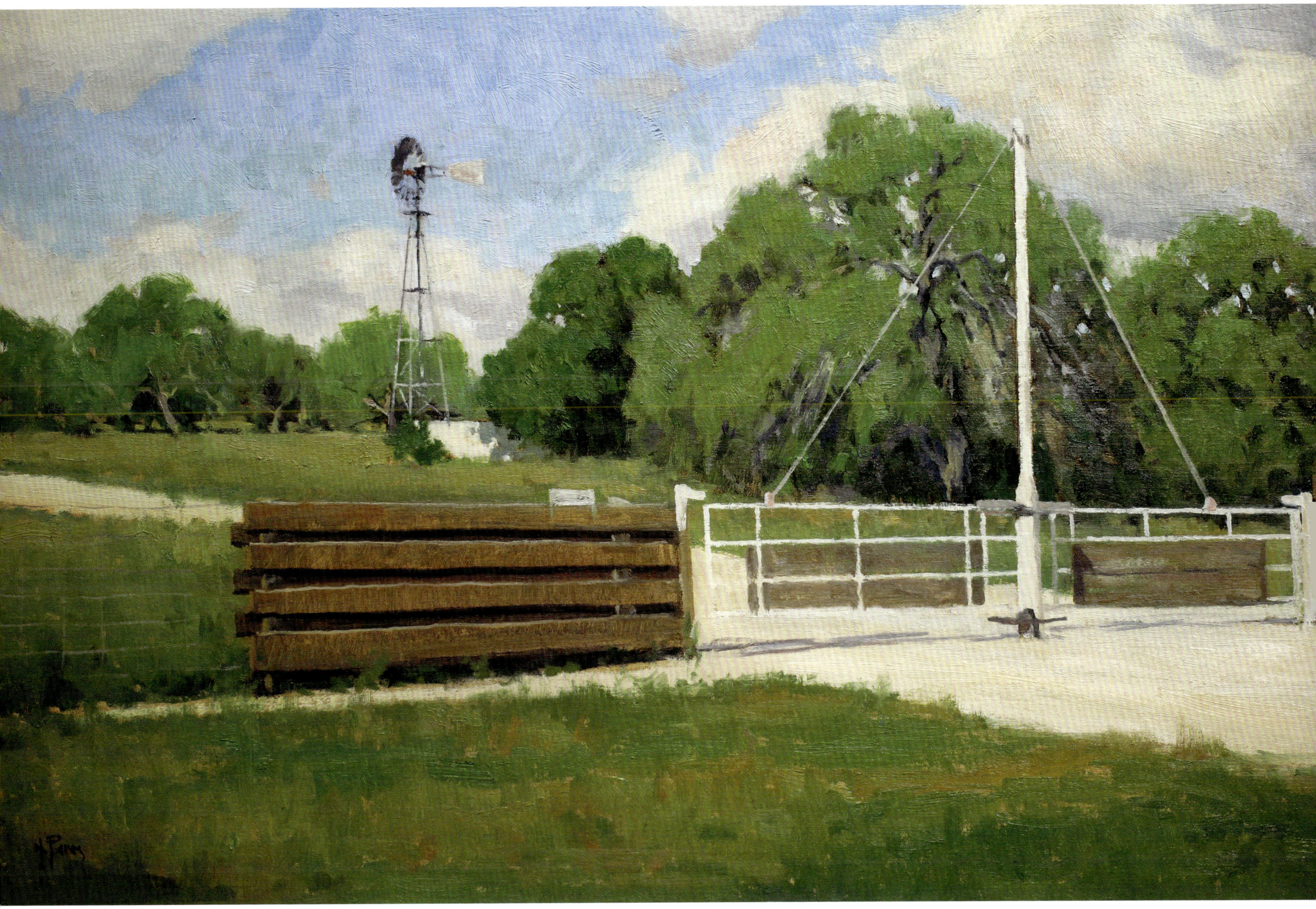

**27**

*Bump Gate at the Caldwell Windmill* (*Santa Gertrudis*), 2019
Oil on canvas, 16 × 24 inches
Courtesy of the artist

## Los Mojados Windmill

Here I was affected by an isolated windmill and water trap at the Norias Division. More than three hundred windmills and solar-powered wells pump precious water on the four divisions of King Ranch.

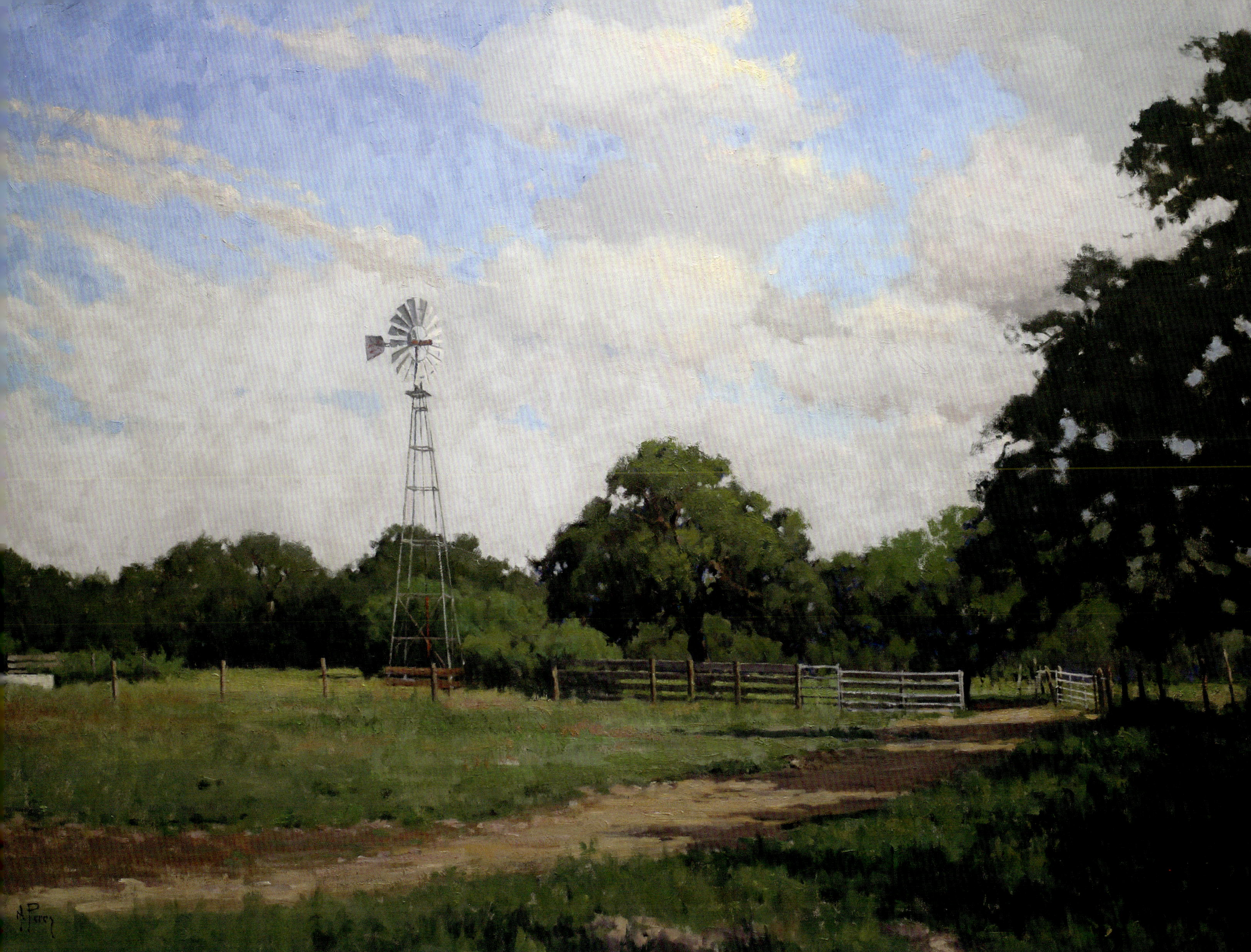

28

*Los Mojados Windmill (Norias)*, 2018
Oil on canvas, 36 × 48 inches
Courtesy of the artist

## Molino Las Mujeres

This windmill is located on the remote stretch of coastal prairie along the Laguna Madre on the Norias Division. *Molino* is the Spanish word for windmill. A distant dune is visible behind the windmill, highlighting its proximity to the coast. When I grew up in South Texas, ranch windmills were a common sight, which is no longer the case anymore. Windmill scenes such as this one will probably soon be rare.

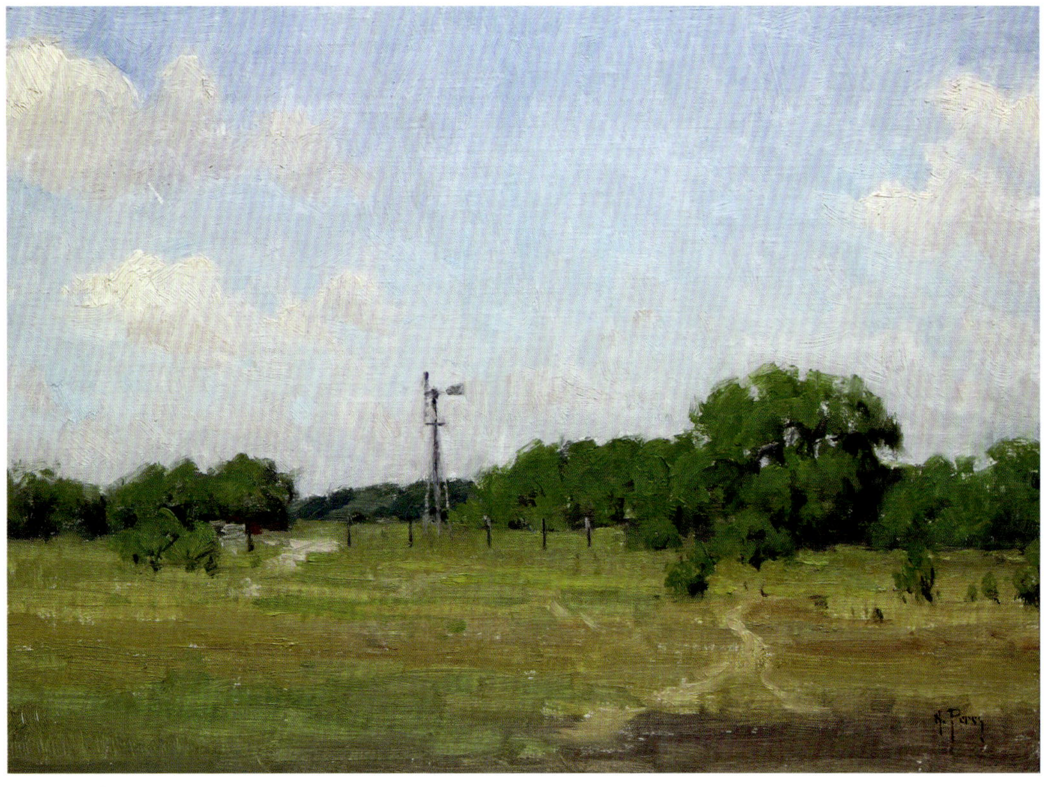

**29**

Study for *Molino Las Mujeres (Norias)*, 2019
Oil on canvas, 12 × 16 inches
Courtesy of the artist

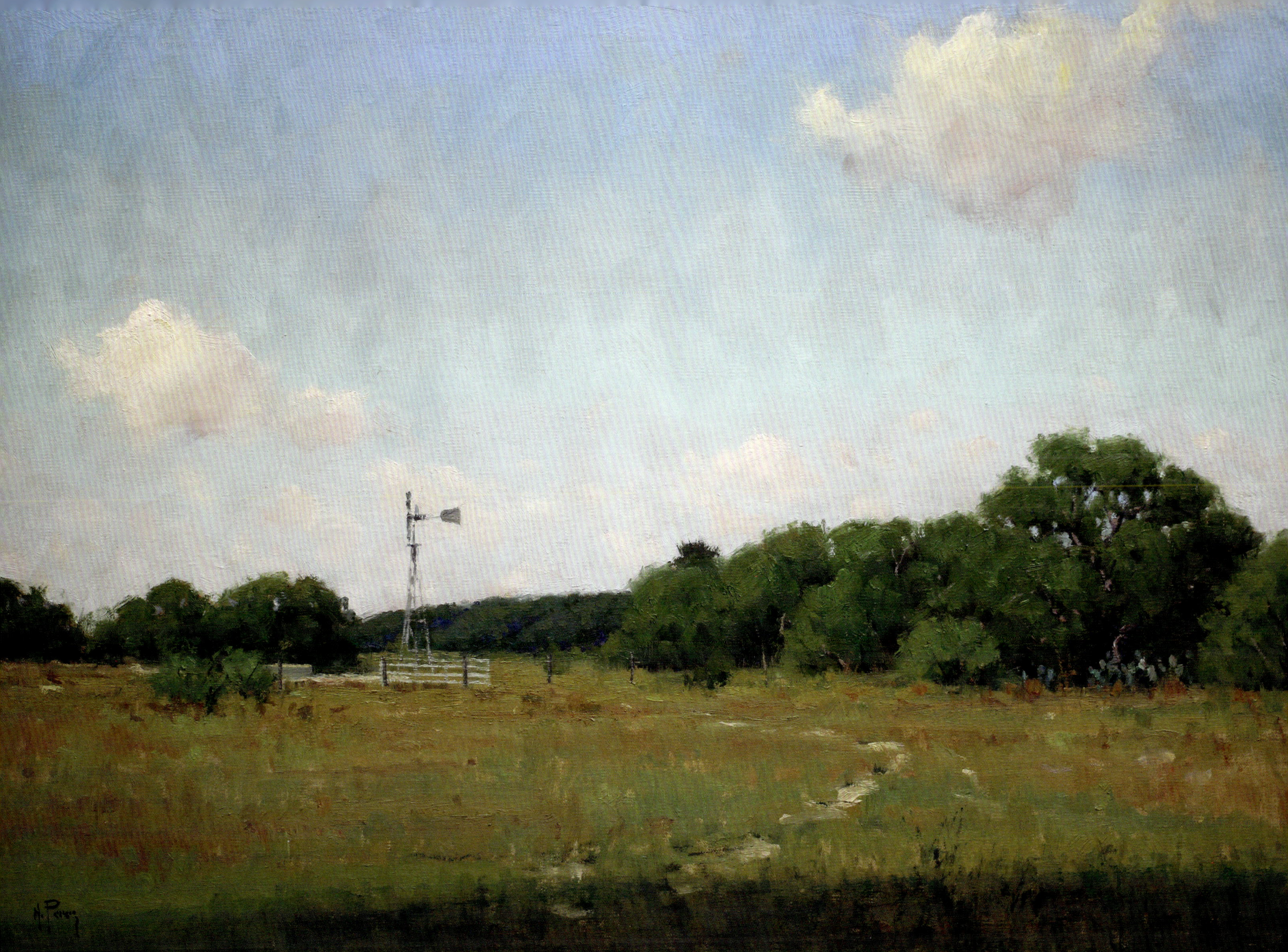

30

*Molino Las Mujeres (Norias)*, 2019
Oil on canvas, 18 × 24 inches
Courtesy of the artist

## Sunset on Ebanos Windmill

I seldom do sunsets, because it is such a strong subject that can take over a composition with little consideration of the artistic merit behind it. But on the evening that I saw this, I knew I had to try. When I do this type of subject matter, I try to balance the beautiful colors with the dry gray grasses of the foreground and the bare mesquite full of thorns and no leaves. I try to portray contrasts throughout the canvas, interspersing thick and thin paint, soft and hard edges, color and gray, and so forth.

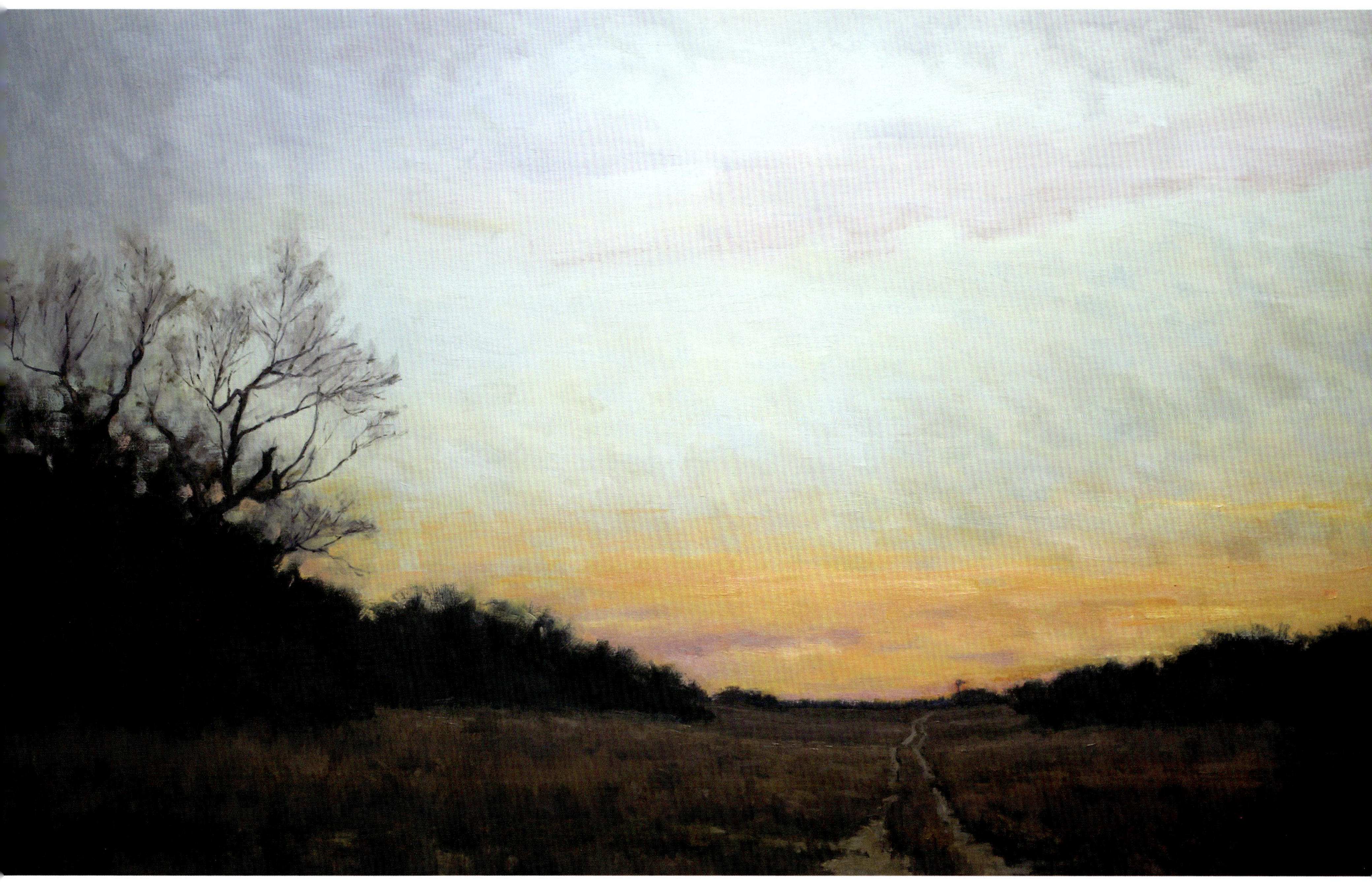

**31**

*Sunset on Ebanos Windmill (Santa Gertrudis)*, 2019
Oil on canvas, 30 × 48 inches
Courtesy of the artist

## Norias Dunes

The dunes at Norias are really a sight to behold. I had not seen them firsthand until this project. From a distance, they almost appear as snow-covered hills. It was a challenge to get the scale of their size and capture their brilliance against the South Texas midday sun.

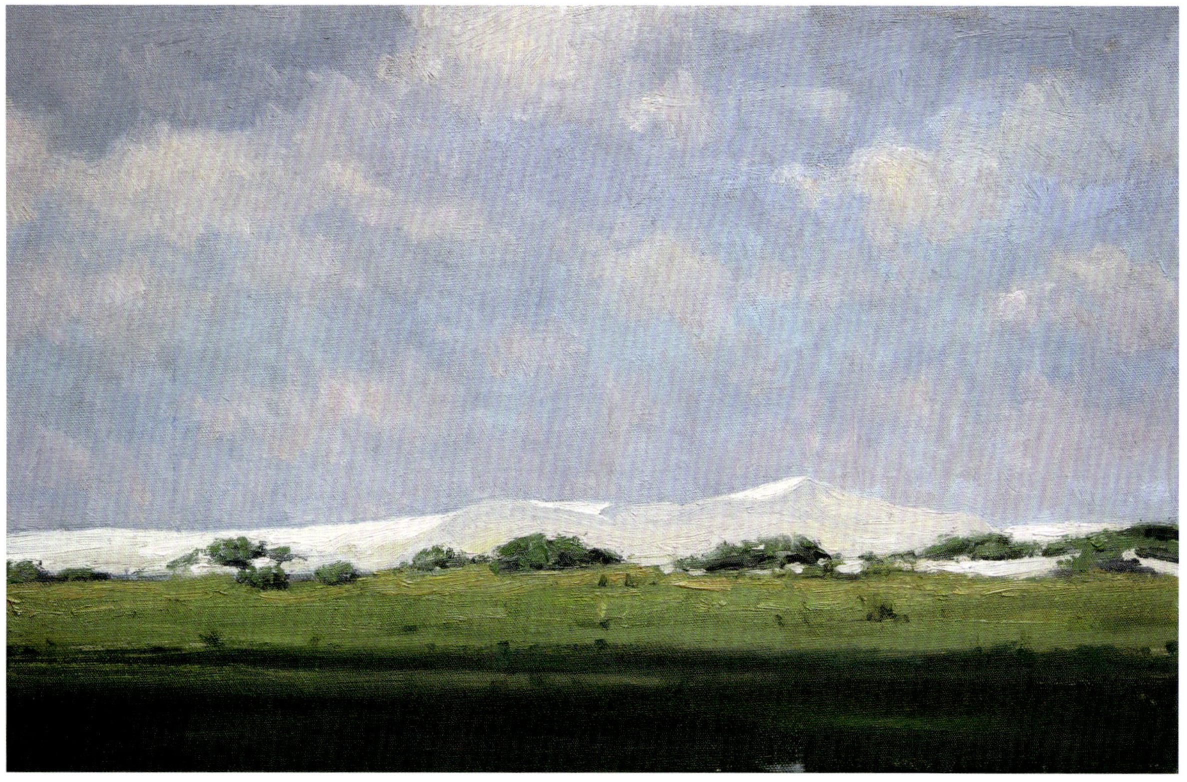

## 32

Study for *Norias Dunes* (*Norias*), 2019
Oil on canvas, 12 × 18 inches
Courtesy of the artist

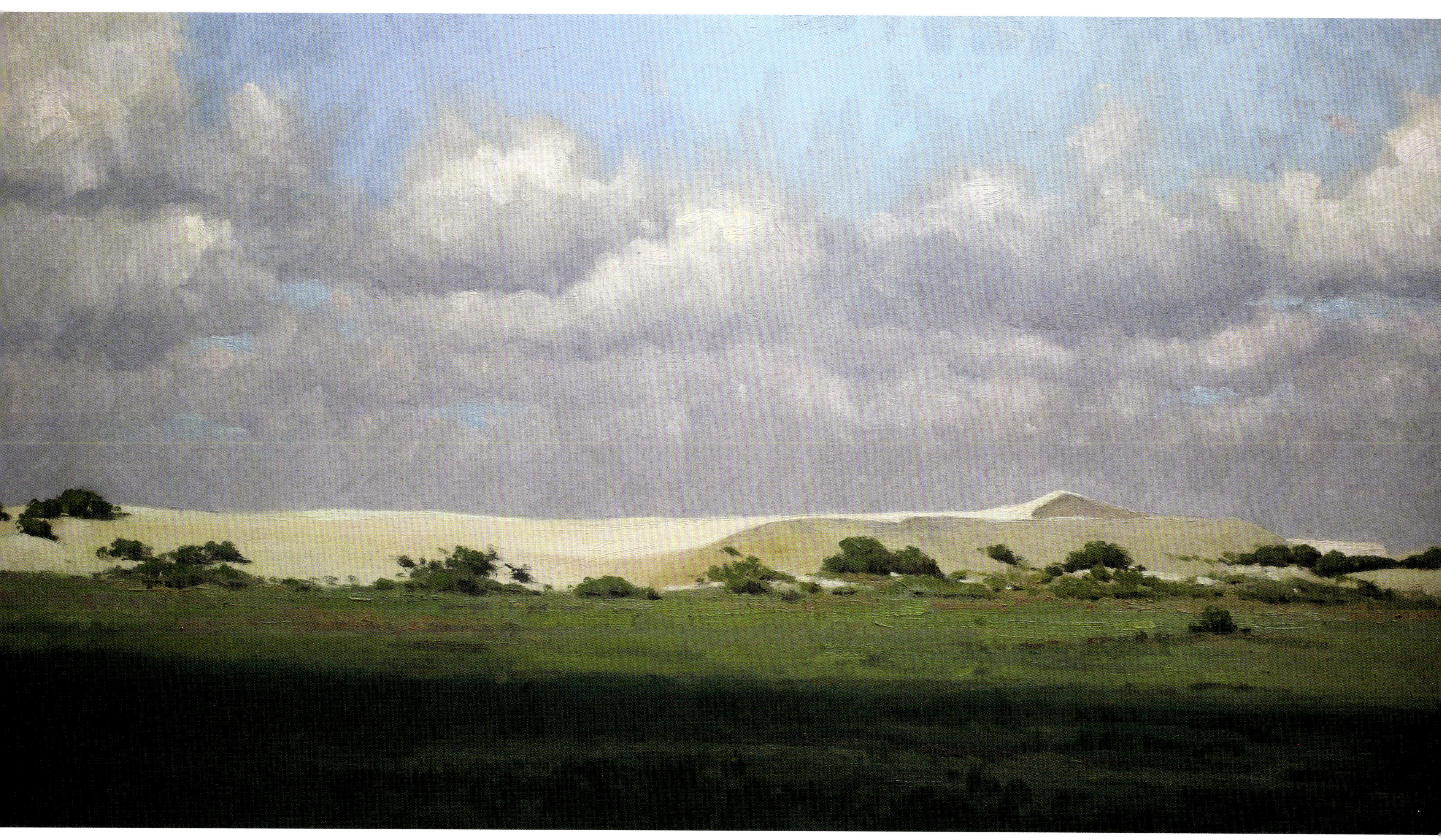

33

*Norias Dunes* (*Norias*), 2019
Oil on canvas, 20 × 36 inches
Courtesy of the artist

## Coastal Plain

This scene highlights the vast open country and beautiful, wide sky that makes this area of South Texas so special.

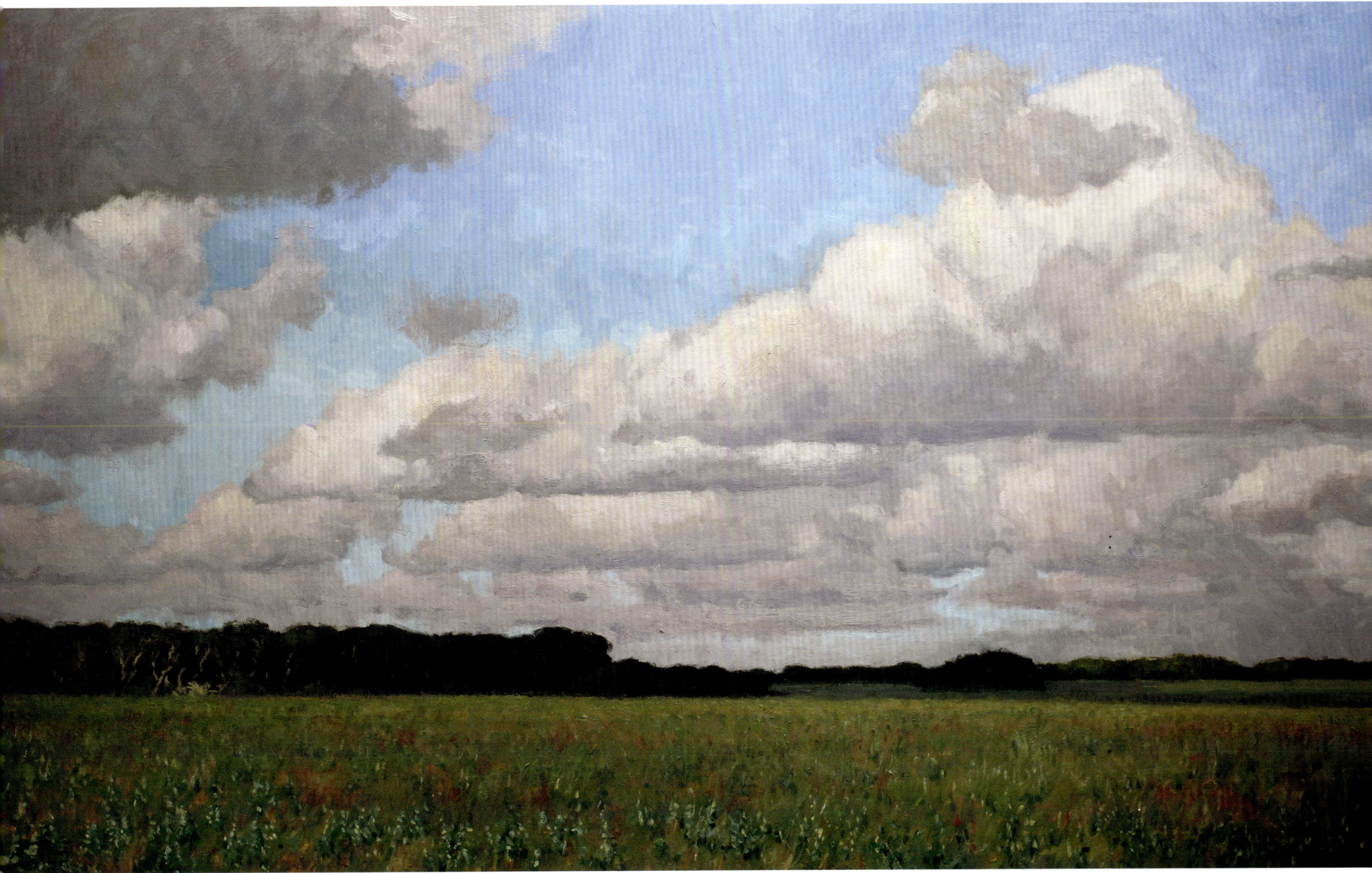

34

*Coastal Plains (Norias)*, 2019
Oil on canvas, 30 × 48 inches
Courtesy of the artist

## Clouds over Oak Motte

I love the coastal plains at Norias. The country is wide and flat, and on a good day, I find myself looking toward the skies. This day had interesting cloud patterns everywhere I looked—I had to do my best to capture it.

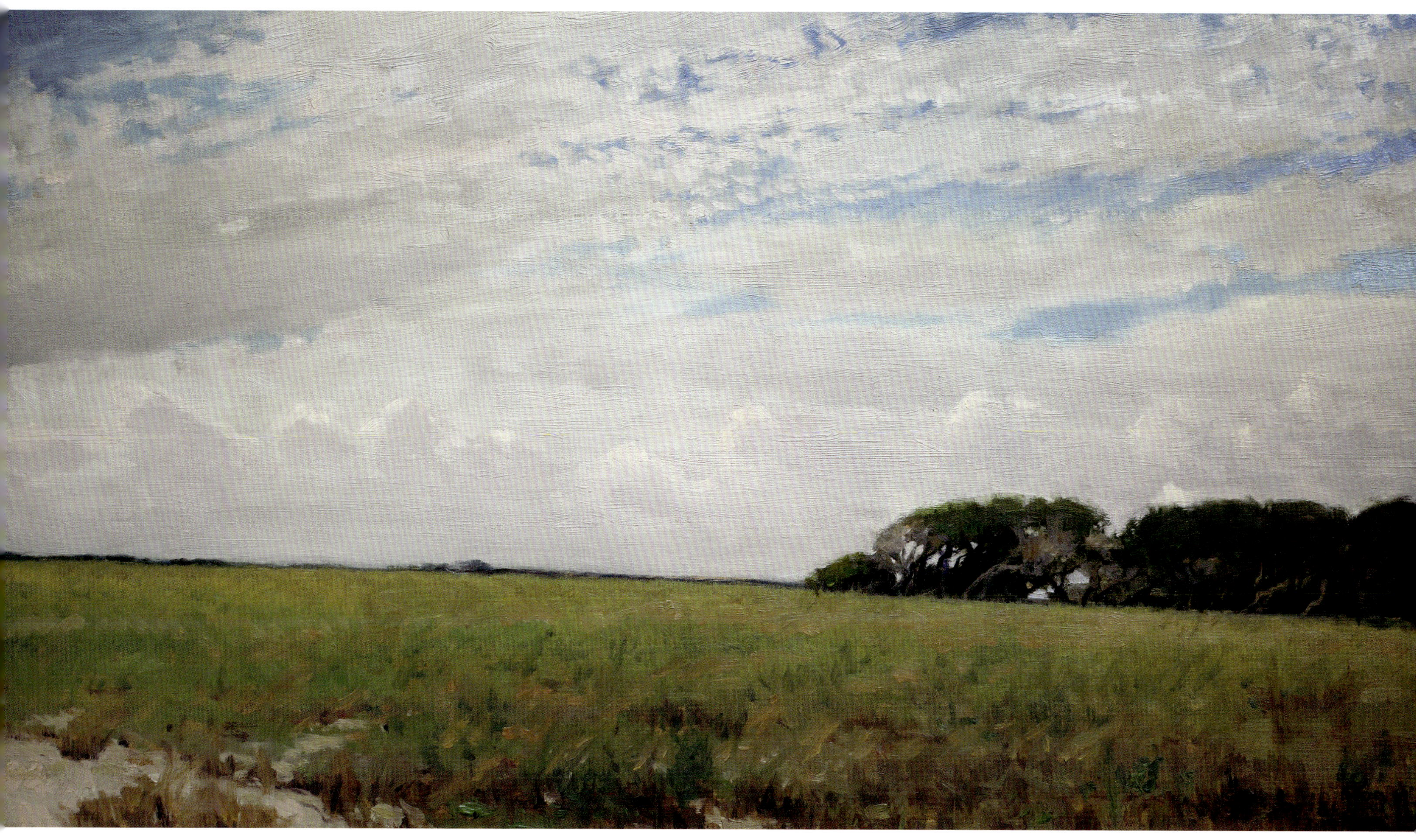

**35**

*Clouds over Oak Motte (Norias)*, 2018
Oil on canvas, 14 × 24 inches
Courtesy of the artist

## Triste Windswept Oaks

If you know my work at all, you'll notice that I love to paint oak trees. To me, they represent strength and character and are aesthetically beautiful. The windswept oaks near the coast are my favorite. The scattered oak mottes along the Norias coast offer an endless supply of great subject matter.

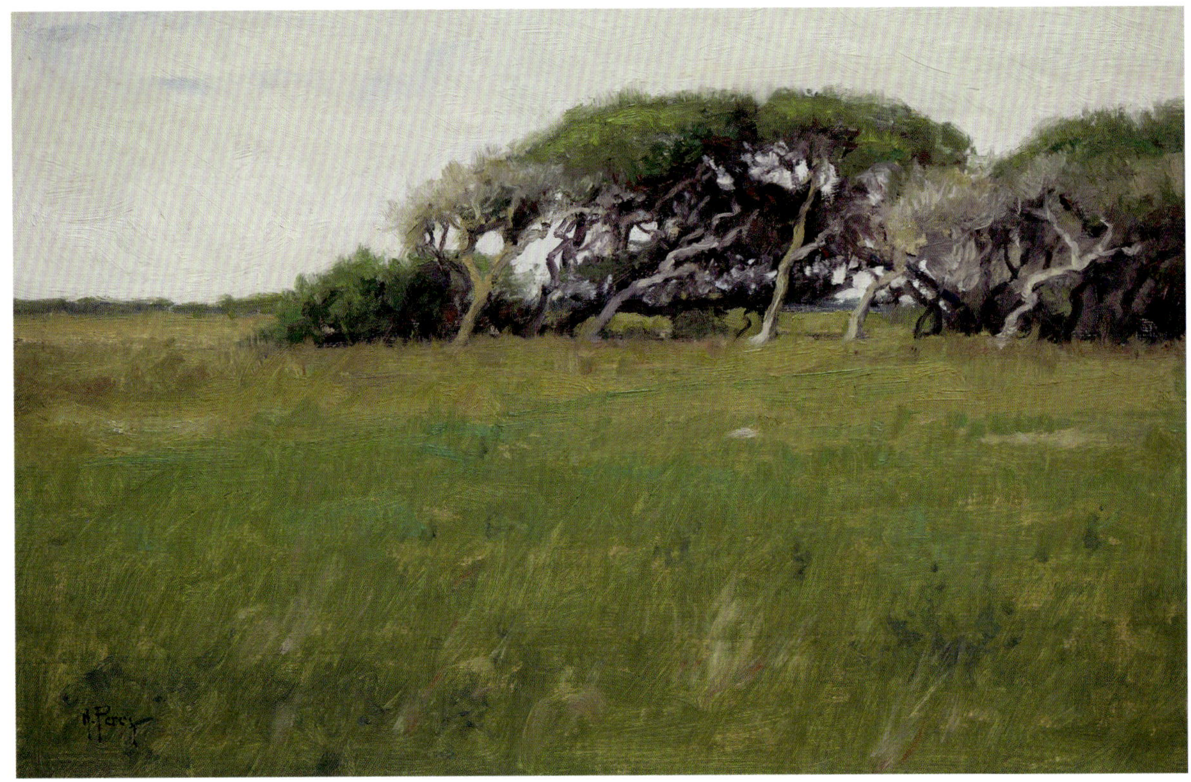

**36**

Study for *Triste Windswept Oaks (Norias)*, 2019
Oil on canvas, 12 × 18 inches
Courtesy of the artist

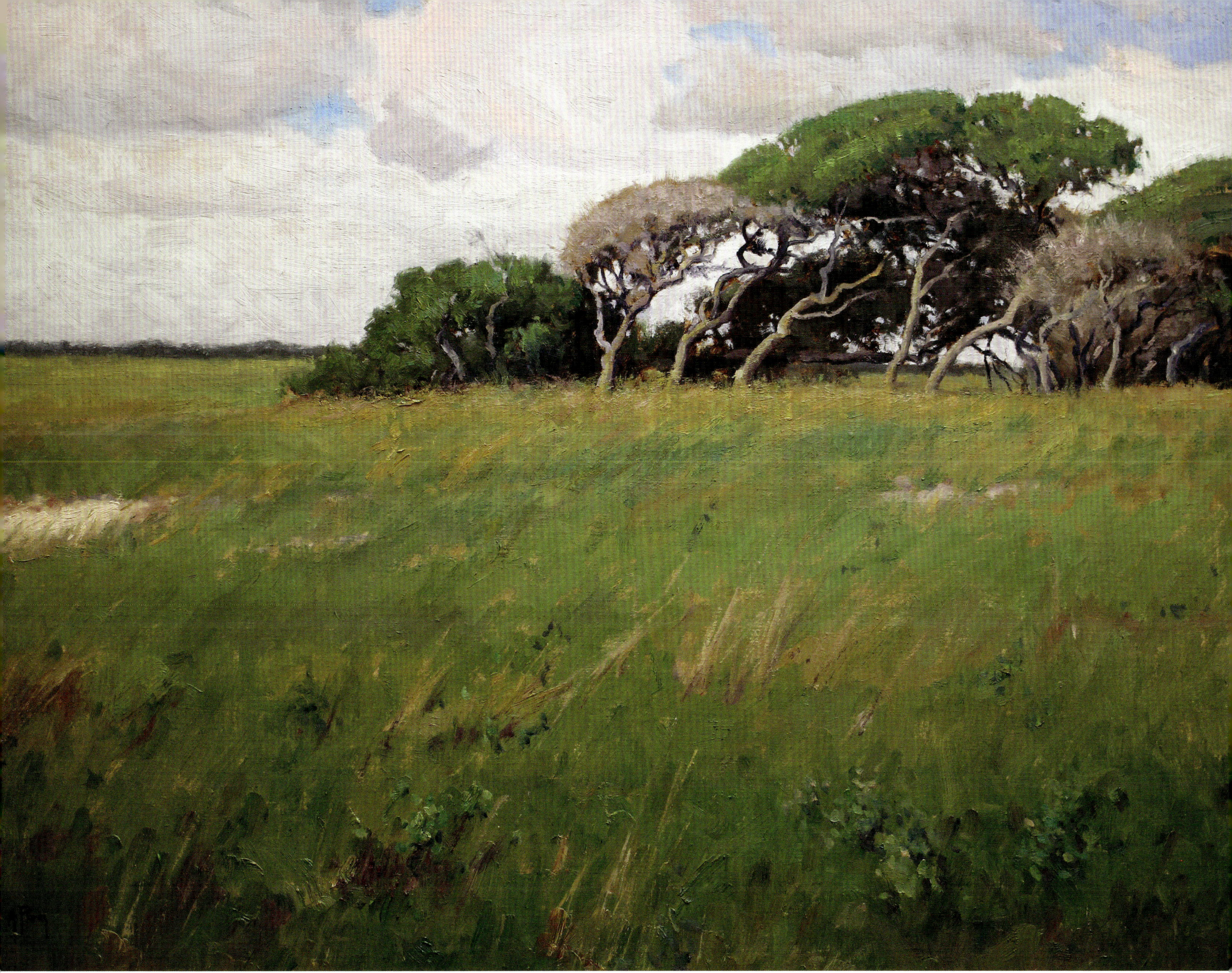

**37**

*Triste Windswept Oaks (Norias)*, 2019
Oil on canvas, 26 × 32 inches
Courtesy of the artist

## Road through the Oaks

Spread across Norias is one of the largest native oak mottes between the Rio Grande and the Nueces River. It is an incredible phenomenon but a really challenging subject to capture in a painting. You find yourself in the middle of oak trees all around—tight, with very little variation in scenery. I had to push to design a workable composition for this amazing oak forest.

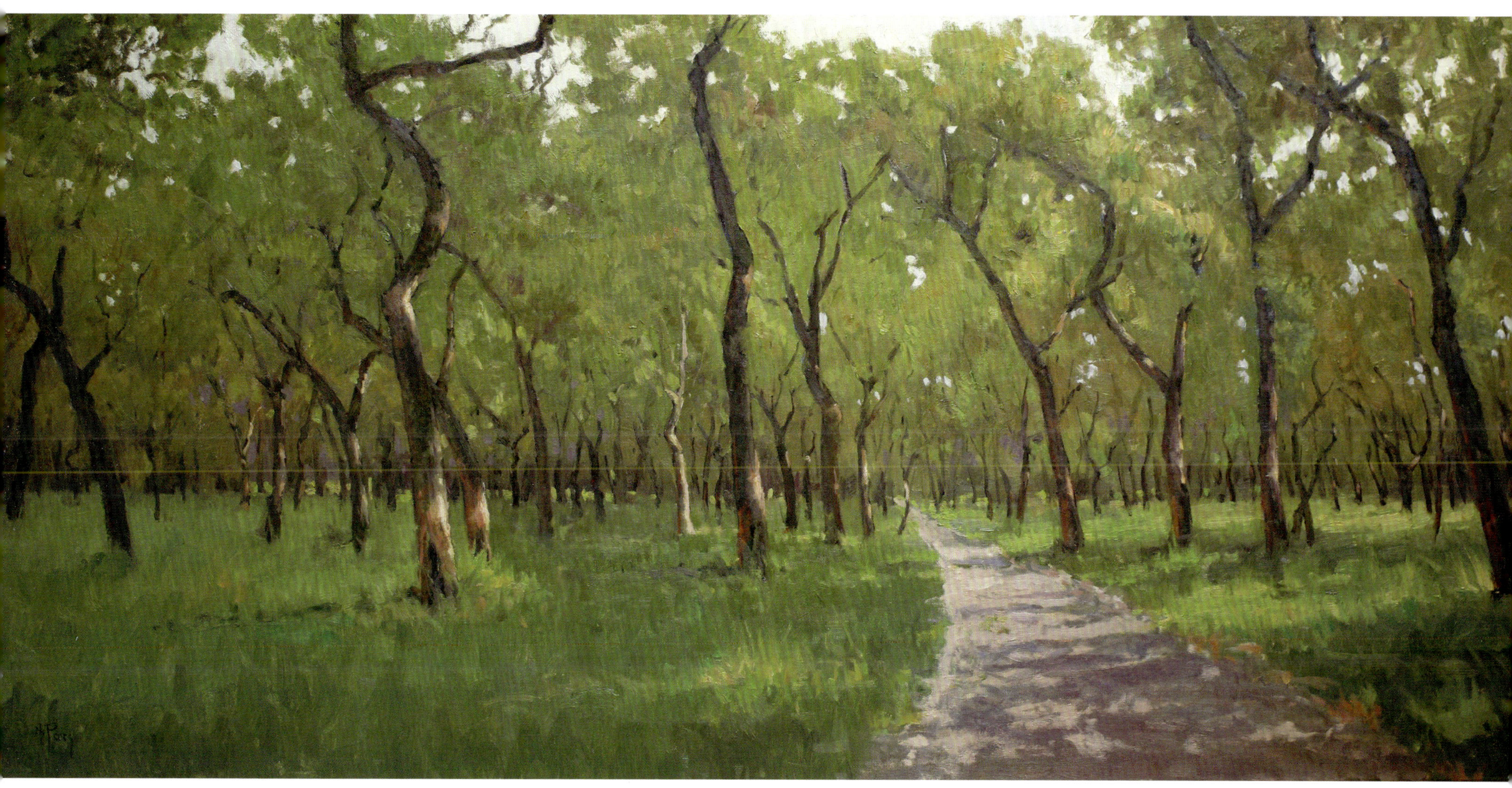

38

*Road through the Oaks (Norias)*, 2019
Oil on canvas, 24 × 48 inches
Courtesy of the artist

## Laureles Headquarters Camp House

We had a really early start and got to see the sun come up over the historic Laureles colony. It was mostly cloudy, but the clouds broke long enough for us to see the skies light up, if only for a brief moment.

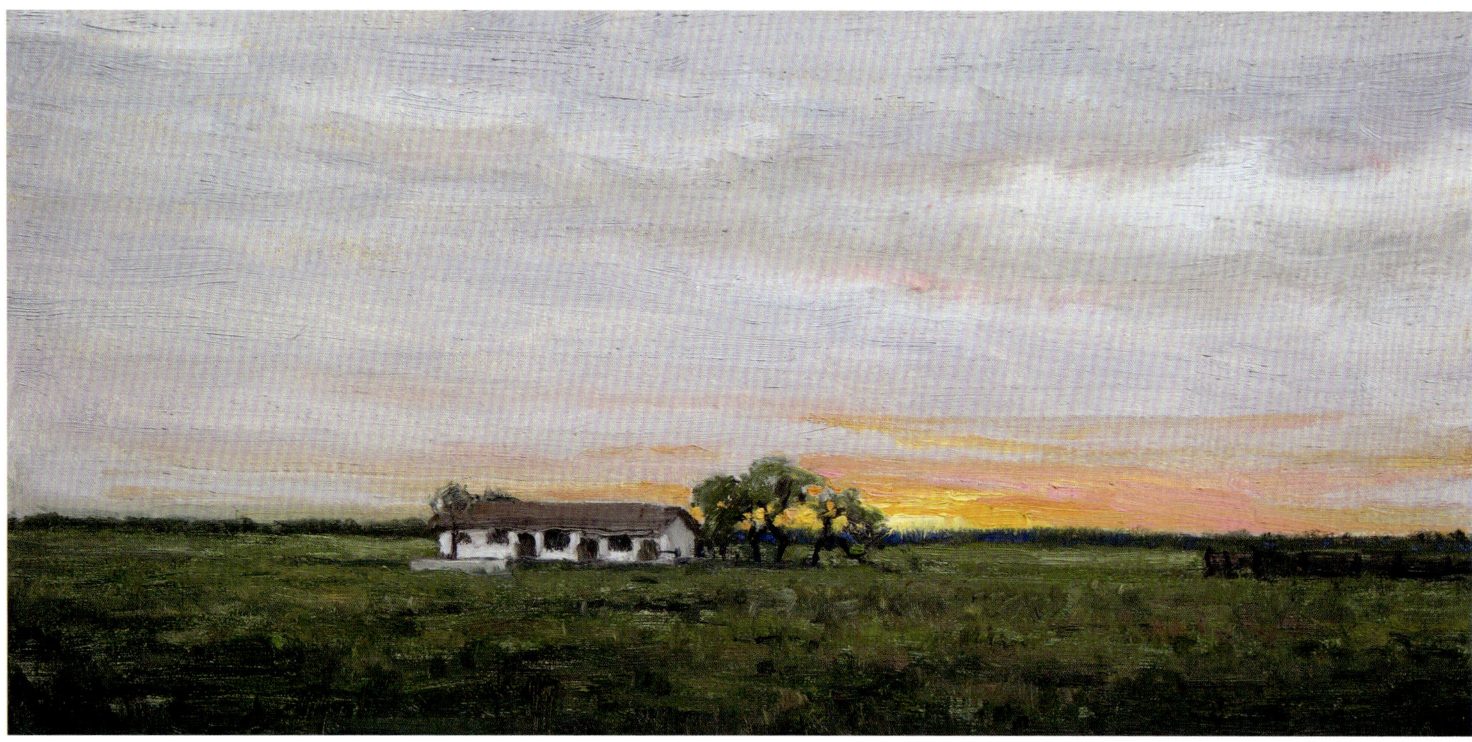

### 39

Study for *Laureles Headquarters Camp House* (*Laureles*), 2019
Oil on canvas, 8 × 16 inches
Courtesy of the artist

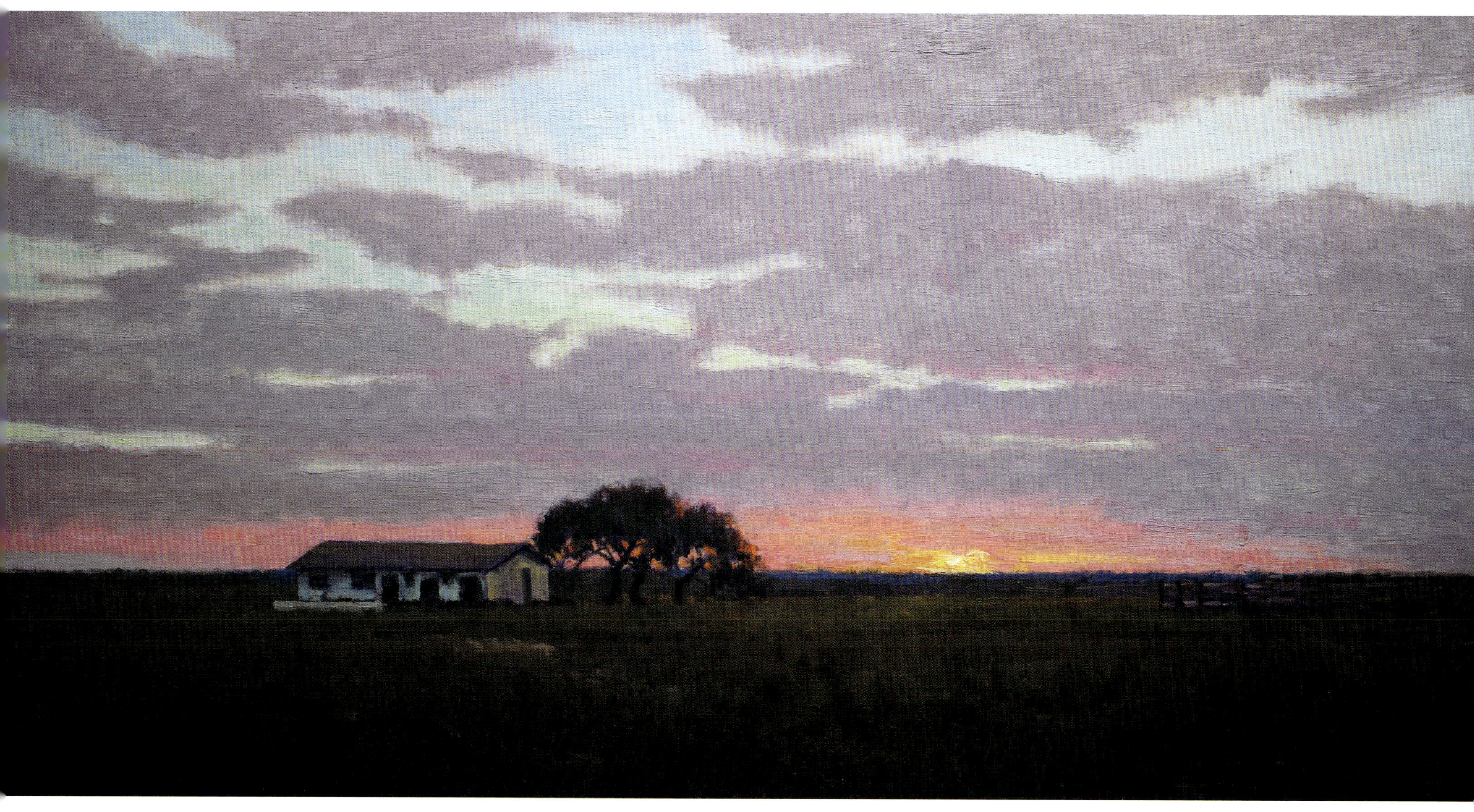

**40**

*Laureles Headquarters Camp House (Laureles)*, 2019
Oil on canvas, 16 × 30 inches
Courtesy of the artist

## Morning Clouds over Álazán Bay

Alazán Bay is a small bay opening on Baffin Bay at the mouth of Petronila Creek. It is surrounded by the Laureles Division. I tried to capture the humidity and heat so typical in this area on a summer morning.

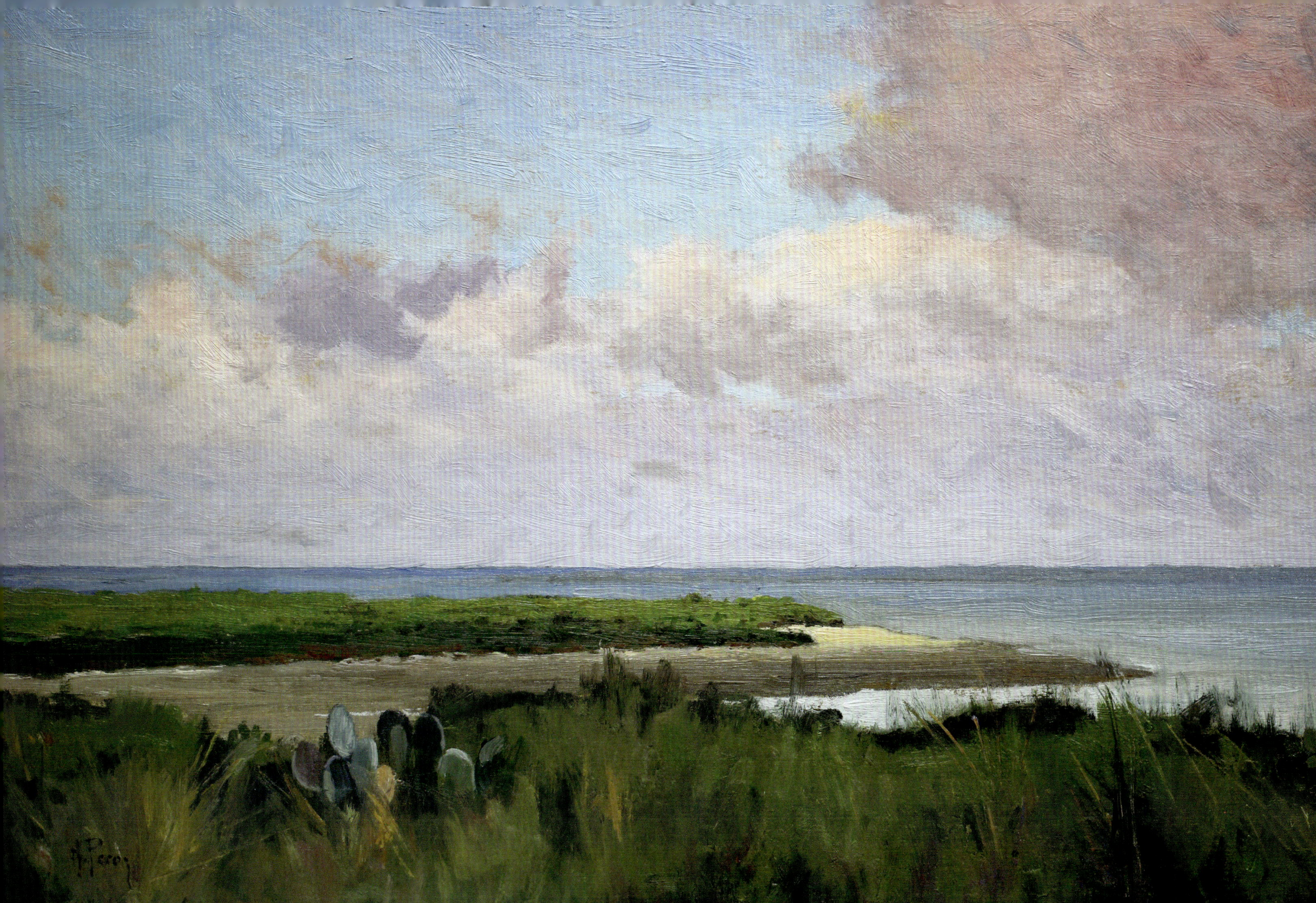

41

*Morning Clouds over Alazán Bay (Laureles)*, 2019
Oil on canvas, 14 × 20 inches
Courtesy of the artist

## El Martillo Camp

The Martillo camp is one of the most remote cow camps on King Ranch. El Martillo lies on a peninsula between Alazán and Baffin Bays.

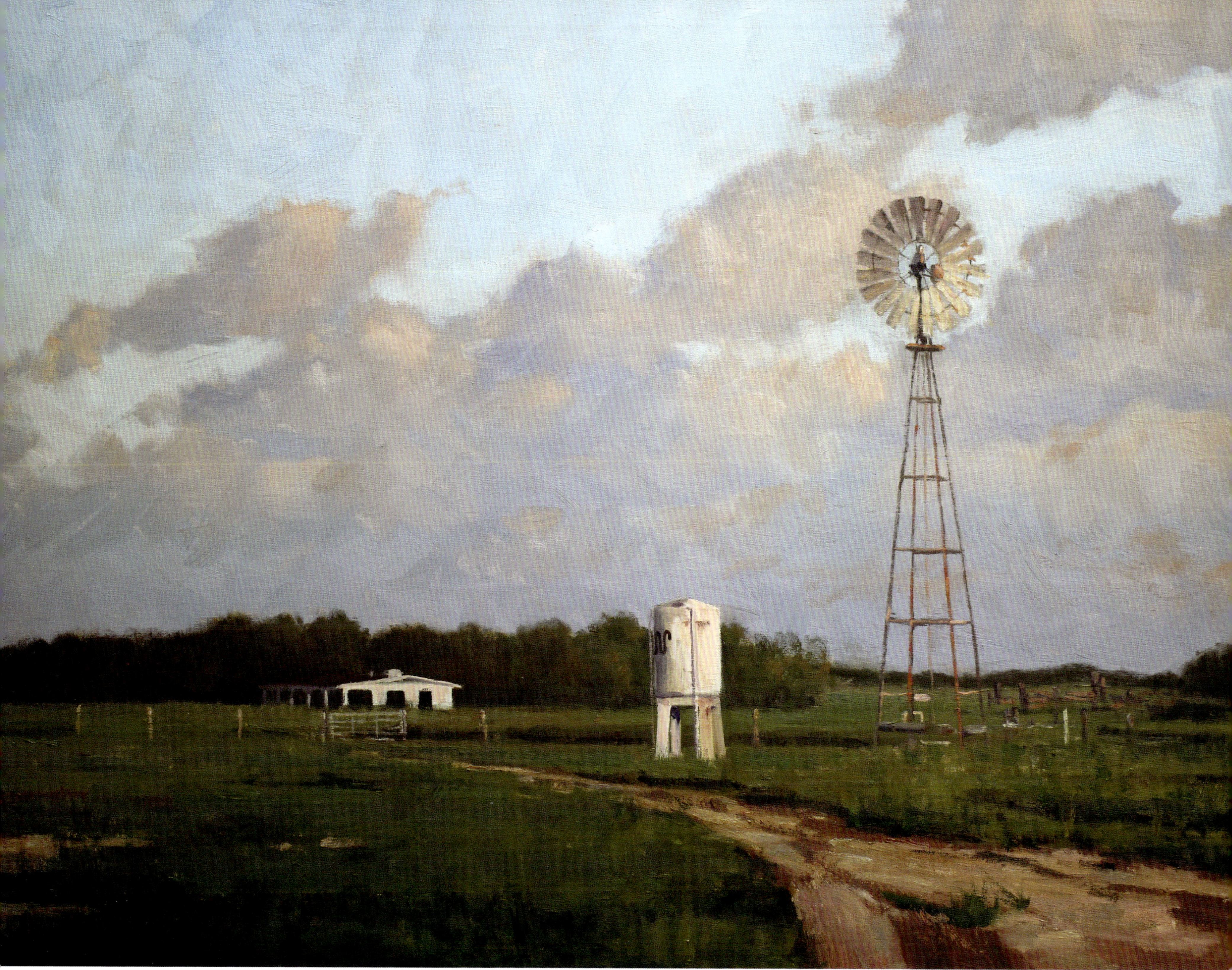

42

*El Martillo Camp (Laureles)*, 2019
Oil on canvas, 24 × 30 inches
Courtesy of the artist

## Evanito Camp House

This is an old cow camp in southern Santa Gertrudis. The Evanito Ranch was once owned by John Fitch, renowned trail driver and headman for Captain King.

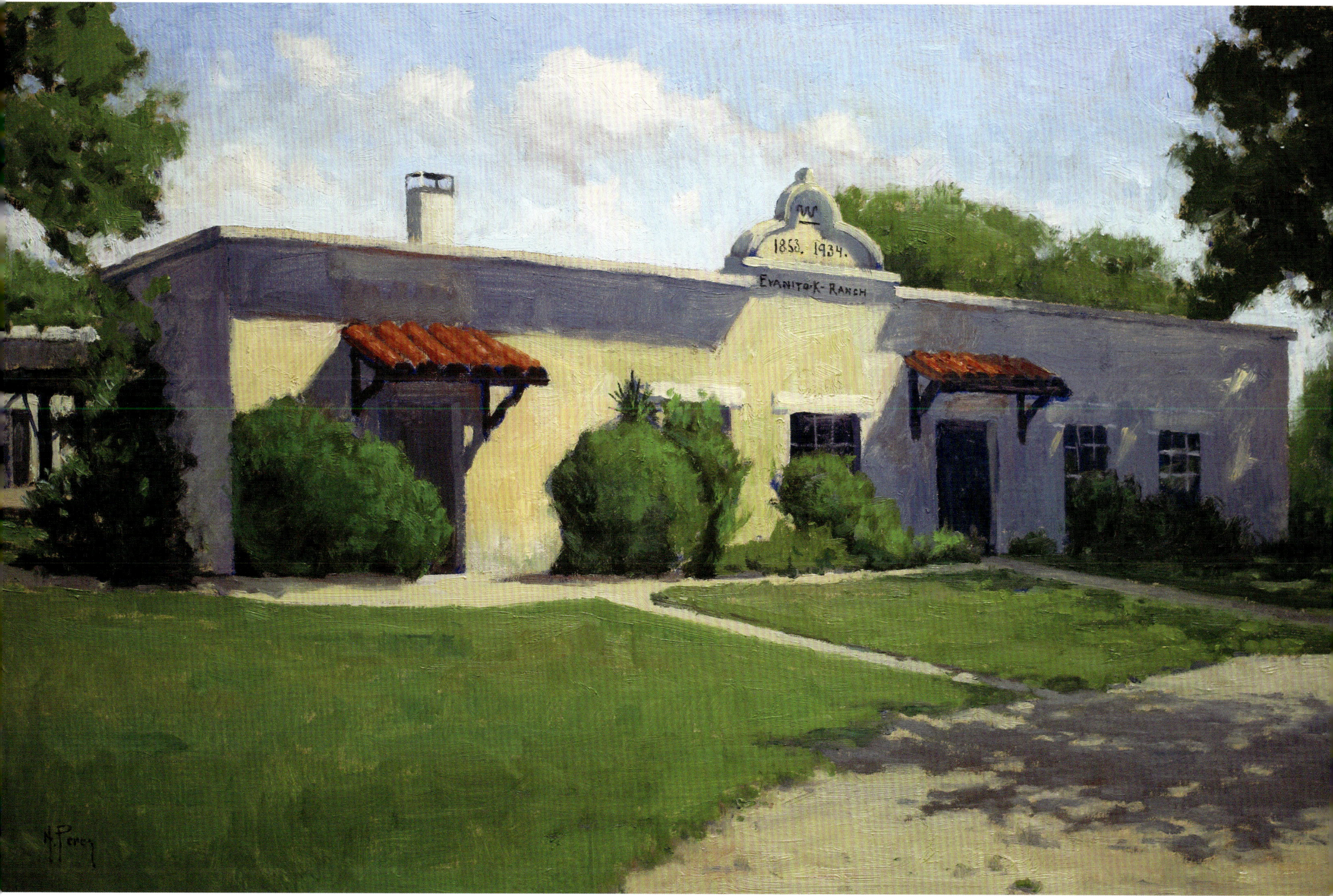


## 43

*Evanito Camp House (Santa Gertrudis)*, 2019
Oil on canvas, 16 × 24 inches
Courtesy of the artist

## Las Palmas Camp House

An early morning trip to Laureles put me in front of this beautiful camp house, sitting in the middle of the 65,000-acre King Ranch farm. This was my chance to capture a nocturne of a white structure, and I took it.

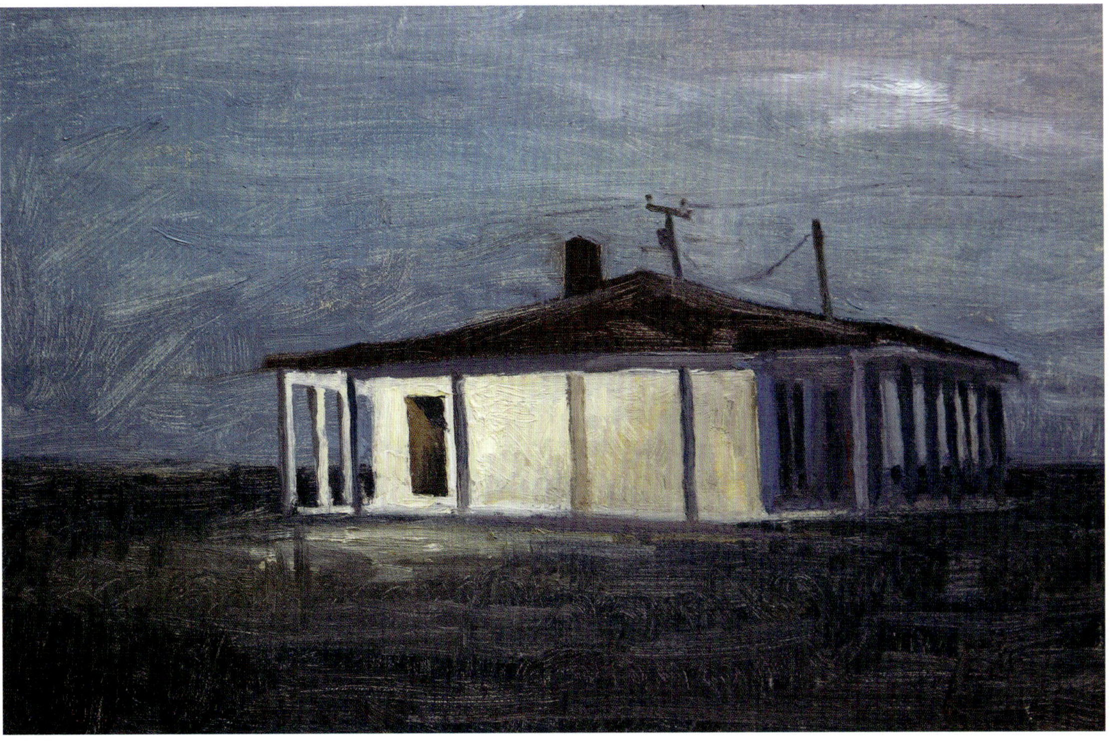

**44**

Study for *Las Palmas Camp House (Laureles)*, 2019
Oil on canvas, 8 × 12 inches
Courtesy of the artist

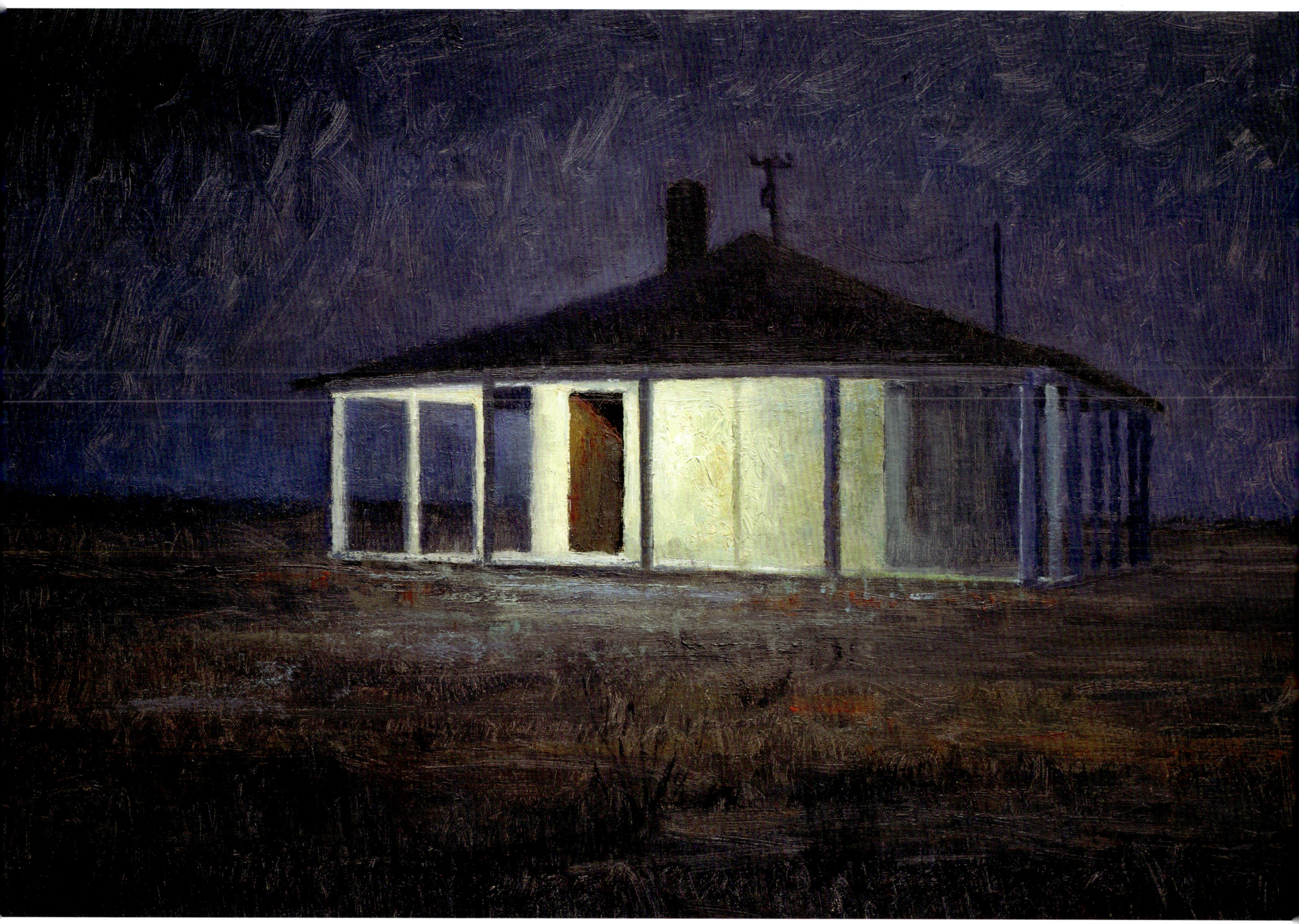

45

*Las Palmas Camp House (Laureles)*, 2019
Oil on canvas, 14 × 20 inches
Courtesy of the artist

## Young Nilgai Bulls

Exotic Indian antelope were introduced by Caesar Kleberg in 1925 at Norias. The small herd purchased from the San Diego Zoo has grown to more than 19,000. I am not a wildlife painter, but this was an opportunity to try my hand.

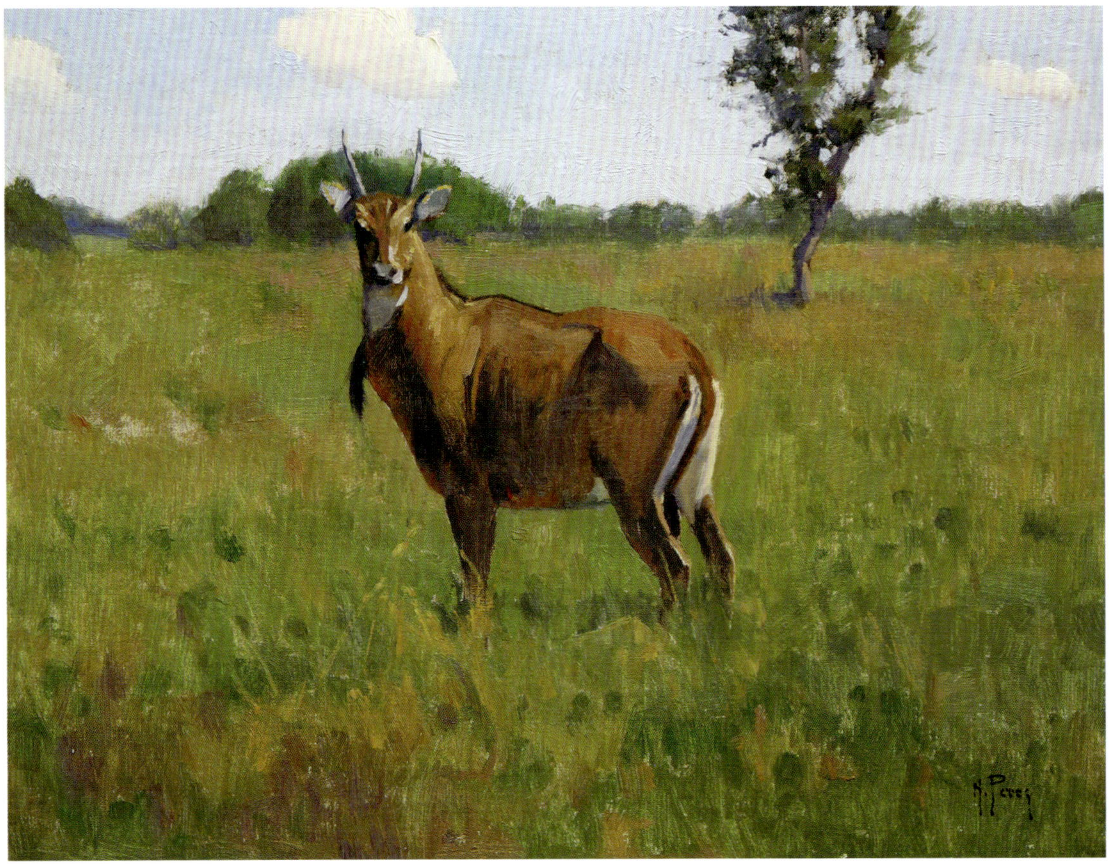

**46**

Study for *Young Nilgai Bulls (Norias)*, 2019
Oil on canvas, 11 × 14 inches
Courtesy of the artist

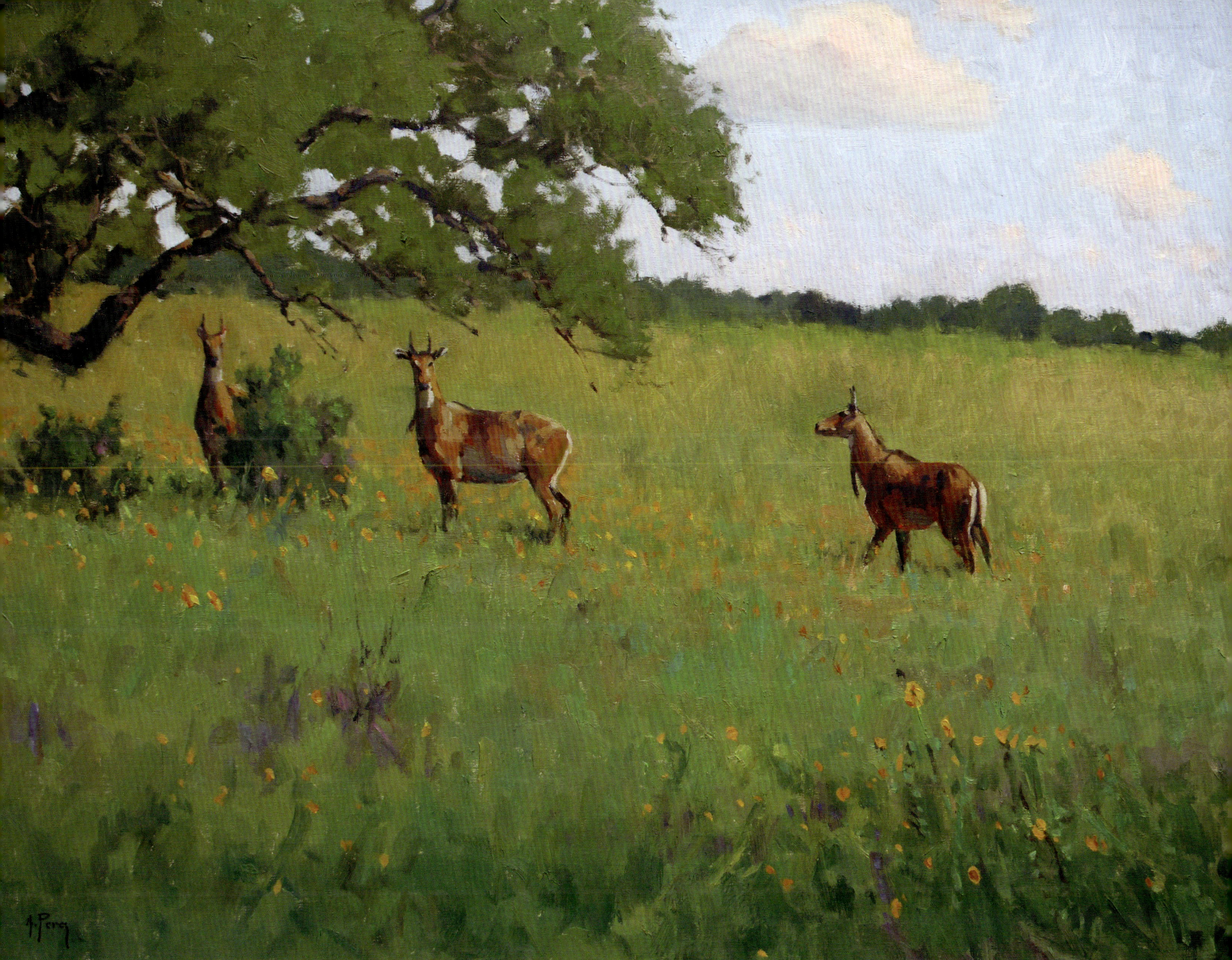

47

*Young Nilgai Bulls (Norias)*, 2019
Oil on canvas, 24 × 30 inches
Courtesy of the artist

## Old Ranch Colony Turkeys

On one of my first trips to Norias, we saw these turkeys near the entrance, at the site of the old Norias colony. The Rio Grande turkey population was limited at one time but now flourishes throughout the Norias Division.

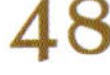

48

*Old Ranch Colony Turkeys (Norias)*, 2019
Oil on canvas, 18 × 18 inches
Courtesy of the artist

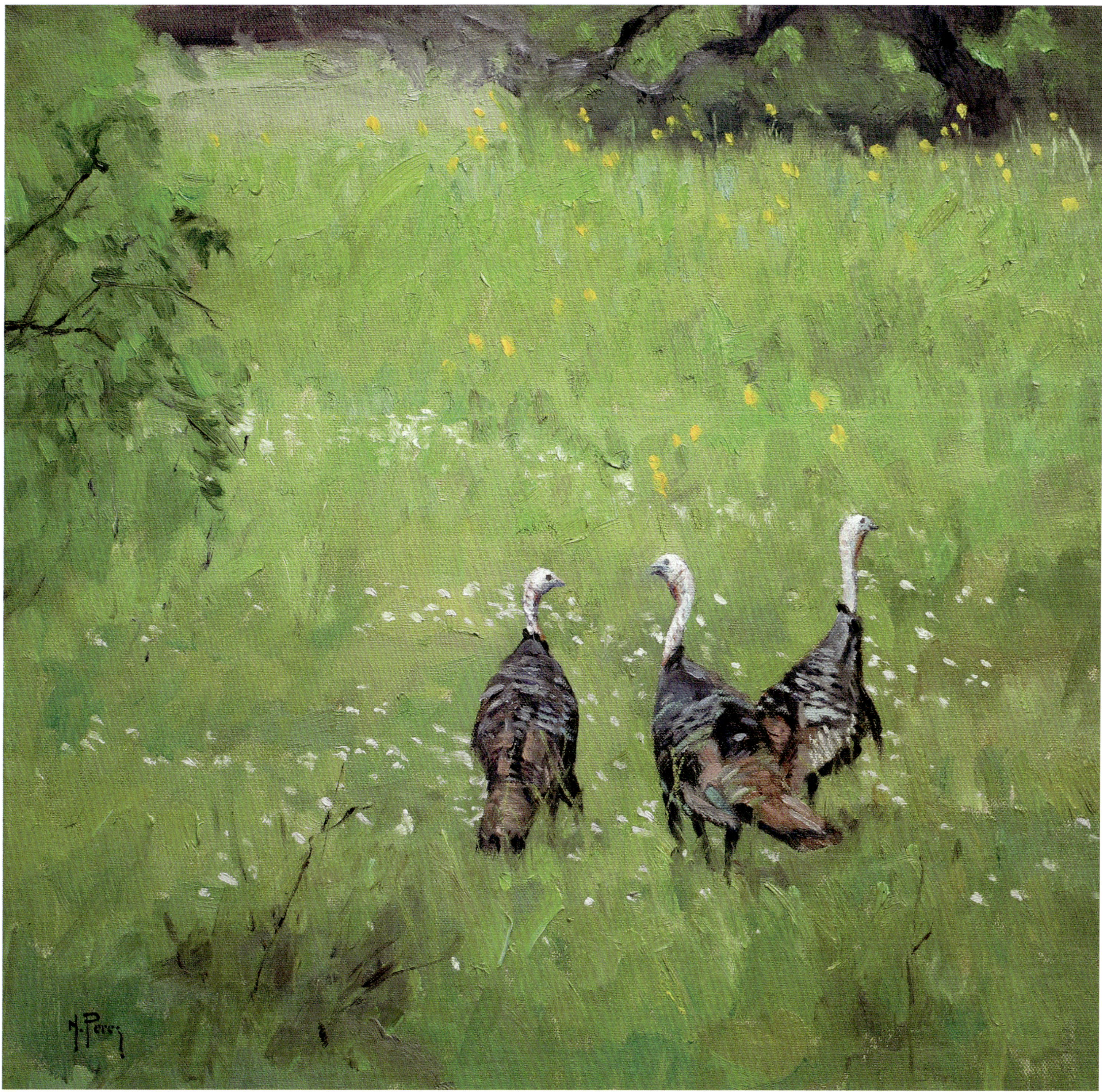

## Venada Camp

This is a remote camp in the northwestern corner of the Encino Division. *Encino* means "oak tree" in Spanish, and the oak trees here were a sight to behold. Even though I painted the camp house, my main interest here was the central oak tree holding court. A close second was the sunlight filtering through, which created interesting patterns on the ground.

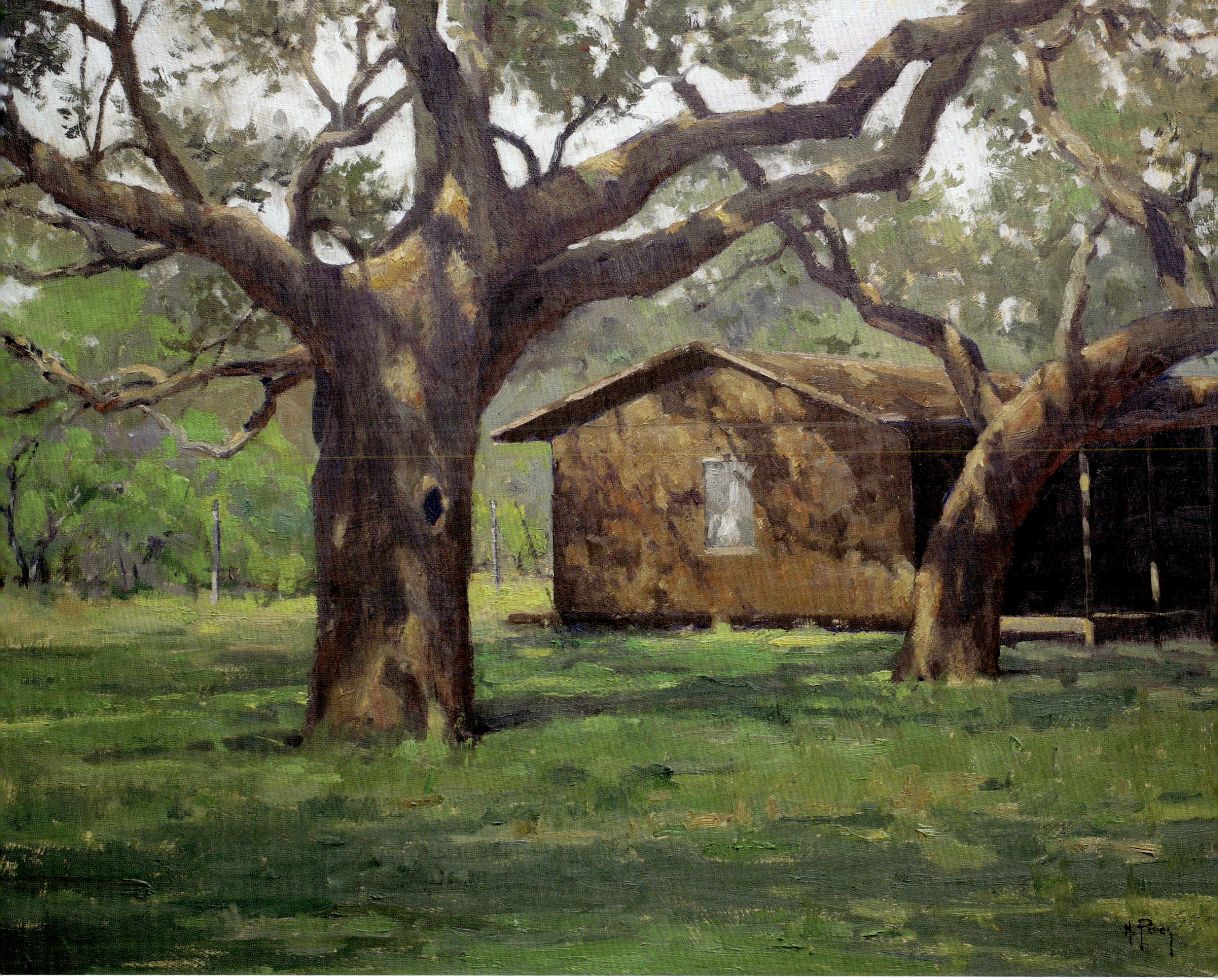

**49**

*Venada Camp (Encino)*, 2019
Oil on canvas, 19¼ × 24 inches
Courtesy of the artist

## Summer Clouds

Even though this painting has some summer flowers in the foreground, my thought was to focus on the clouds by lowering the horizon line and giving the clouds the commanding role in this drama, shadowing the distant tree line.

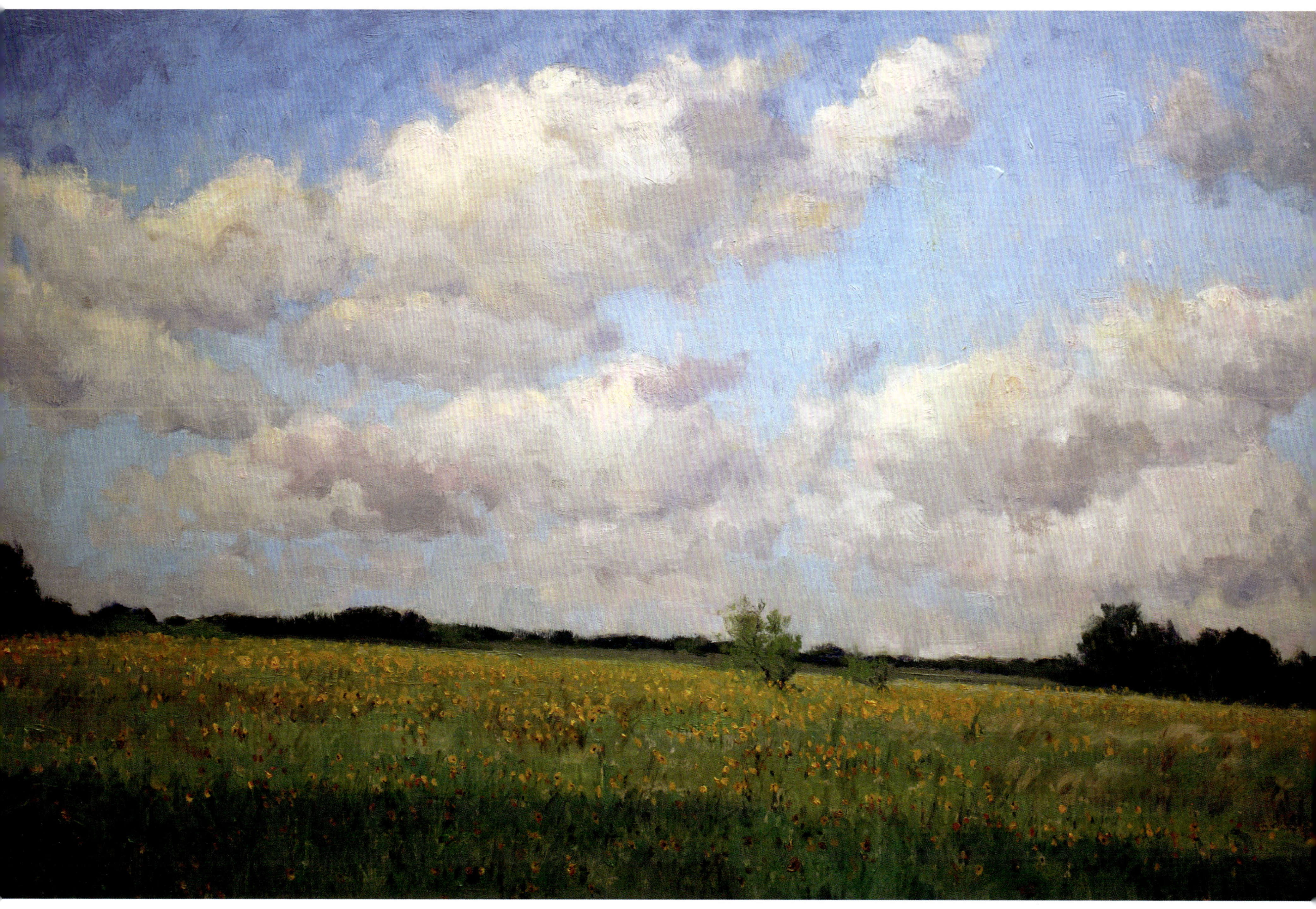

**50**

*Summer Clouds (Norias)*, 2019
Oil on canvas, 20 × 30 inches
Courtesy of the artist

## Spring Flowers at Encino

This simple scene reminds me of visiting area ranches when I was growing up—a sandy lane running along a fence line, late-season flowers holding on, and mesquites with fresh, bright foliage make for a typical South Texas spring.

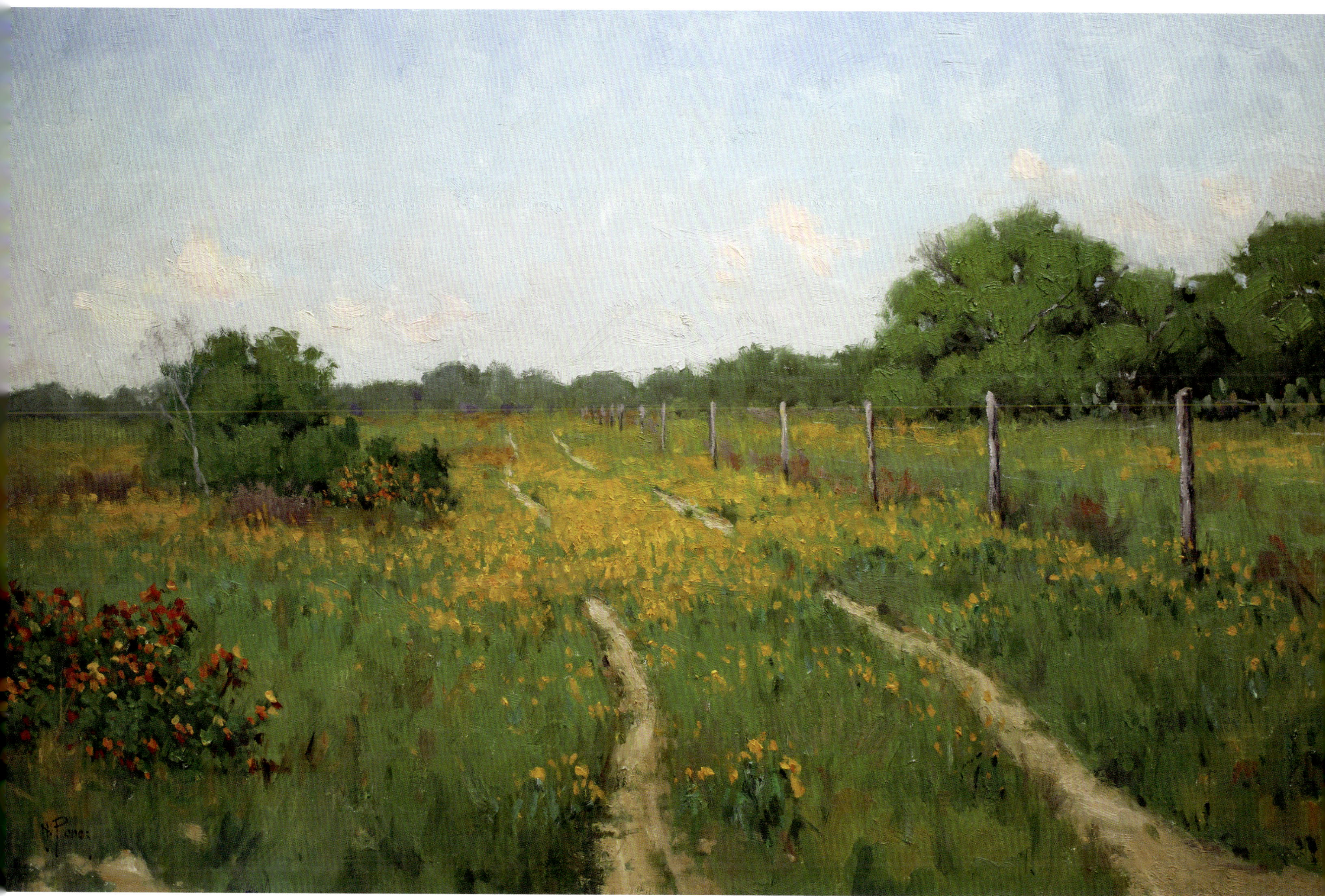

**51**

*Spring Flowers at Encino (Encino)*, 2019
Oil on canvas, 20 × 30 inches
Courtesy of the artist

## Lauro's Field Prickly Pear

My fascination with prickly pear cactus as a subject matter is right up there with oak trees. There is so much to capture that it's hard to stay simple. I try to showcase the beauty of the cactus without getting too bogged down with details. Then again, that is the challenge with just about any work of art. This is a common scene around the Santa Gertrudis headquarters in spring, and this painting is a nod to the early masters of the Texas landscape—Dawson Dawson-Watson (1864–1939), Jose Arpa (1858–1952), and Porfirio Salinas (1910–73).

**52**

*Lauro's Field Prickly Pear (Santa Gertrudis)*, 2019
Oil on canvas, 40 × 30 inches
Courtesy of the artist

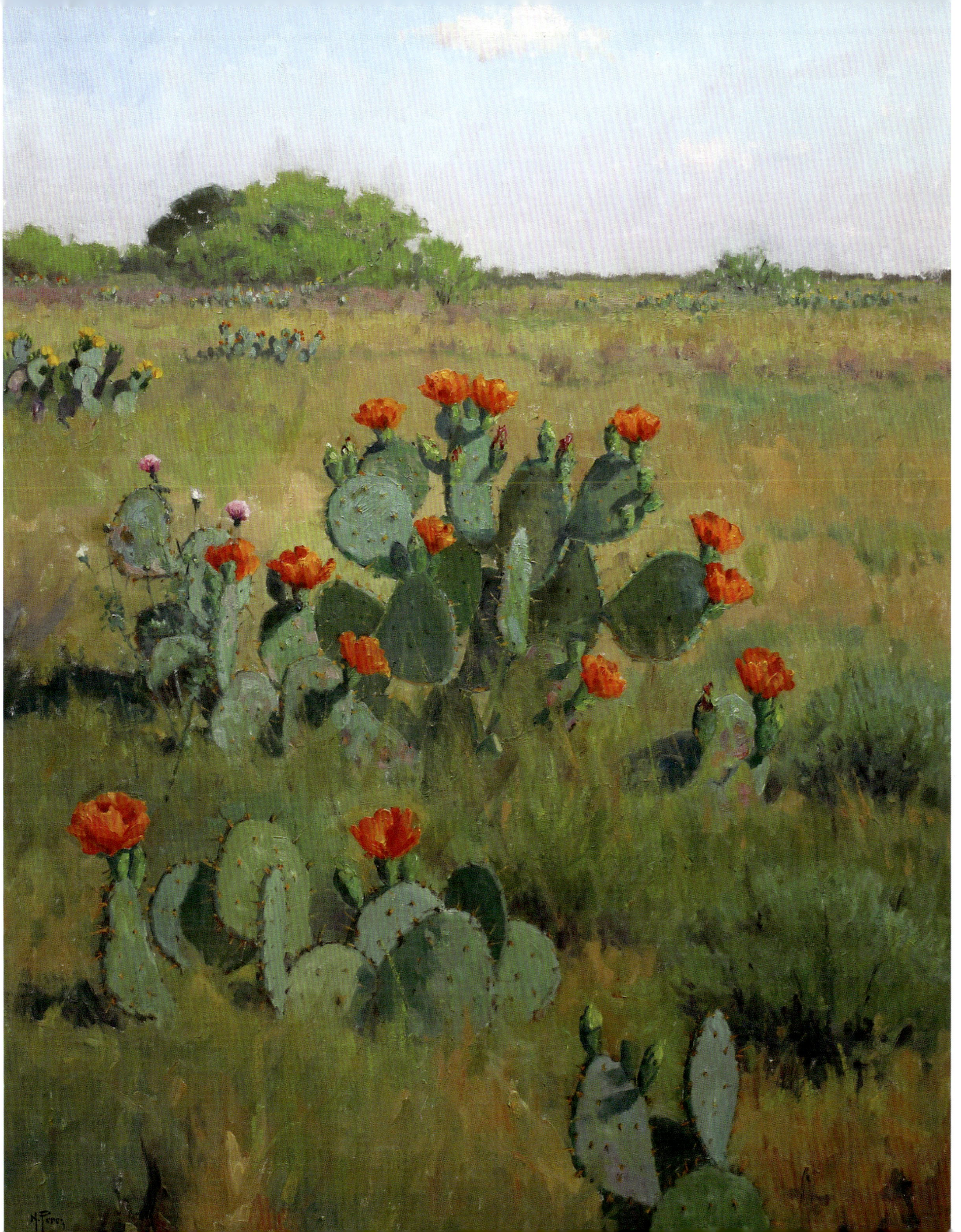

## Seep Springs

Santa Gertrudis Creek is the location of the ancient seep springs as Captain King might have seen it. As I drove around the headquarters at Santa Gertrudis, the backlit clouds and shimmering creek were an obvious choice of subject matter.

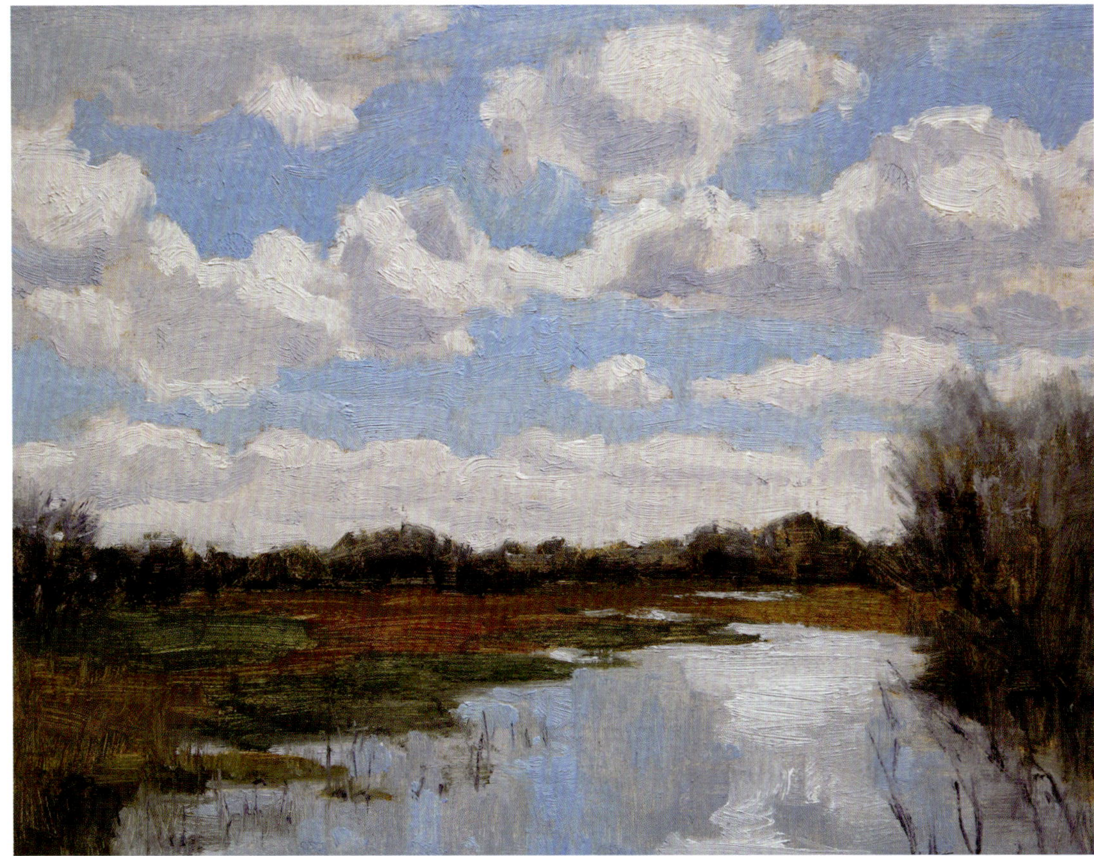

**53**

Study for *Seep Springs (Santa Gertrudis)*, 2019
Oil on canvas, 11 × 14 inches
Courtesy of the artist

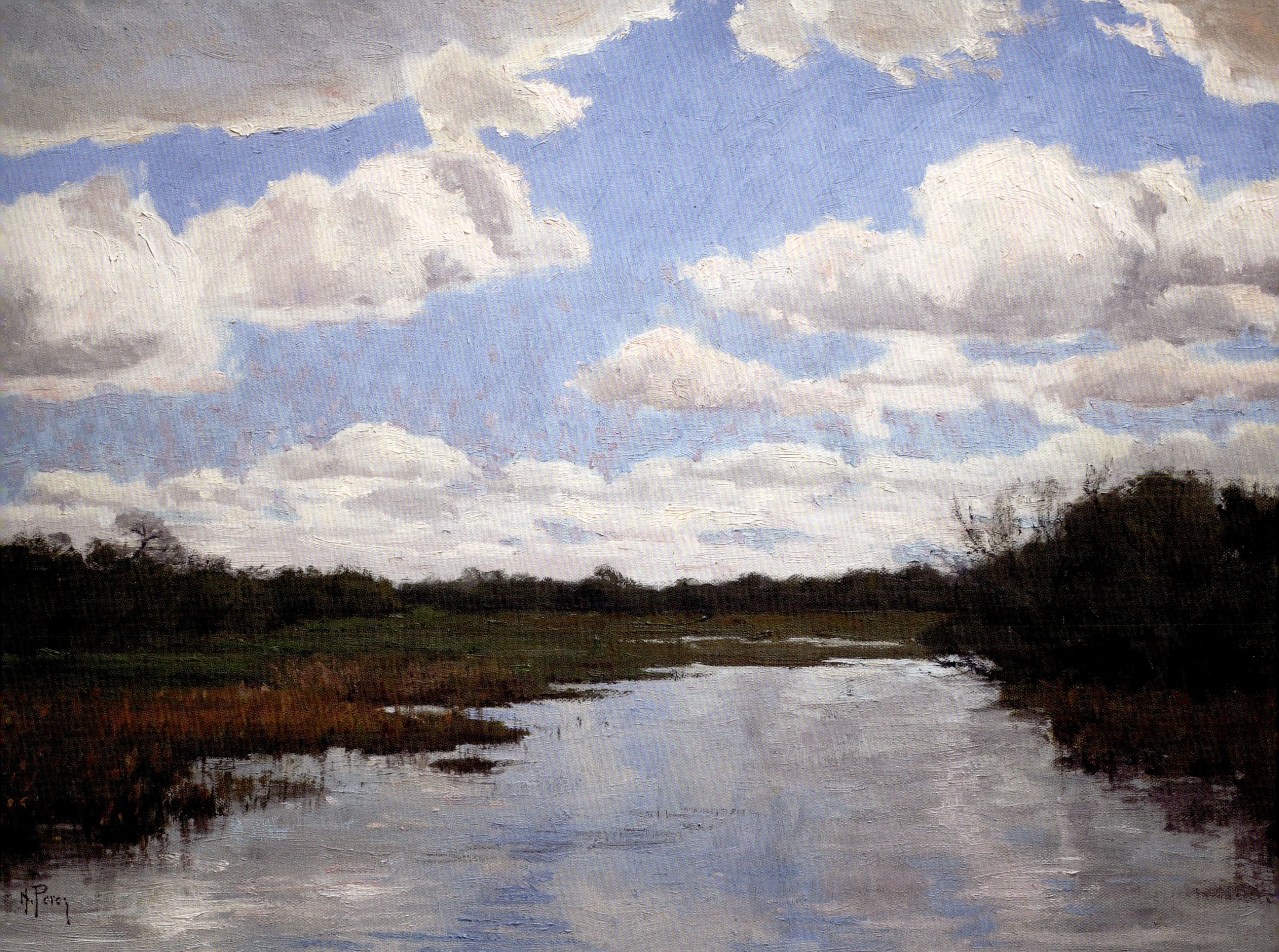

**54**

*Seep Springs* (*Santa Gertrudis*), 2019
Oil on canvas, 18 × 24 inches
Courtesy of the artist

## Bridge over Santa Gertrudis Creek

I was immediately attracted to this bridge, built by Austin Bridge Company in 1935, because of its structural grace and lightweight strength. These types of structures can be difficult to paint. Ultimately, I was attracted by the blue-green color of the palm leaves and the hint of the Santa Gertrudis as it exits on the right side of the frame. It is located near the historic cotton road.

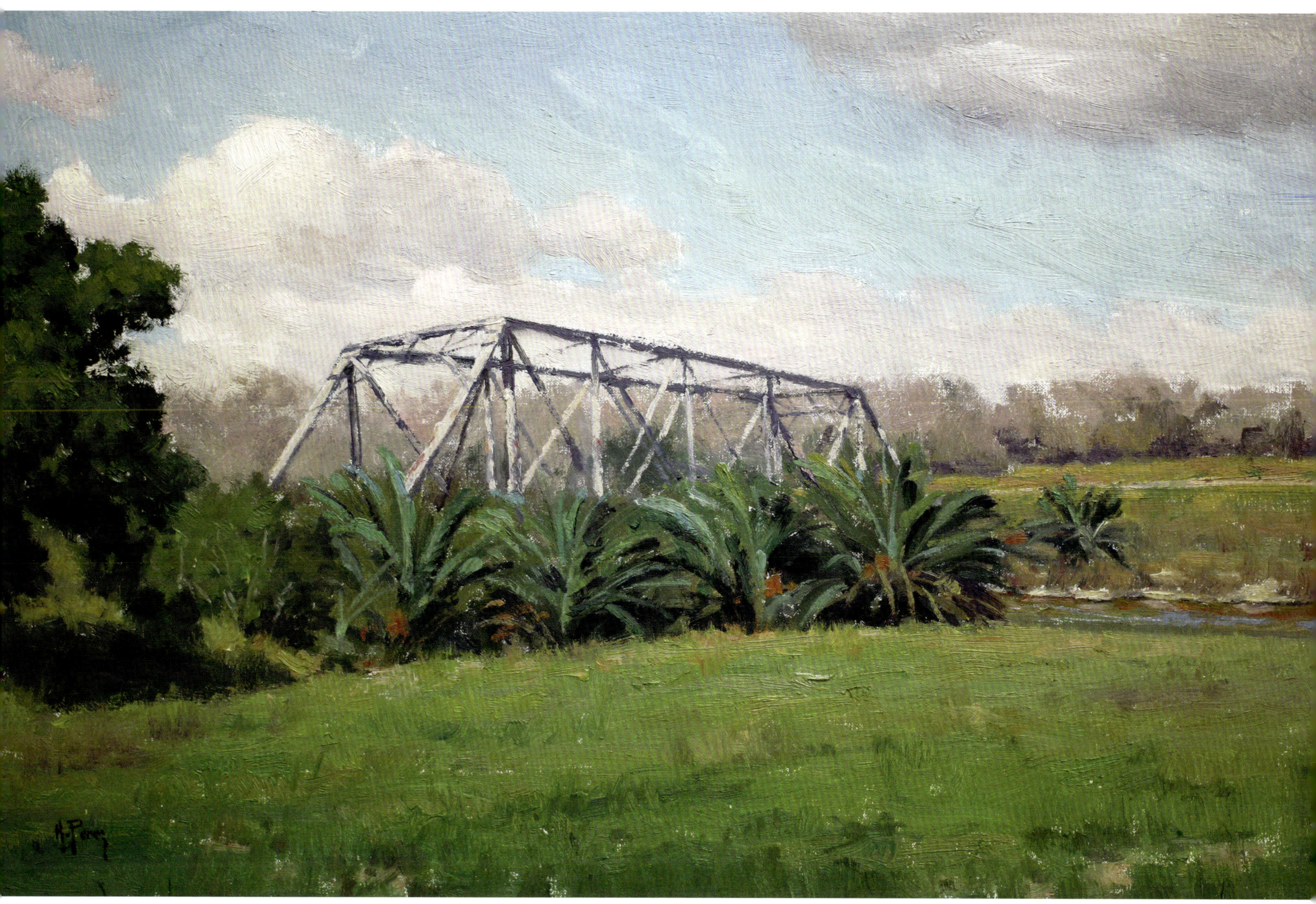

55

*Bridge over Santa Gertrudis Creek (Santa Gertrudis)*, 2019
Oil on canvas, 11½ × 17 inches
Courtesy of the artist

## Una Mañana en el Árroyo Santa Gertrudis

This scene reveals the Santa Gertrudis as the first light of day lands on the mesquites bordering the iconic creek on King Ranch.

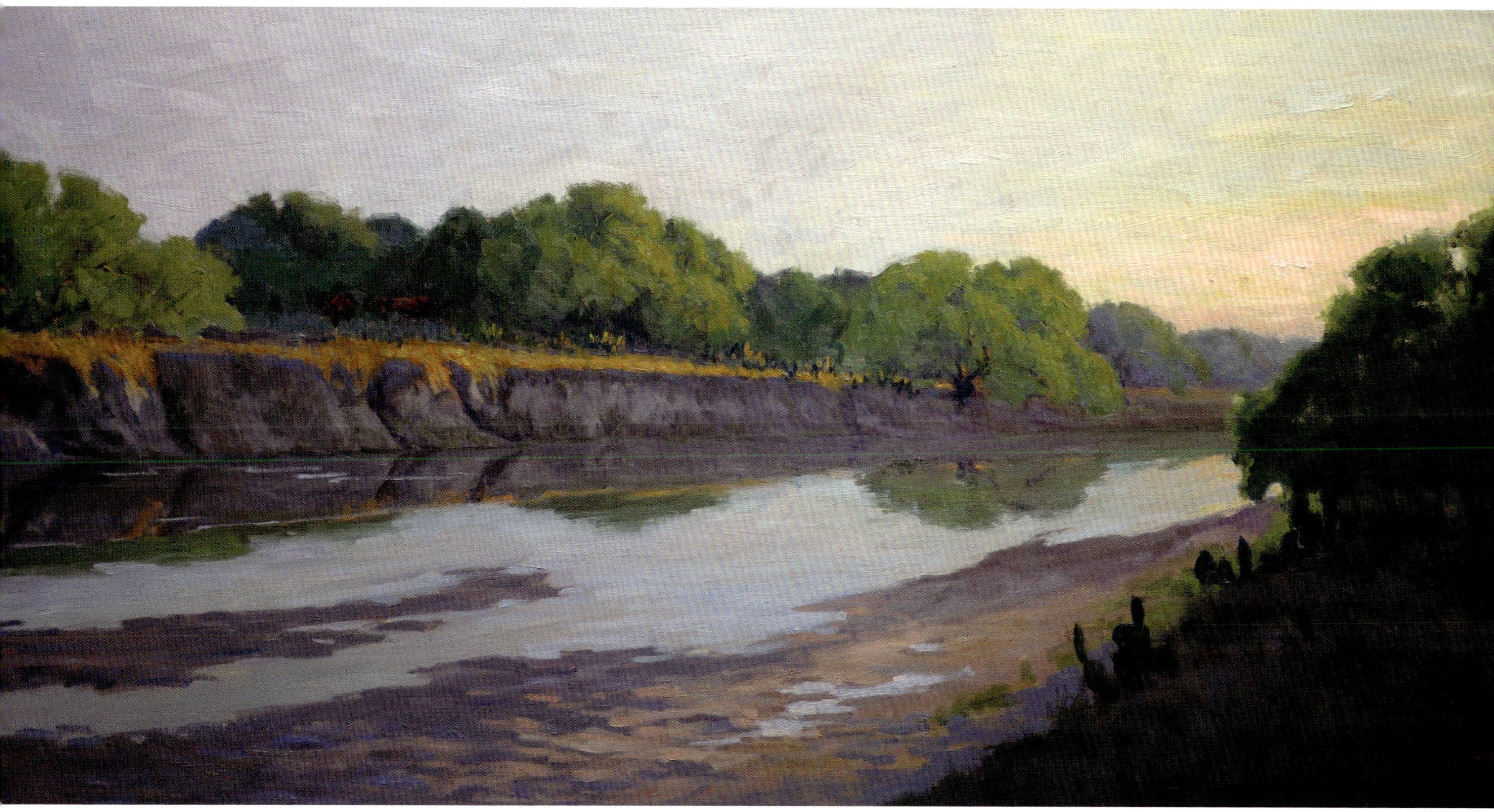

56

*Una Mañana en el Arroyo Santa Gertrudis*, 2016
Oil on canvas, 24 × 48 inches
Collection of Judy and Jamey Clement
Courtesy of the artist

## Winter Mesquite

A small group of us involved in this project got to spend the night at King Ranch in February 2019. In the morning, I walked around and took pictures of the start of a cool, foggy day. This mesquite has such great character, with the classic shape of this hearty breed of South Texas trees. This was a welcome departure from the sunny scenes that I am usually drawn to.

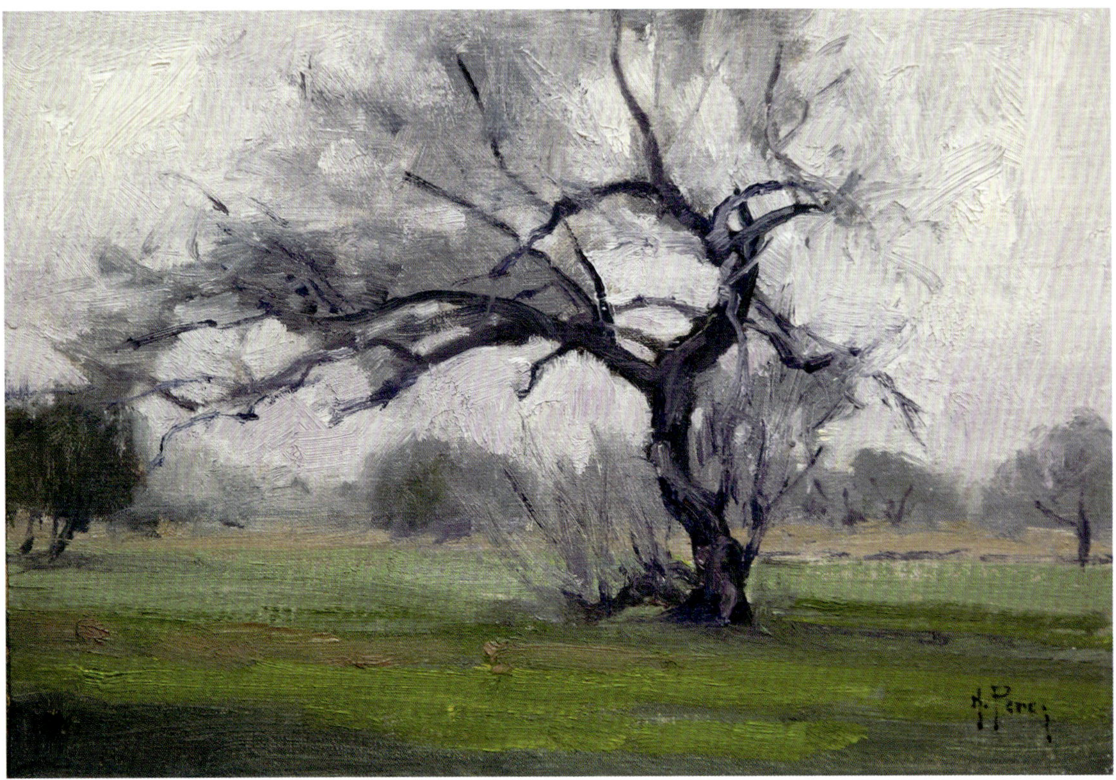

**57**

Study for *Winter Mesquite (Santa Gertrudis)*, 2019
Oil on canvas, 7 × 10 inches
Courtesy of the artist

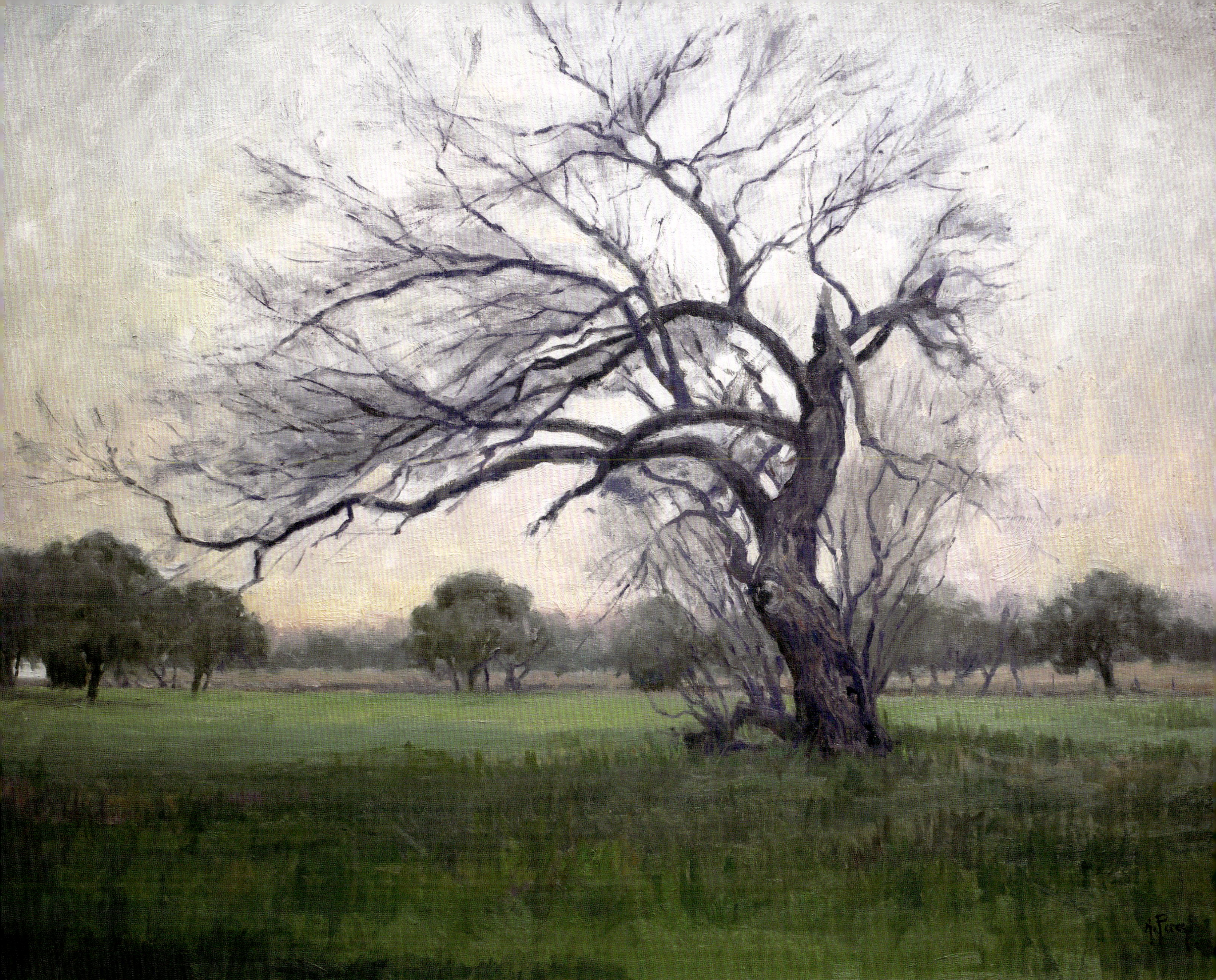

58

*Winter Mesquite (Santa Gertrudis)*, 2019
Oil on canvas, 24 × 30 inches
Courtesy of the artist

## Olmos Mesquites at Dusk

On a holiday trip to Falfurrias, I timed my return so I could drive through Kingsville at dusk, and the payoff was better than I'd hoped. We had a beautiful sunset, and I was able to capture some great photos. This scene is located on the western edge of the original Santa Gertrudis de la Garza land grant.

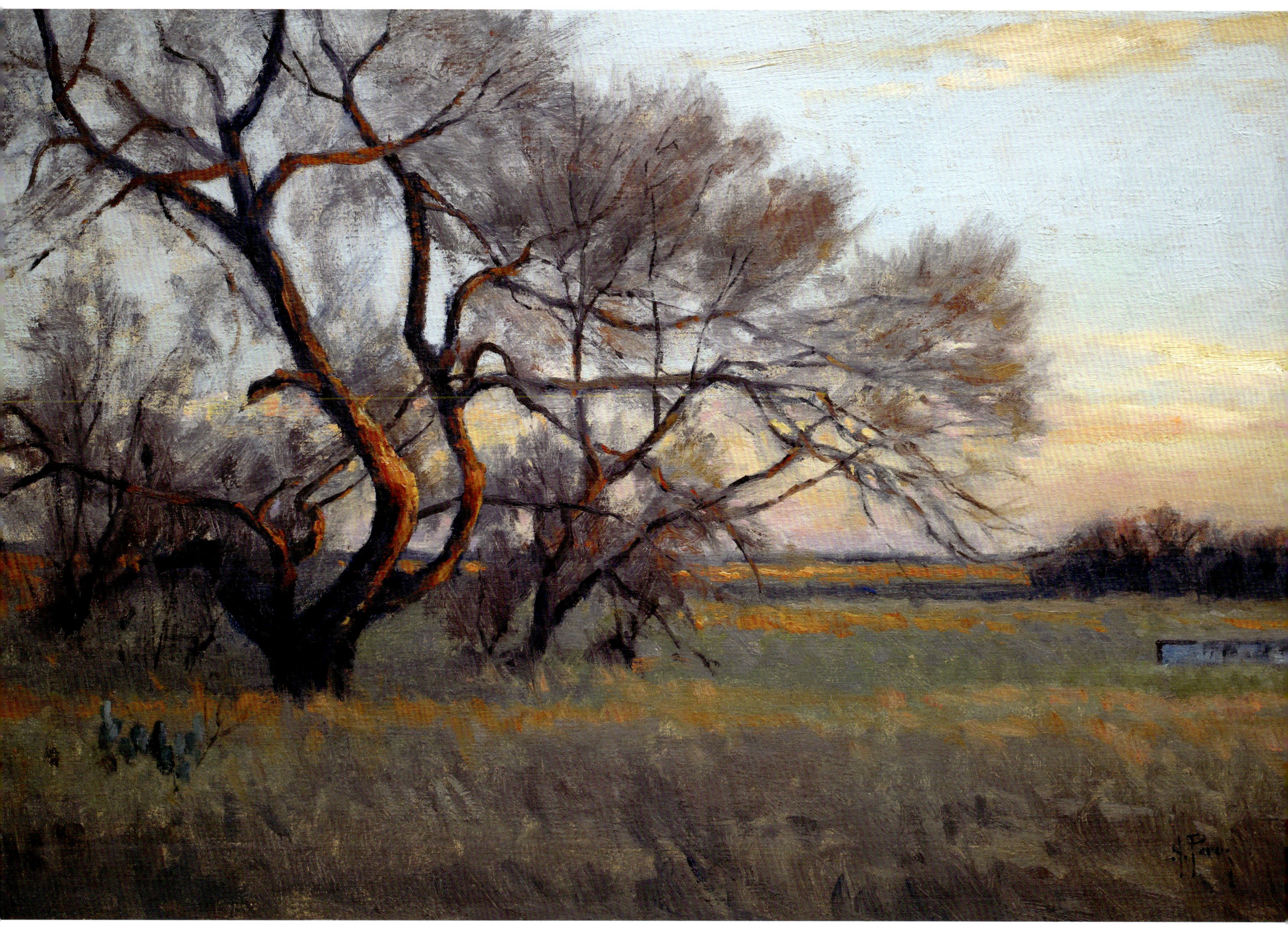

59

*Olmos Mesquites at Dusk (Santa Gertrudis)*, 2019
Oil on canvas, 14 × 20 inches
Courtesy of the artist

## Gate at Spohn Pens

When I visited, the pens were not active but still presented a place where my imagination saw cattle, Kineños, and quarter horses—all at the top of their game. Little remains, including this gate, of the original Spohn cattle pens, named for Dr. Arthur Spohn. This was one of the major shipping points along the St. Louis, Brownsville, and Mexico railway on south Santa Gertrudis.

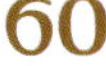


*Gate at Spohn Pens* (*Santa Gertrudis*), 2019
Oil on canvas, 30 × 30 inches
Courtesy of the artist

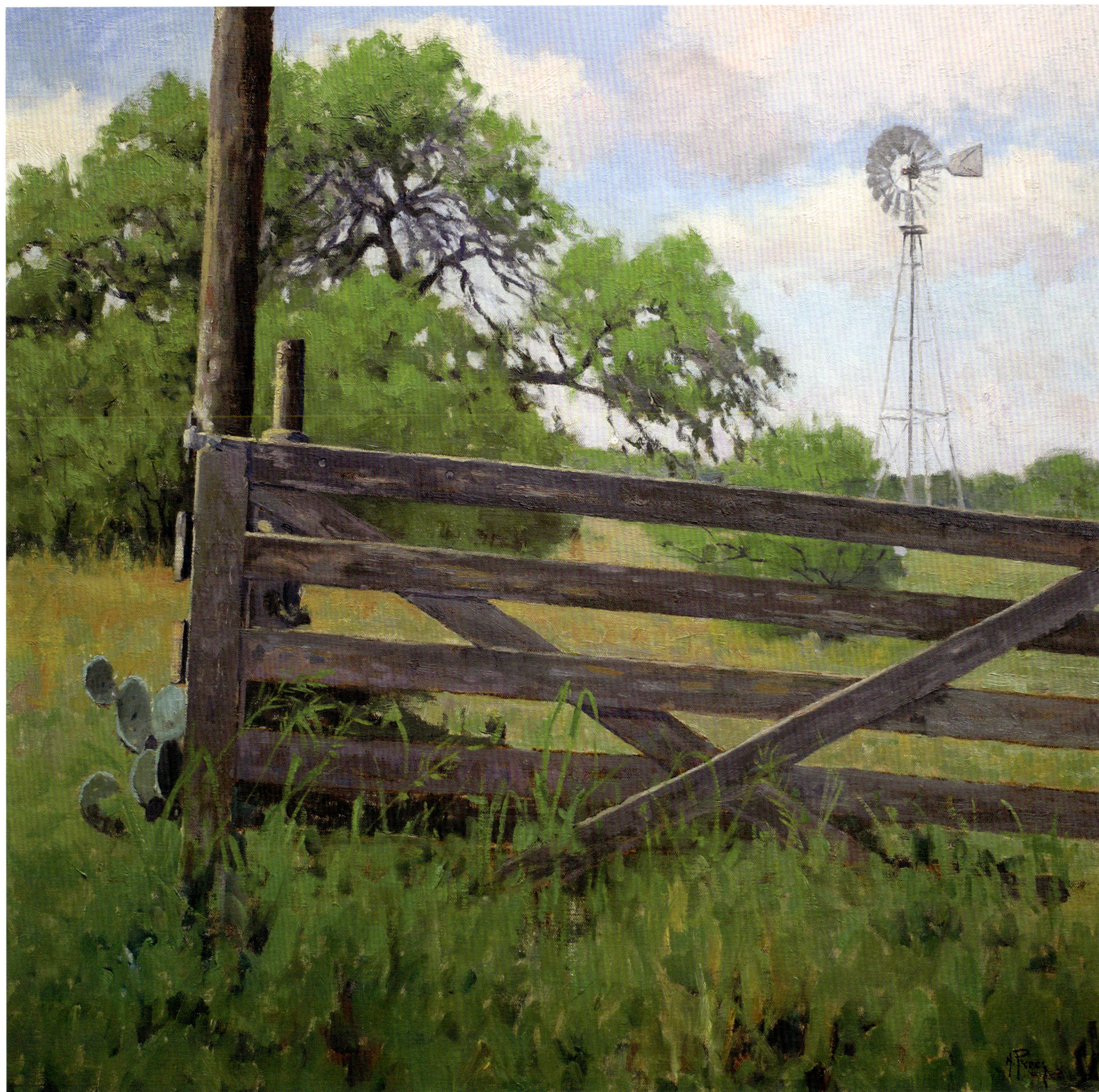

## Mare Study

I did this study of a mare I encountered and intended to use it in a larger painting of horses in a corral.

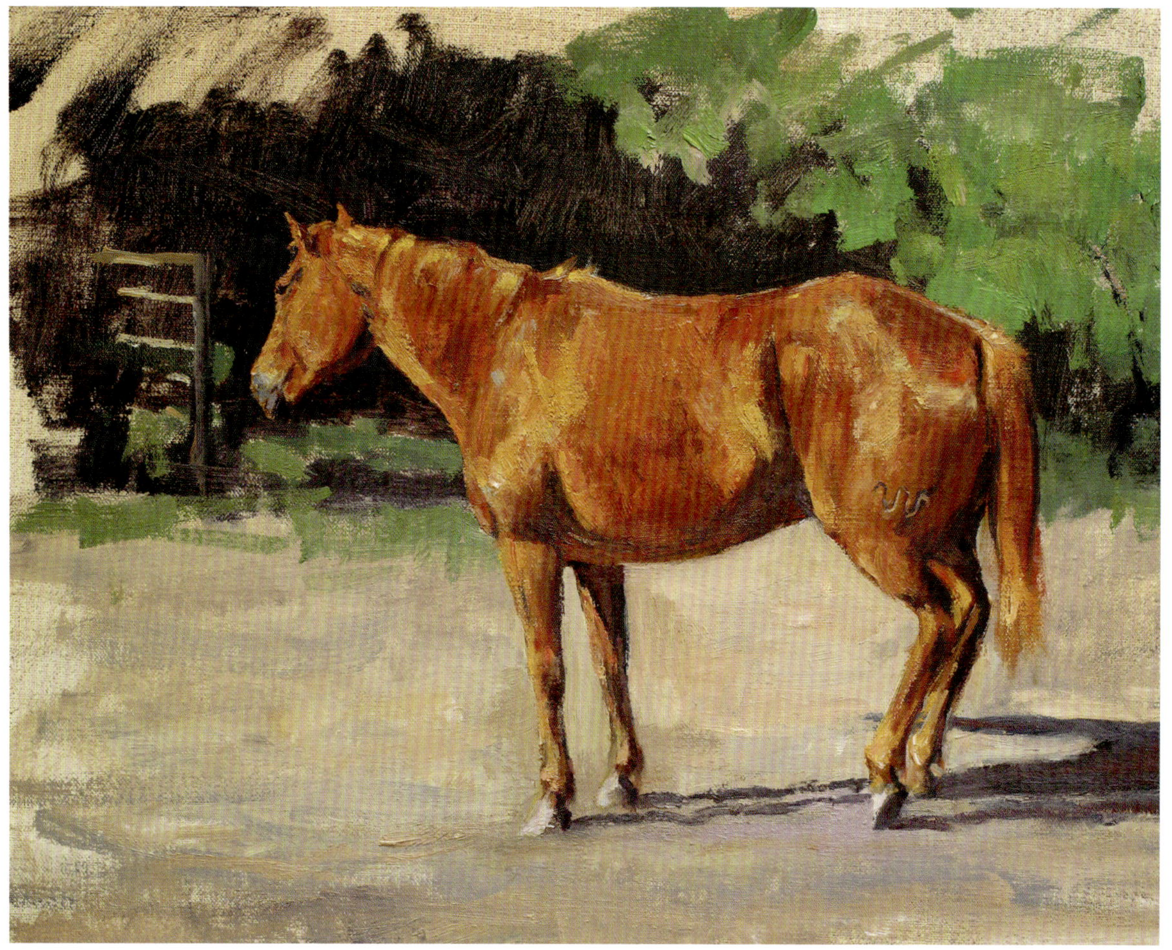

**61**

*Mare Study*, 2019
Oil on canvas, 11 × 13 inches
Courtesy of the artist

## Horse's Head Study

This is a horse "portrait" I did as a warm-up one morning.

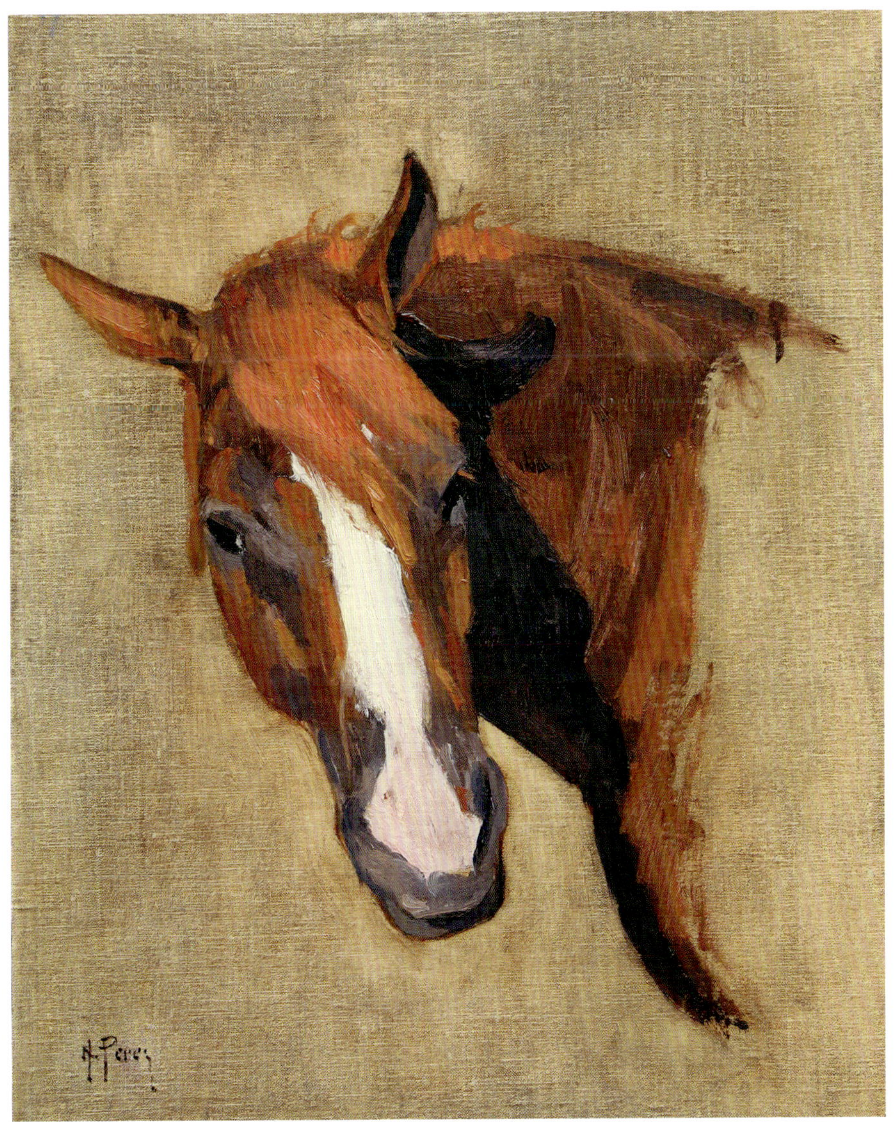

**62**

*Horse's Head Study*, 2019
Oil on canvas, 14⅝ × 11¼ inches
Courtesy of the artist

## Blooming Huisache Study

I intended to do a blooming huisache painting but just couldn't find an arrangement I liked—this was one idea.

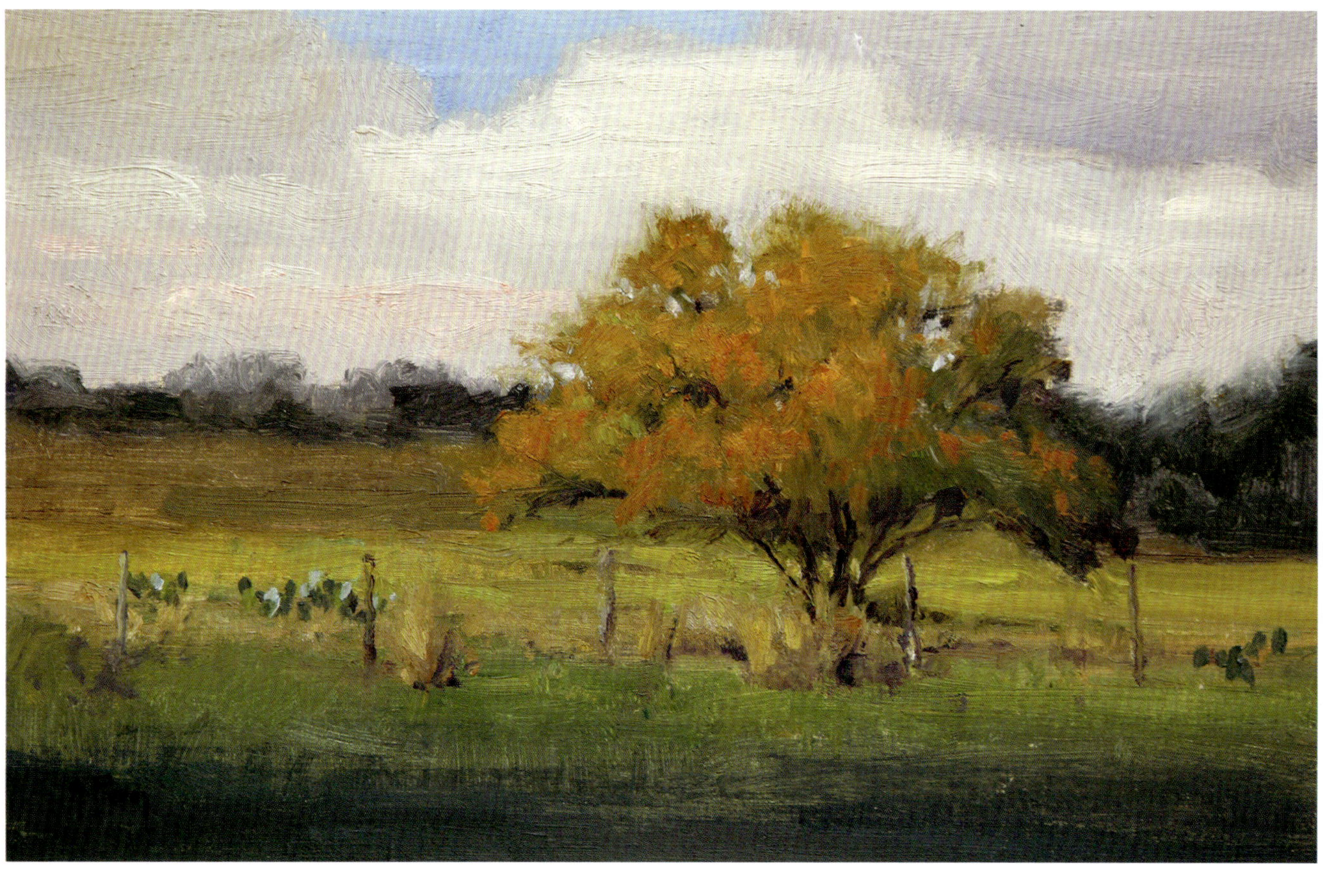

**63**

*Blooming Huisache Study*, 2019
Oil on canvas, 8 × 12 inches
Courtesy of the artist

## Blooming Cactus Plein Air Study

I did this little plein air painting on a beautiful day when I had brought my paints out to the ranch. Because you must act quickly, plein air sketching is a great way to capture what is before you without overthinking. I never tire of blooming cacti, and capturing them *en plein air* is the best education. I usually keep these plein air paintings as research for future works.

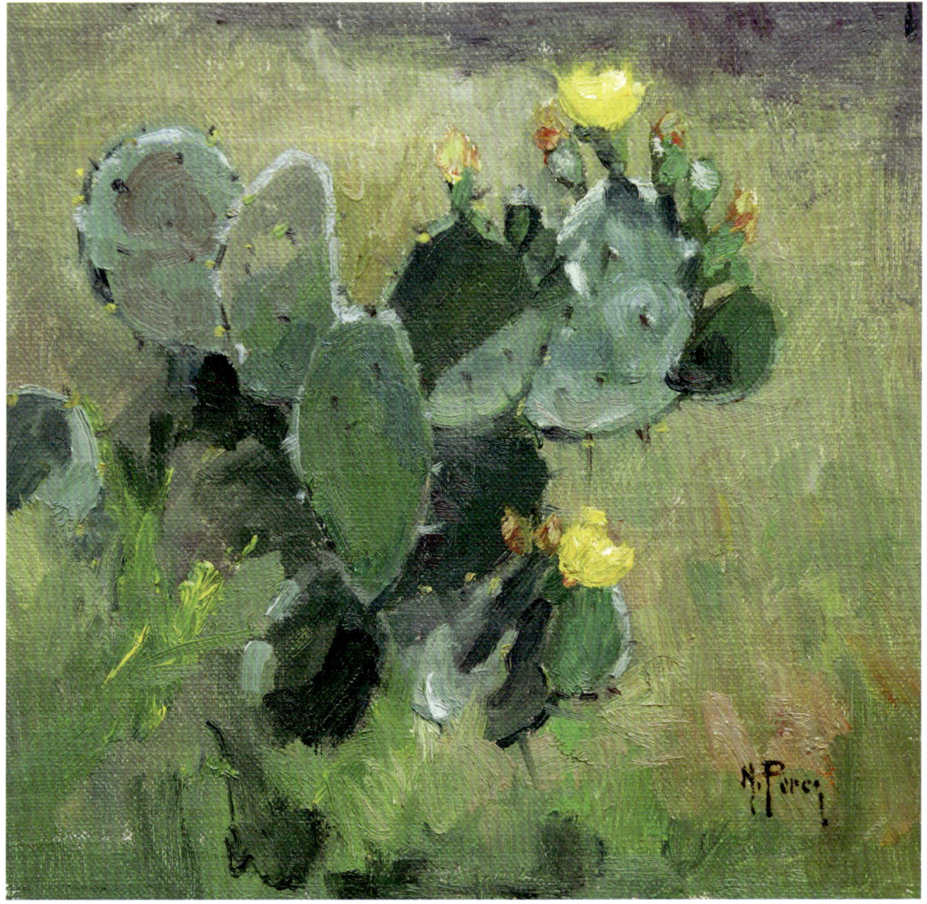

**64**

*Blooming Cactus Plein Air Study*, 2019
Oil on canvas, 8 × 8 inches
Courtesy of the artist

## Santa Gertrudis Bull Study

I really wanted to do a Santa Gertrudis bull for this project, but I never saw one with the look that I was after. This is one I liked, but I was never able to follow through with the idea before the painting project ended.

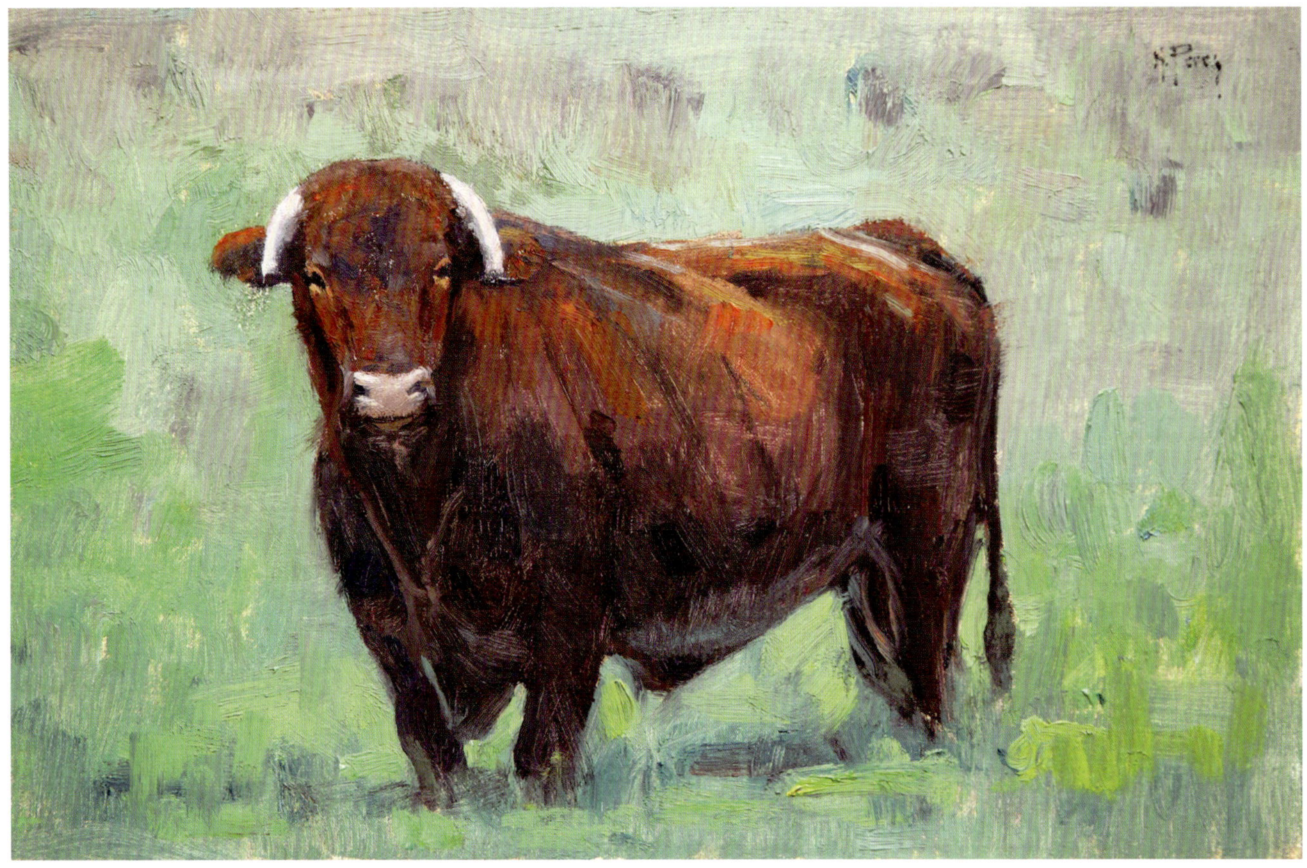

**65**

*Santa Gertrudis Bull Study*, 2019
Oil on canvas, 8 × 12 inches
Courtesy of the artist

## Sunset Study 1 and Sunset Study 2

I did two small studies, trying to work out a composition for a larger painting, but the studies didn't go any further. I liked them enough to include them here.

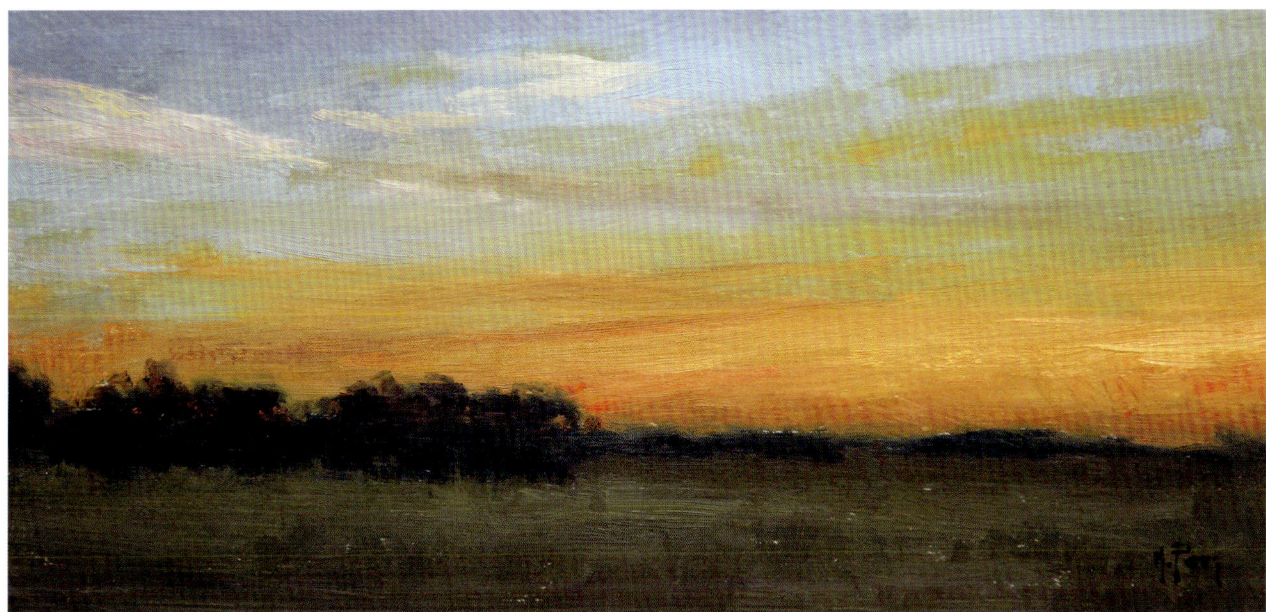

66

*Sunset Study 1*, 2019
Oil on canvas, 6 × 12 inches
Courtesy of the artist

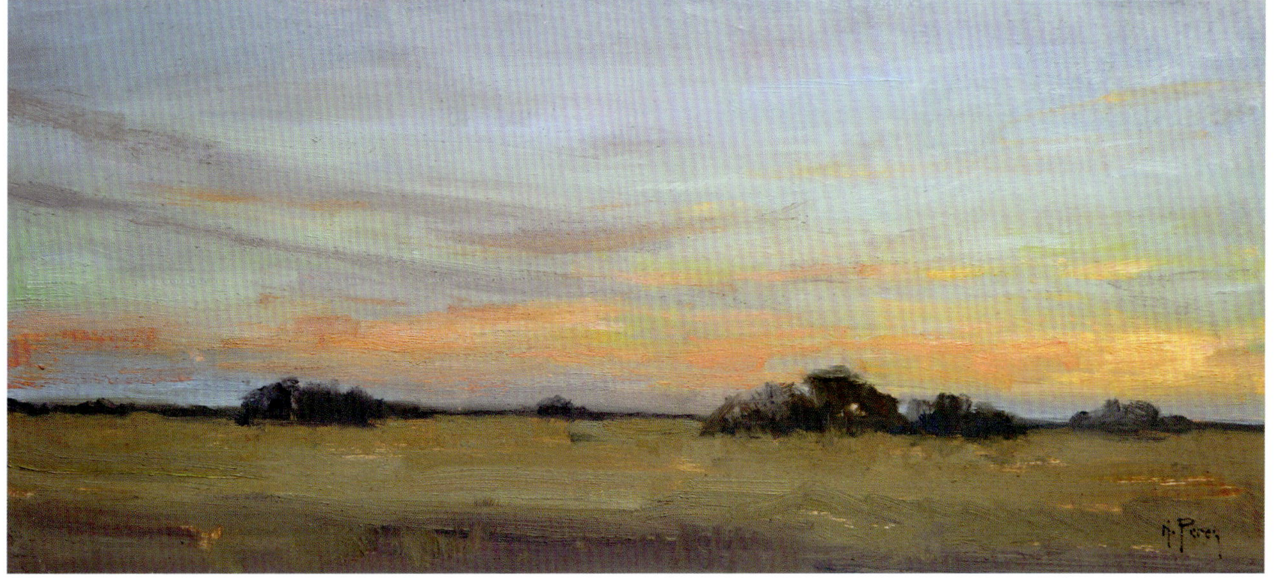

67

*Sunset Study 2*, 2019
Oil on canvas, 7 × 15 inches
Courtesy of the artist

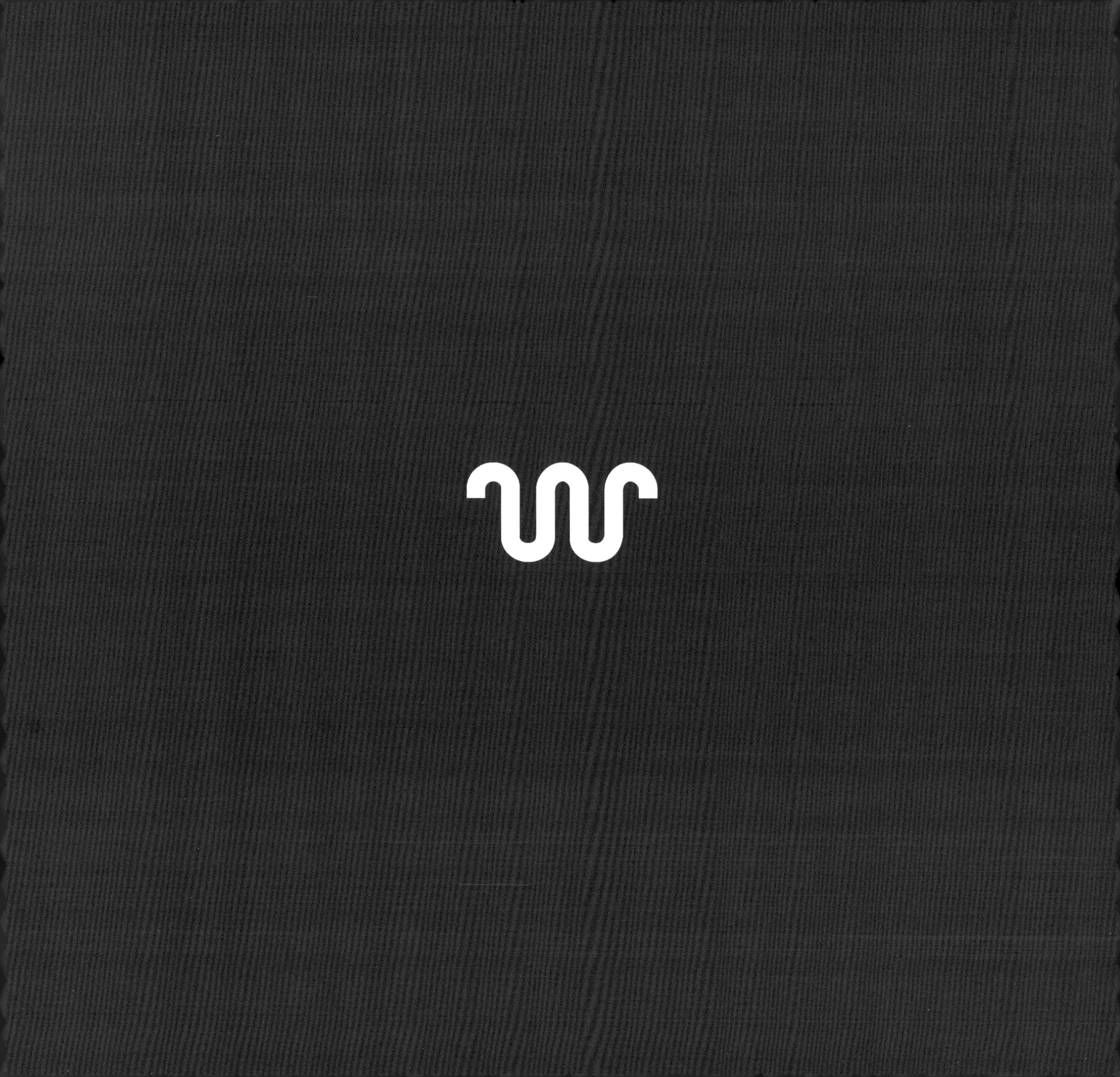

# Index

NOTE: Page numbers in *italic* type indicate information contained in images or image captions and descriptions.

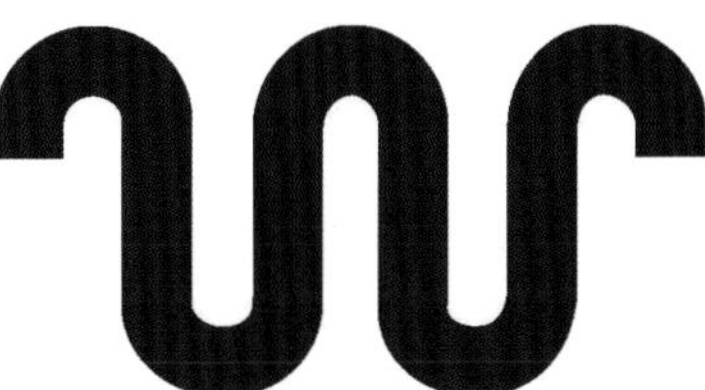

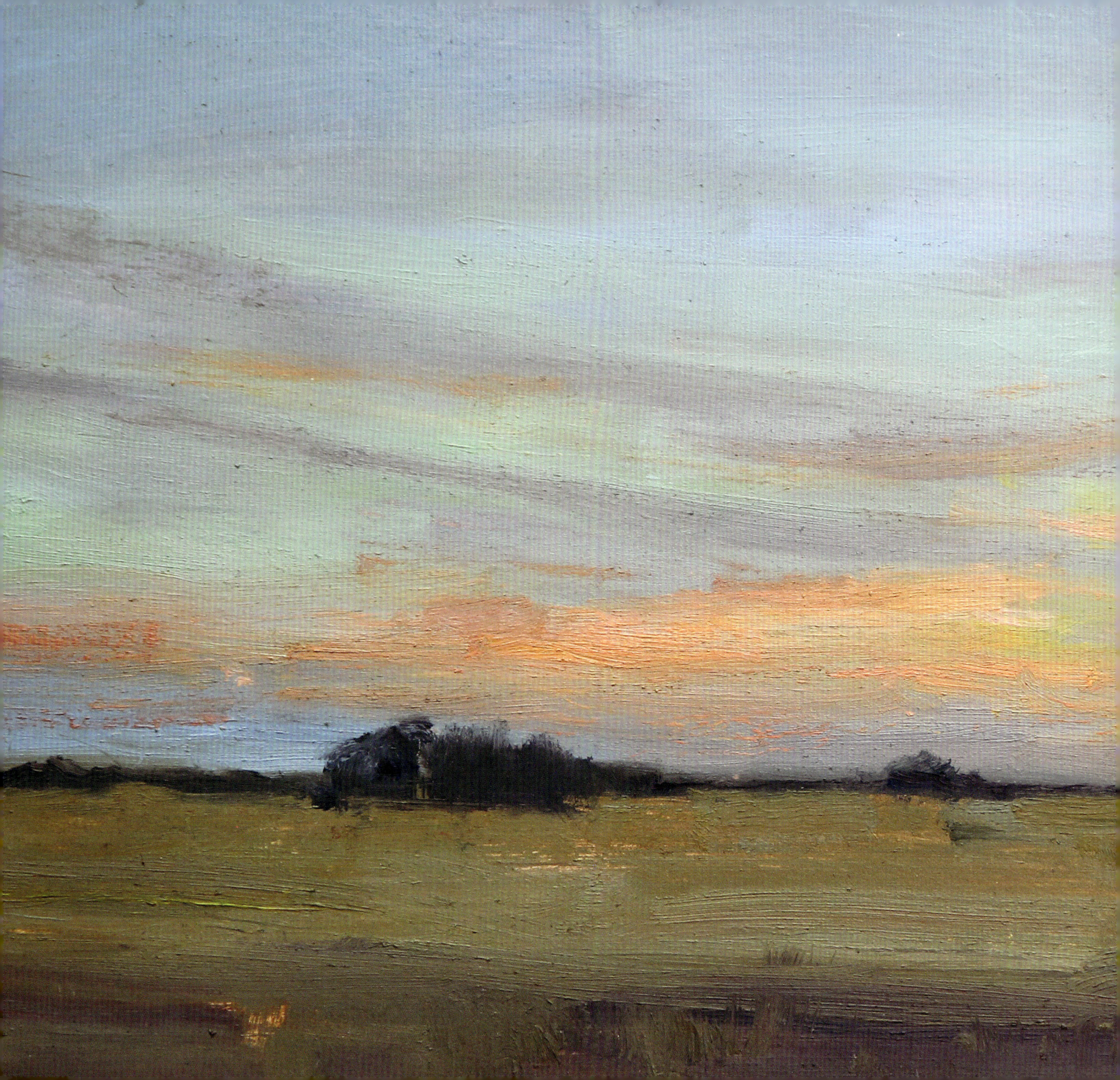

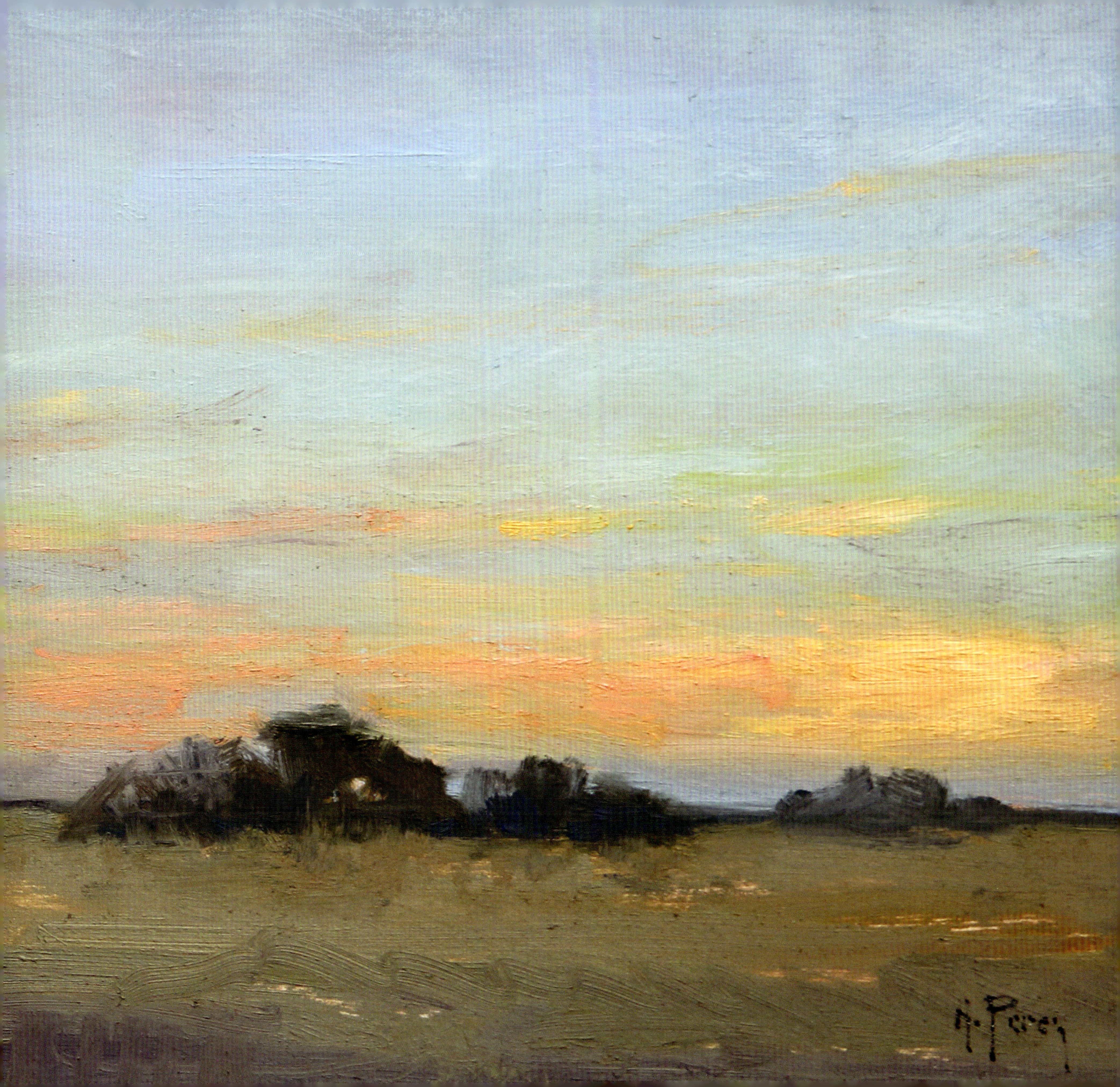